Environmental Equity in China and Beyond

Bloomsbury Introductions to World Philosophies

Series Editor:
Monika Kirloskar-Steinbach

Assistant Series Editor:
Leah Kalmanson

Regional Editors:
Nader El-Bizri, James Madaio, Ann A. Pang-White,
Takeshi Morisato, Pascah Mungwini, Mickaella Perina, Omar Rivera
and Georgina Stewart

Bloomsbury Introductions to World Philosophies delivers primers reflecting exciting new developments in the trajectory of world philosophies. Instead of privileging a single philosophical approach as the basis of comparison, the series provides a platform for diverse philosophical perspectives to accommodate the different dimensions of cross-cultural philosophizing. While introducing thinkers, texts and themes emanating from different world philosophies, each book, in an imaginative and path-breaking way, makes clear how it departs from a conventional treatment of the subject matter.

Titles in the Series:

A Practical Guide to World Philosophies,
by Monika Kirloskar-Steinbach and Leah Kalmanson
Daya Krishna and Twentieth-Century Indian Philosophy,
by Daniel Raveh
Māori Philosophy, by Georgina Tuari Stewart
Philosophy of Science and The Kyoto School, by Dean Anthony Brink
Tanabe Hajime and the Kyoto School, by Takeshi Morisato
African Philosophy, by Pascah Mungwini
The Zen Buddhist Philosophy of D. T. Suzuki,
by Rossa Ó Muireartaigh
Sikh Philosophy, by Arvind-Pal Singh Mandair
The Philosophy of the Brahma-sūtra, by Aleksandar Uskokov
The Philosophy of the Yogasūtra, by Karen O'Brien-Kop
The Life and Thought of H. Odera Oruka, by Gail M. Presbey
Mexican Philosophy for the 21st Century, by Carlos Alberto Sánchez
Buddhist Ethics and the Bodhisattva Path, by Stephen Harris
Contextualizing Angela Davis, by Joy James

Environmental Equity in China and Beyond

Past, Present, and Future

Michael Nylan and Thomas Hahn

BLOOMSBURY ACADEMIC
LONDON • NEW YORK • OXFORD • NEW DELHI • SYDNEY

BLOOMSBURY ACADEMIC

Bloomsbury Publishing Plc, 50 Bedford Square, London, WC1B 3DP, UK
Bloomsbury Publishing Inc, 1359 Broadway, New York, NY 10018, USA
Bloomsbury Publishing Ireland, 29 Earlsfort Terrace, Dublin 2, D02 AY28, Ireland

BLOOMSBURY, BLOOMSBURY ACADEMIC and the Diana logo are trademarks of Bloomsbury Publishing Plc

First published in Great Britain 2026

Copyright © Michael Nylan and Thomas Hahn, 2026

Michael Nylan and Thomas Hahn have asserted their right under the Copyright, Designs and Patents Act, 1988, to be identified as Authors of this work.

For legal purposes the Acknowledgements on p. vii constitute an extension of this copyright page.

Series design by Louise Dugdale
Cover image: Irina/Adobe Stock

All rights reserved. No part of this publication may be: i) reproduced or transmitted in any form, electronic or mechanical, including photocopying, recording or by means of any information storage or retrieval system without prior permission in writing from the publishers; or ii) used or reproduced in any way for the training, development or operation of artificial intelligence (AI) technologies, including generative AI technologies. The rights holders expressly reserve this publication from the text and data mining exception as per Article 4(3) of the Digital Single Market Directive (EU) 2019/790.

Bloomsbury Publishing Plc does not have any control over, or responsibility for, any third-party websites referred to or in this book. All internet addresses given in this book were correct at the time of going to press. The author and publisher regret any inconvenience caused if addresses have changed or sites have ceased to exist, but can accept no responsibility for any such changes.

A catalogue record for this book is available from the British Library.

ISBN: HB: 978-1-3505-2753-9
PB: 978-1-3505-2752-2
ePDF: 978-1-3505-2755-3
eBook: 978-1-3505-2754-6

Typeset by Deanta Global Publishing Services, Chennai, India
Printed and bound in Great Britain

For product safety related questions contact productsafety@bloomsbury.com.

To find out more about our authors and books visit www.bloomsbury.com and sign up for our newsletters.

Contents

Acknowledgements	vii
Dedication	viii
Series Editor preface	ix
Authors' Foreword	x

1	The Recalcitrance of Anglo-American Law	1
	A Brief History of Revisionist Environmental Law	18
	Some New Developments (unresolved)	28
	Three Cases	28
	"Greenpeace Tries New Tactic in Dakota Pipeline Suit"	32
	The End of Impunity for Tech Giants?	34
	Interim Conclusion	36
2	Intergenerational Equity during the Early Empires in China	39
	Underlying Theories of the Body and Body Politic	46
	Seasonality for the Body Politic, as for the Body	55
	Case Study: The Xuanquan Edict of AD 5	60
	"Instructions" on Seasonal Disbursements	68
	Exhibit A: Care of the Aged	73
	Exhibit B: Debt Relief for the Poor	77

3 The World We Want	83
Some Numbers and Dates: 2035, 2045, 2050, 2060	114
Joint Conclusion	137
Further Readings	141
Chronology	161
Bibliography	167
Index	194

Acknowledgments

The authors would like to thank (in no particular order) Eric Henry, Sally McMullen, Maia Kemp-Welch, and her mother Alice Kemp-Welch, Tan Sor-Hoon, Jianye He, Deborah Rudolph, and Robin Workman. All the members of this group (mainly women) have given us research help and cheered us on in the several years that we have spent writing this book. In addition, Michael Nylan would also like to thank Roger T. Ames for getting the two of us involved in the project in the first place, and Gerald P. Boswell, Esq., for teaching Nylan the law.

Monika Kirloskar-Steinbach has been an exemplary editor, at once encouraging, probing, and impatient with generalities. Because this project is so interdisciplinary (in imitation of the early Chinese sources), it has taken a thinker who thinks well "outside the box" to realize that this is indeed a philosophical exploration, in this precise sense: it asks how we are to live, which is the earliest philosophical question we know. We recall that less capacious minds have chided us for not doing philosophy when we write as we do here. We thank Tan Sor-hoon and Hans Sluga for encouraging us to keep working on the project after withering criticism.

We must also thank the anonymous reviewers for Bloomsbury Press. Nearly every single comment they provided was constructive, and the manuscript is much improved, thanks to them.

Dedication

We co-authors think a book about intergenerational equity should be dedicated to the very young and the older generation. With that in mind, we dedicate this book to Blake Nele 霞 Manning, Emery Bea Lan 嵐 Manning, and to Frank Gooding (representing the younger generation) and to Marty Verhoeven (to honor an oldster in the trenches like us). By Nylan's desk sits the exquisite calligraphy penned by a student of thirty years ago, citing the *Analects*' injunction "To put the elderly at ease, to be of good faith to friends, and to cherish the young" 老者安之，朋友信之，少者懷之. And, as Kongzi reportedly remarked in *Analects* 9/23:

"The young ones should be held in high esteem. Who is to say that the future generation will not measure up to the present one?" Indeed.

Series Editor Preface

Bloomsbury Introductions to World Philosophies offers plural, hitherto unexplored pathways into the study of world philosophies. Instead of privileging a single philosophical approach as the basis of comparison, the series provides a platform for diverse philosophical perspectives to accommodate the many different dimensions of cross-cultural philosophizing. While the choice of terms used by the individual volumes may indeed carry a local inflection, they do not foreclose critical thinking about philosophical plurality. Each individual volume strikes a balance between locality and globality.

Environmental Equity in China and Beyond: Past, Present, and Future reframes ancient Chinese thinking for the present. It explores ways to implement and adapt past and present notions of intergenerational equity to better realize the dignity of (human) beings, now and in the future. Co-authors Michael Nylan and Thomas Hahn urge us to engage in radical rethinking to relocate people's niche in the cosmic order, since standard theories preoccupied with ascertaining the right 'rational' choices regarding resource acquisition and optimization cannot get us to reduce the toxicity of the total environment whose air we breathe. Rather, we will have to take a step back, learn from our ancestors, and begin working with each other across differences to move toward zero-waste, improved food science, fairer voting methods, and sounder medical approaches.

Their book will appeal to readers across disciplinary divides and to a broader audience outside the academy.

Monika Kirloskar-Steinbach

Authors' Foreword

[Michael Nylan on behalf of both authors]

We live in a world that has begun to reckon with the terrible consequences of climate change. Endless wars, worldwide pandemics, mass migrations, desertification, rising seas, and dying oceans, diminishing biodiversity, mountains of nuclear and plastic waste, homes across Euro-America that have become uninsurable, stark inequalities in access to education[1] and meaningful work, a stunning lack of trust in nearly all institutions, from the family to the neighborhood to the modern nation-state, not to mention in fellow human beings (nearly all political and corporate leaders among them)—this constellation of disasters is no longer the "new normal," in Jerry Brown's memorable phrase, since the pace and scale of disasters exponentially accelerates, presenting profound challenges to all who hope to ensure lives of dignity, quality, and purpose for themselves and for future generations.[2] Climate change is a force multiplier of instability and chaos, and few people welcome chaos.

Nearly every day now, the newspaper headlines tell the same story. When we wrote the first draft of this book in the summer of 2023, *The New York Times*, as the US paper of record, steadily noted the sorry state of planet Earth. For example, on July 6 of 2023 it confronted

---

[1] Lest one be in any doubt, "Extreme Weather Threatens Global Gains in Education," as per *The New York Times*, Aug. 15, 2024, A10 (byline Somini Sengupta).

[2] During the pandemic, nation-states openly discussed "acceptable casualty thresholds" (meaning, the ratio of their citizens whom they were prepared to see die), in a startling coarsening of even public pretenses. This practice continues.

readers with "Heat Records are Broken in Places across the Globe, FAST"; on July 11, 2023, with "Extreme Weather Fueled by Climate Change is [the] 'New Normal.'" On July 19, 2023, when John Kerry met with Chinese leaders to "push China" on climate change, the front page screamed, "A Milestone Sears Phoenix: At Least 110 Degrees, 19 Days in a Row" and inside the same paper, "Canada's Epic Wildfire Season." On September 13, the biggest "national news" in the United States was "The Glaciers of Rainer are 'Forever' No More." On September 22, readers had their suspicions confirmed: "Hottest August on Record Caps a Scorching Summer." As we finished the second draft of this manuscript in the 2024, the year brought still worse: the environmental catastrophes never seem to stop.[3] Hurricane Milton followed Hurricane Helene, both said to be "worst of the century."[4] The summer of 2024 was the hottest on record (no surprise there).[5] Temperatures in the Coral Sea were at their highest in 400 years (August 8), so we can expect the Great Barrier Reef to be dead within a generation. Elsewhere, beset by drought, the Panama Canal was too shallow for some seagoing vessels to pass through (September 5), and the electric grid was itself now a wildfire hazard, prompting upgrading and the burying of power lines.[6] It hardly mattered where one lived: Phoenix, Arizona endured 100 days of temperatures at or over 100 degrees Fahrenheit; in Saudi Arabia, some 1500 pilgrims died while making the Hajj; global warming made lethal rains in Europe twice as likely";[7] and "renegades of Silicon Valley" polluted the sky "to save the planet" (September 30),[8] while in some places in Africa and

---

[3] For instance, "Extreme Heat Harms Mental Health, With Link to a Rise in Suicides, Scientists Say," *New York Times*, sec. A1. On July 10, 2023, John Kerry said to reporters that some eight million people die from climate change each year. The news clip came from Amy Goodman's TV show, "Democracy Now."
[4] Public Broadcasting Service (US), "News Hour," Oct. 8, 2024.
[5] *The New York Times*, International, Friday, Sept. 6, A8.
[6] *The New York Times*, Opinion (Michael E. Webber), Aug. 22, 2024, A22.
[7] *The New York Times*, Aug. 27, 2024, A 4 (by-line Austyn Gaffney).
[8] *The New York Times*, Sept. 30, B1-b2 (by-line David Gelles).

Asia monkeys and bats tumbled out of trees from heat exhaustion.[9] Trump's campaign was "Drill, Baby, Drill," and under Trump, climate change has become a hoax, with predictable consequences already.

No single panacea can solve such multifaceted problems in a world long accustomed to the "acquisition and optimization" of resources (the corporate catchphrase for raping the land) accelerated by AI and to acceptable "casualty tolerance thresholds," the number of human beings whom socioeconomic strategists reckon they are willing to sacrifice, rather than rethink their current exploitative ways and means.[10] One nightmare scenario: that Trump, delighted to ignore long-standing international law, will allow strip mining of the deep sea for minerals and metals, destroying entire ecosystems.[11] Plainly, swift rethinking will have to take place in many sectors and tiers of decision-making, including international organizations, if we are to move quickly toward zero-waste, improved food science, and security,[12] sounder medical practices, fairer voting methods, more educational opportunities, and policies to foster greater social justice, all factors in the *quotidien* that would contribute to lives worth living. At present, discrete academic departments and rival political entities ruminate on such issues, while identity politics (intentionally?) has made it appreciably harder for groups to look past their ethnic differences to identify their common interests and struggles.[13] Dysfunction inevitably is the result, because problems of this scope

---

[9] *The New York Times*, Opinion (Nicholas Kristof), Sept. 15, 2024, A4.
[10] Bridle 2022, Introduction, esp. 4–6. AI helps fracking efforts, to take one example. On "thresholds," see, e.g., Wells 2016.
[11] Marx 2025.
[12] Increasingly, toxic "forever" chemicals turn up in farms in the United States, in part because of contaminants in sludge fertilizer (i.e., urban sewage), bought cheaply. See *The New York Times*, Sept. 1, 2024, 1.
[13] Malouf 1998; Sennet 2012. Many would argue that the Black Panther Fred Hampton at age twenty-one paid for his life in an FBI raid in December, 1969, because he was so successful at mobilizing both poor white and black folk to work together for social justice, even forging alliances with Chicago street gangs. The movie *Judas and the Black Messiah* gets most of the story right.

require steady, coordinated cooperation at multiple transboundary and cross-disciplinary sites. In the United States, David Brooks, no wild-eyed radical, has already called for a civic uprising, where individuals and groups, arm and arm, commit to civilization.[14] Yet, as presently configured, it seems doubtful that our political, legal, and academic institutions are up to the task.[15]

Climate change has been an incontrovertible fact since the 1980s.[16] This book therefore calls upon sophisticated notions of intergenerational equity, past and present, as the single best entry point into the issue of environmental equity. What the latter phrase requires is conceptually simple: we should leave behind as few traces of rupture as possible, acting as stewards of the places we travel through in life, even if a deed plainly states we own it, because this alone will allow succeeding generations to enjoy opportunities roughly comparable to those we have known. It is no coincidence, we co-authors contend, that now it is the elders and the young who have joined forces to try to scare the reigning powers-that-be, since the powerful are evidently happy to keep on polluting the planet as if there will be no tomorrow, greenwashing if they must to salvage reputations or careers while insisting that climate change is overstated or unproven.[17] The older ones, in retirement, have more time to reflect

---

[14] Brooks 2025.
[15] Here in Trumpland, a few of us argue that Trump has done us all an inadvertent favor by inducing this much chaos this quickly; he is garnering attention from many quarters that would have ignored him had he taken a more gradualist approach.
[16] For an early warning by a NASA scientist, see Hansen et al., 1981; cf. Begley 2007. Rachel Carson's *Silent Spring* was first published earlier, in 1962.
[17] Greenwashing refers to "whitewashing" one's reputation with respect to environmental action. The list of "greenwashing" businesses is lengthy, but the big oil companies, Volkswagen, Coca-Cola, Starbucks, bottled water companies, and "fast fashion" businesses usually top the lists of malefactors. In addition, the big banks are still lending hefty sums to the industries that contribute the most to global warming, while pretending to be leaders in the green transition. Among conspiracy theories, Nieboer 2023 is one of the most outrageous examples. And then there are cases where it's hard to tell how bad the greenwashing is, as with Tritan Renew, which claims its products contain "up to" 50 percent recycled material, although some products contain far less, which the company

upon what they value in their lives, having made it (or not) in their careers. The young, as movements like Fridays for Future and The Last Generation attest, have not yet become inured to the daily instability they witness helplessly. Sweet reason tells us that all sentient beings from time immemorial have shared a common interest in preserving the health of the biosphere on which all human beings in all ages have depended—we should not bite the hand that feeds us—but reason, facts, and logic are feeble tools easily manipulated by those touting the virtues of business-as-usual. Even Steve Chiang, my neighbor's super-smart kid, remarks that "it's sorta sad" that his generation will never have the chance to be nearly as profligate in their consumption habits as his parents' generation, since the clock is ticking. And then we co-authors come along, hoping to persuade you that greater glory lies in having the guts to resist some impulses, if only because the modern propensity to dally with the twin fictions that "the past is past" and that a person can "have it all" and so need never trouble to "learn what is enough"[18] are major contributing factors in the mess, certainly. To state the obvious, "politics" by definition concerns the pursuit of what is deemed good (albeit often in blind, disputed, or self-interested ways) in particular instances by agents having limited powers and resources, where the choice to pursue one direction usually *precludes pursuit of another*.[19] However, to arrive at what is

---

justifies by talking of "mass balance accounting." See *The New York Times*, Business, Thursday, Sept. 5, 2024, B5.

[18] The phrase *zhi zu* 知足 ("learn what is enough") is common to texts deemed Confucian, Daoist, and Legalist. It appears no fewer than 24x in pre-Han and Han literature, not counting the *Wenxuan* or Yan Kejun's modern compendium of texts, according to CHANT/ ICS Concordance https://www.chant.org/result/Basic/ ee659d37-0263-4640-9e04-c78eeac0f317

[19] Geuss 2008, 30 (mod. 1–2); Shklar 2019, Introduction. Hampshire 2018 adds that political obligations generally result in conflicts, and not only because loyalties are owed to more than one group. NB: 'politics' does not neatly map onto modern academic definitions of the 'political', as so many ritual matters (burial of emperors, posthumous titles, divinations, omen readings, etc.) held grave political importance in the past.

usually understood as the "common good" requires more than savvy politicking via catchy slogans.

Growing up on a small farm in Kentucky, in a family of civil rights advocates, and trained as a historian to follow the money, it is no accident that Michael Nylan came to embrace feminist care ethics, role ethics, and political realism as guiding lights.[20] An orphan at ten, she knows life is short and she trusts her antique Chinese sources' intuitions, which insist that the deepest, most satisfying, and most enduring pleasures are to be had from friends in every corner, books on every topic, music and gardens and good food, fulfilling work performed with integrity, and home. To sustain this plenitude requires effort, clearly, but she feels that her investment is safe, so long as she puts in that effort. Thomas Hahn, from Frankfurt, Germany, began to research China's sacred mountains (usually Daoist) and from there has gone on to relate the geological and ecological histories that mountains, forests, medicinal plants, waters, and minerals readily reveal to those with persistent curiosity. An accomplished photographer and cultural geographer, his love of the get-ups and tales that people devise for themselves make his Leica images, as well as his prose, testaments to the irrepressible human spirit. So, yes, we co-authors speak in different voices, but any complex ecosystem needs a plurality of resources to attain true resilience. Besides, we co-authors agree on this conclusion: humans have made this crisis, and there is just time for them to undo the worst, but the longer they hem and

---

[20] As there are so many different philosophers who call themselves "political realists," I should say I follow Raymond Geuss's *Philosophy and Political Realism*. I deplore many forms of so-called Realtpolitik, partly on the grounds that as Isabel Hull has shown in her *Absolute Destruction* (2006), steely-minded policies of destruction so seldom work. (Hull shows how Clausewitz's theories failed to save imperial Germany in any of its wars against other Great Powers or in Africa.) Henry Rosemont, Jr. was mentor and friend, and it is he who taught me the basic theory of role ethics (pitted against the dominant "virtue ethics" as first espoused [but later emended] by Alasdair MacIntyre 1981). With Donald Swearer, I accept that caregiving is "the quotidian context in which we are most fully human"; see Molina and Swearer 2010, ix.

haw, the more draconian the constraints. Yes, there is time to fend off the worst-case scenarios.[21] Improvements are coming.[22] While we are told we "have no choice but to set off on the darkening roads that stretch out before and behind us in the here and now,"[23] on good days we (mostly) believe that a brighter future could be in the collective offing, so long as we refuse to succumb to futuristic fantasies—either that new technologies will "save" us or that new terrains to conquer (e.g., Mars, or cryonics) represent viable exit strategies from earthly predicaments.[24] (The key problems with technological fixes are three: the scale of the problem; the years or decades needed to test solutions, before scaling up; and the fact that all new technologies differentially benefit and harm different groups.)[25] Neither pious prayers nor cryptocurrency nor "creative" accounting can repay the debts once

---

[21] For rays of hope, see below.
[22] An electric revolution is underway in California, which could mean the beginning of the end for polluting and dangerous diesel trucks. See *Sierra* magazine comments: "Clean truck standards are key to reducing carbon pollution from the freight sector. Nationally, transportation accounts for nearly one-third of carbon emissions and heavy-duty trucking is responsible for a quarter of that, adding more than 400 million metric tons of greenhouse gases to the earth's atmosphere every year. *That's the equivalent of 103 coal plants*" (italics in the original); also, "San Pedro Bay port communities, heavily working-class and Latino, suffer the worst diesel-particulate-matter pollution in the state. That's starting to change. Los Angeles's sister port in Long Beach now bills itself as 'the Green Port.'"
[23] See Neil Badmington 2022.
[24] Plainly, one's own decisions to act (I much prefer that phrasing to "choices" with its neoliberal ring) are made within the context of multiple constraints, including imperfect knowledge of the present and future situations, as Zhuangzi's metaphor of the caged bird registered two millennia ago. But it is a different matter when today many neoliberal and libertarian thinkers profess themselves perplexed over what future generations will think is in their best interest, seeing in that a good excuse to shirk their present responsibilities. My question is, Is their perplexity real or feigned? So far as we know, "post-humans" are as much a figment of the imagination as flying pigs.
[25] For this reason, I am dubious about growing new coral reefs in a lab, unlike Carly D. Kenkel, and about launching gigantic sun shields. Almost 500 leading scientists and more than 2000 civil society organizations world-wide are calling for a non-use agreement in solar geoengineering (tried to much fanfare at the Beijing Olympics). "Claims that solar radiation modification, or S.R.M., could control the sun's warming effects ignore the immense risks and reality of sudden temperature spikes, if deployment is stopped. This technology could never 'restore' the climate but would further destabilize an already disturbed climate system, leading to unforeseen and irreversible ecological disasters," writes Lili Fuhr, the Berlin director of the economy program at the Center for International Environmental Law, in *The New York Times*, Aug. 14, 2024, A23.

incurred, and it is always much more expensive to clean up messes than it is to tread lightly in the first place. Moreover, we authors both mean to challenge two shopworn narratives: outside China, that China has no history or understanding of the rule of law, and inside China, that environmental consciousness is a "Western" preoccupation and hence part and parcel of the "imperialist/ colonial racist" agenda that China must overturn, if it is to become and remain a superpower.[26]

Note that the authors lodge no Orientalist claims that China represents a unique situation, whether uniquely good or uniquely bad.[27] They simply wish to speak of what they know, as a way of starting some conversations and continuing others. Were the co-authors of this volume not China experts, they would doubtless be highlighting equally interesting phenomenon elsewhere in the world. Still, discussing China at this juncture makes good sense, in light of the instrumental role that the PRC will play, for better or worse, in determining the fate of all going forward.[28] Additionally, all other geopolitical calculations being equal, China feels politically and ideologically compelled to take the lead in environmentally-friendly

---

Chinese thinkers in the early empires already saw the problem with new technologies. Guo Xiang 郭象 (ca. 265–ca. 312), for example, in his commentary on the *Zhuangzi*, observed that creating new technologies leads to increased competition and social strife. See Chapman (forthcoming).

[26] Increasingly, people outside China are speaking of a "China Peak," the idea that China is not likely to supersede the US, as was predicted by many before, during, and shortly after the 2008 Olympics. For those who can read Chinese, the justifications offered for censoring Xu Hong's book (scheduled for publication in July, 2023), whose title sensibly described the Shang as an empire in the classical sense, reveal the intensity of the culture fevers being orchestrated by the PRC propaganda machines. Social media accounts announced that only the evil EuroAmericans and Japanese can be imperialists, despite China's ambitious Belt and Road project. Yeats, in the "Widening Gyre," wrote that "the best lack all conviction."

[27] Contra Vaclav Smil 1993, Judith Shapiro 2001, etc. Granted, the scale and speed of China's recent development are unprecedented in the history of mankind, but more on this below.

[28] In general, the substantial divisions of capitalist society render the notion of a "common good" for all individuals, groups, and classes elusive. Yet, as Schumpeter 1950, 256, once noted, a common threat often allows an unusually high degree of cohesion.

energy production technologies,[29] finally countering its own record of spectacular environmental degradation during the last century, and both its backward and forward lurches in that respect are fully in line with other nations' wrestling with the unintended consequences of "trickle-down" economics and expansionist ambitions. Admittedly, China's alliance with Putin has complicated what once seemed a stable trajectory, as China builds hundreds of new coal-burning plants to shore up Russian finances.

This book consists of three parts: Chapter I explores Anglo-American law and American formulations of the model penal code, as the chief basis for modern international law, since the developed nations, on local, national, and international legal fronts, must introduce and coordinate constructive change.[30] After all, democratic countries, short of ousting or recalling its leaders at the ballot box, have left it primarily to the courts to make bad actors suffer the consequences for their wrongdoing; the public is relatively powerless, if armed solely or primarily with moral outrage. Chapter II presents the exemplary case of the early empires in China, which more than the contemporaneous Roman empire prioritized the care of the earth

---

[29] The PRC government announced a "war against pollution" in 2014 and had been making progress until 2022, if their self-reported figures are reliable. But unsurprisingly, the sharpest decline in China's PM2.5 pollution happened in 2020, when the coronavirus pandemic forced much of the country's economic activity to slow or shut down. In 2023, the last year for which WTO has figures, there was a notable 6.3 percent increase in China's air pollution compared with 2022. Likewise, Beijing experienced a 14 percent increase in PM2.5 pollution in 2023. Its support for Russia has not helped, for several reasons, among them the considerations that contributed to China's decision to build up to or more than 300 new coal-burning plants, which are either under construction, permitted, or awaiting permitting. China is now responsible for 95 percent of new coal plant construction in the world, according to Carbon Brief (2024). That represents a fourfold rise since 2019. Elsewhere, coal plant retirements are outstripping new coal plant construction.

[30] This book will not go into great detail to defend the claim that "international law" is predominantly Anglo-American law, but Daniel Friedman (Yale Law; Berkeley Ph.D.), in his growing body of work, especially 2024, provides much-needed evidence to support this book's claim, insofar as the American Law Institute and the Rockefeller Foundation are responsible for many formulations upon which international law depends today.

and the disadvantaged. While the complex vision that we find in early China shares some insights with other some antique civilizations, its commonsensical stipulations for social and cosmic order were unique, if broadly shared across many philosophical traditions in China envisioning good rule. (Strictly speaking, they were neither Confucian, Daoist, or Legalist, although their benevolent attitudes and practices strike many today as "Confucian.") The signal lack of sectarian divides in antiquity is itself exemplary, for sectarian divides (like class, status, and gender divides) generally keep people from striving together to realize laudable agendas. For some readers at least, this part of the book may summon the "power of enchantment" in the Foucauldian sense, juxtaposing "things that have [or hitherto have been thought to have] no relation to one another," things in this case as varied as the environment, care ethics, debt relief, political legitimacy, and mining.[31] Chapter III outlines policymaking and policy implementation in the People's Republic of China today, as the PRC seeks to project a meaningful future for itself through five-year and fifty-year ecological and institutional plans. By turns clear and ambiguous, the language of these plans is crafted with infinite care with an eye to domestic and international sensitivities. As a result of a range of recently redefined "red lines," "ecological civilization" in the form of Ecology-Oriented Development (EOD) takes its place in history not so long after Mao's "Away with All Pests." (Chapters I and II are mainly by Michael Nylan, with an assist from Thomas Hahn, and Chapter III is mainly by Thomas Hahn, with an assist from Michael Nylan.)

Read in tandem, all parts of the book build the case that Chinese leaders need never reject such notions as human rights, the rule

---

[31] Foucault used the term "power of enchantment" with this definition, in his "Preface" to *The Order of Things*. Thanks to Liu Ming 2022, 3–74, we understand the ties between these disparate topics, some of which will be discussed below and others omitted, in the interests of keeping a manageable length for the book.

of law, or economic equity on the grounds that these are "Western inventions" utterly foreign and thus antithetical to Chinese ways of life. To the contrary, these basic notions existed in antiquity in the area we now know as China—more so than in other antique empires, judging from the evidence at hand. Consequently, today's citizens in the PRC and Sinosphere have a surplus of resources to allow them to adjust antique ideas to today's local conditions, contra the prevailing propaganda touting among the citizenry "Asian values," Chinese exceptionalism, or policies equipped "with Chinese characteristics."[32] Some antique ideas, suitably reframed, offer a viable path forward that is neither irrational, altruistic, nor exploitative, when engaged and enlightened governments promote constructive values suited to the particularities of local communities.[33] For the antique ideas do not put the economic and political burdens on the poor and defenseless. They rather establish viable organizations fostering good environmental legacies (to bequeath and inherit), in the knowledge that these enhance the quality of "the very air we breathe" in this precise sense: by the antique resonance theories, every encounter that a person has with another of the myriad things represents an exchange of life-breath, of *qi*, to the person's benefit or harm, so those with whom we have the most interactions, the members of our communities in our habitats, constitute a disproportionate amount of the "air we breathe"—a finding that modern neuro-science and pop culture have just begun to accept (as when describing a person as toxic). Moreover, to experience a sense of well-being, every generation before ours in history has prioritized what philosophers call "life-transcending projects." Simply put, we humans, when we have enduring commitments, wish to arrange things so that after our

---

[32] Solnit and Lutunatabua 2023 accept that solutions must be, to some degree, rooted in local conditions, if they are to advance national and international solutions.
[33] See Solnit's Foreword to Solnit and Lutunatabua 2023.

deaths they go well for our loved ones, including our community, our friends, our children and even our children's children. Many rest easier, without regrets, if they believe some part of them will positively impact present and future generations.[34] Then, too, as Joel Feinberg has put it, "[Despite] their present facelessness and namelessness," we know that future generations will exist, and "this imposes a duty on us not to throw bombs in their direction."[35] To desist from bomb-throwing while imagining a larger presence,[36] humans pin their hopes on stable organizations and institutions seeing to the husbanding and appropriate transfers of resources, with echoes of "stewardship" in Burke's language. When the present structures do not provide for these basic human impulses, they must and will be created by those operating outside those structures (more on this below).

But step no. one is this:[37] doing away with the fond fictions of "agency," "autonomy," and "choice," as the world discourse today typically uses these terms, because (a) human beings have limited agency, with so much of their lives spent in inherited or imposed constructs and many studies have shown how conformist human beings are, by nature and by upbringing; (b) every careful scientific study has shown that human beings don't have "autonomy," if that means that their judgments are truly "independent" of the experiences they have had—experiences that in many cases they did not mandate or desire; (c) so much talk about choices boils down to "consumer choices" rather than "values and commitments" and it is wildly misleading to analogize judgments

---

[34] *Mencius* 1A/3.
[35] See Feinberg 1980, 18,1–82.
[36] Here I think of the *Analects* line (15/29): "Human beings can enlarge the Way; it is not the Way that enlarges people" 人能弘道. 非道弘人; and that Adorno's phrase "especially if one loves them" reminds us that the manner in which we relate to people enhances and even extends what we are capable of seeing, as noted in Hallisey, in Molina and Swearer 2010, 55. For that reason, I am less enamored of Vallor 2016 than many.
[37] Noam Shpancer in *Psychology Today* summarizes the findings: "Individually, we are designed to pick up social cues and coordinate and align our behavior with those around us. Recent research has shown that social disapproval provokes the brain's danger circuits. Conformity soothes." Cf. Morgan and Laland 2012.

and actions with earth-shattering consequences to "game theory" and "rational choice" theory.[38] (The objection to both of these is that the theories bear remarkably little resemblance to the way human beings conceive of their decisions and actions within their situational options, as they construe them. Unlike game theory, real-life decisions are seldom zero-sum; moreover, game theory is predicated on rational actors who maximize their payoffs, financial or otherwise, ignoring all other considerations that may matter to ordinary human beings.)[39] Finally, there is the small matter of environmental epigenetics and "the transgenerational effects of ancestral exposure to toxicants." Environmental epigenetics, a relatively new field of scientific inquiry across a number of relevant disciplines such as neurophysiology, psychology, and the behavioral sciences, poses questions about the transmission of cell-based responses to pollutants, both in response to single traumatic events and to long-term conditions. To date, the findings are consistent across multiple studies: the consequences of environmental degradation stressors on whole populations over time are huge,[40] in that the negative impacts "experienced by parents can influence their offspring's vulnerability to many pathological conditions, including psychopathologies . . . . [And] these effects may even endure for several generations."[41] In what world can choice, autonomy, and agency find expression when nature's responses imprint individuals' cell structures over long generations?

---

[38] Libertarianism is one philosophical strain that values, above all, choice protection.
[39] For one view of this, see Kreps 1990. Kreps concludes, "the theory fails to help us understand how individuals react to counter-theoreticals in dynamic interactions." Cf. "How Games and Game Theory Have Changed the World," in *The Economist* (June 20, 2024).
[40] They "ultimately may increase disease susceptibility in following generations. [. . .] In this context, since environmentally-induced changes to the epigenome of somatic and germ cells can influence gene expression and the emergence of phenotypes, they could also be used as biomarkers of disease predisposition." See Arzate-Mejía and Mansuy 2022, 21.
[41] Lacal and Rossella 2018.

Human beings are adept at detecting patterns, but poor at discerning which patterns are operative in their own lives. Computers are incalculably quicker to detect patterns, but worse at recognizing workable solutions to human predicaments, since "what matters" in human lives has little to do with game theory and/or rational choice. Big data feeds not on rich values, but instead on information and misinformation alike.[42] Besides, to well-informed people, the dual-use of any advanced technology presents real conundrums.[43] To date, "modernity's imperative rests on an inadequate and skewed picture of the relationship between human happiness, authenticity, and freedom, on the one hand, and time, on the other, utterly disregarding [the fact] that [wise] values . . . necessarily engage the past and future as well as the present."[44] The issue is, then, not when human life begins but what conditions will allow it to thrive eventually.[45] If philosophy since its inception asks how are we to live, the two most pressings questions are, as always, "What Future is Being Imagined for Us by Ourselves and Others?" and "What Is To Be Done?"

There is no dearth of people who accept that "each of us has a responsibility to try to ensure that today's children and future generations inherit a global environment not appreciably worse than the one we ourselves inherited from those who went before."[46] "Thanks

---

[42] Many feminist writers have noted the poverty of these theories (and often their inherent violence).

[43] Nearly all technological advances have civil and military applications. In history, *all* technological advances have profoundly benefited some while disadvantaging others. One might think of computers as an example.

[44] Weston 2008, 402.

[45] See Brown Weiss: "Intergenerational rights are not . . . rights possessed by individuals. They are generational rights, which are held in relation to other generations."

[46] Weston 2008, 376. And, where that goal proves impossible to achieve, to try to mitigate climate change harms, whether abrupt or "normalized." As climate mitigation and amelioration are still possible for us to achieve, it would be irresponsible at this point to only adopt climate mitigation as the goal. See multiple statements issued by the 1987 Brundtland Report on "Our Common Future," prepared for the U.N. World Commission on Environment and Development (WCED); the 1997 UNESCO Declaration on Responsibilities Towards Future Generations, the Paris Accords, etc. See the Chronology

in large part to a growing appreciation of non-Western systems of knowledge" predicated on "the essential cooperation of non-human colleagues and partners," such as trees and shrubs, elephants and octopuses, whales and dolphins, we may yet come to acknowledge the close ties binding the infinitely varied ecosystems' needs for survival and human beings' need to survive. By stages, in rethinking our characteristic modes of being and interacting in the world, we may see that human beings need only to adopt (or return to) the most salient ways of acting, acknowledging "complexity, interrelatedness, interdependence, distribution of control and agency, and a closeness to the earth and sky."[47] One passage sticks with me, as I explore these ideas:

> The problem, it turns out, is not an overabundance of humans but a dearth of humanity. . . . This is why political depression is important: zombies don't feel sad, and they certainly don't feel helpless; they just are. Political depression is, at root, *the experience of a creature that is being prevented from being itself.* . . . If humanity is the capacity to act meaningfully within our surroundings, then we are not really, or not yet, [fully] human.[48]

In arguing that ample resources exist within Chinese traditions (plural) to support efforts to remediate environmental damage and sometimes forestall it, we co-authors do not deny that resources exist within other traditions that might be usefully invoked to a similar end. For example, the Roman law maxim *si utere tuo ut alienum non laedas* ("Use your own property so as not to injure that of another") has been repeatedly invoked by the International Court of Justice to

---

for details. On July 23, 2025, the International Court of Justice ruled that states may be liable for ignoring climate science.

[47] Bridle 2022, 14. Bridle, following the American philosopher David Abram, would have us imagine a "more-than-human world" where we abandon human exceptionalism (17). As Lynn Margulis notes, humans are entangled with non-human life and life in a "far wider system."

[48] See Wallace-Wells 2019 (italics mine).

uphold the principle that one state's use of its sovereign territory may not breach the sovereign rights of a neighboring state.[49] But since the default arguments have, up to now, been largely EuroAmerican in derivation,[50] this book aims to complicate the standing narrative, echoing Bernard Williams' *Shame and Necessity*, which declared,

> The ethical thought of the Ancients was not only different from most modern thought, particularly modern thought influenced by Christianity; *it was also in much better shape*. . . . since this system of ideas basically lacks the concept of [Kantian] morality altogether, in the sense of *a class of reasons or demands which are vitally different from other kinds of reason or demand*. . . . Relatedly . . . the questions of how one's relations to others are to be regulated, both in the context of society and more privately, are not detached [in antiquity] from questions about the kind of life it is worth living.[51]

The punch packed in Williams' passage cannot but strike readers forcibly, if they have been schooled in convention. That indigenous empirical thinking might be able to teach something valuable to moderns priding themselves on technologically more sophisticated communities is almost as unthinkable as the notion that the "West" (i.e., modern Europe and North America) has no monopoly on ideas and practices that conduce to good governing.[52] To the co-authors' ears, the prized language of "universality" is just a dialect spoken by a diminishing few.[53] Accordingly, this book has been written with

---

[49] This was stated in the Corfu Channel case (U.K. v. Alb.) in 1949, the first case to be adjudicated under the Court. This undermined the so-called "reason of state" legal arguments.
[50] Hölscher and Frantzeskaki 2019, an important work on transformative climate-related practices, mentions China once and India once.
[51] Williams 1993, 20, 251. I have substituted "the Ancients" for Williams' original "the Greeks [in antiquity]." As Williams continues, it becomes clear that his target is the Kantian and neo-Kantian divide between morality and pragmatism that he deplores.
[52] See Lewis and Wigen 1997.
[53] I borrow a common assertion made in sociolinguistics.

the *theft (and gift!) of history* in mind, at a time when we seem to be reverting back to the shortsighted Cold War dichotomies.[54]

With so much work to be done, let us see what we can do. And in the struggle, let us be mindful of the rays of hope that we see. For me, these include, a "New Study Re-evaluates Worst Case Scenario for Antarctica's Thwaites Glacier,"[55] and "A Struggling Iowa Farmer Trades His Hogs for Mushrooms."[56] Yes, Antarctica's glaciers are melting, but perhaps not as fast as some had predicted, and not all farmers are resistant to change. Perhaps even fungi will help capture carbon ("A Quest to Clean the Climate by Using Dirt to Capture Carbon," about an experiment in Forbes, Australia).[57] And, in a long-overdue step, under Biden the US Bureau of Land Management agreed that the nation's largest manager of public lands (with some 245 million acres under its control) would begin leasing land to conservation and other public-interest groups to carry out habitat restoration work.[58] Note the "Bridge Meadows" intergenerational set-up in PBS (September 16, 2024), and California Governor Newsom's belated (if fabulous) decision to ban all plastic grocery bags in the state (September 24, 2024), coming right on the heels of the state's decision to back an electric revolution in California, which could mean the beginning of the end for polluting and dangerous diesel trucks, which annually add the equivalent of 103 coal plants in emissions.[59] And the UN is

---

[54] Cf. Goody 2006, passim. On "mentalities," Lloyd 1990 offers insights about the social contexts of communication.
[55] *The New York Times*, Aug. 21, 2024, A10 (byline Raymond Zhong).
[56] *The New York Times*, Aug. 15, 2024, A11 (byline Cara Buckley); cf. *The New York Times*, Sept. 16, 2024.
[57] *The New York Times*, Aug. 14, 2024, A4 (byline Somini Sengupta); cf. *The New York Times*, Opinion, Sept. 16, 2024 (by-line Shawn Regan).
[58] Trump has been too busy putting US citizens and green card holders in a Salvadoran jail to overturn that ruling as of this writing; much may happen before this book goes to press.
[59] For details, see note 22 above. Three new pieces of legislation also give hope: On May 21, 2024, the International Tribunal for the Law of the Sea affirmed that greenhouse gas emissions pollute the marine environment, and ruled that both public actors and private companies can now be sued. On July 4, 2025, the Inter-American Court of Human Rights

negotiating a plastics-ban, according to the BBC.⁶⁰ This past summer, for the first summer in *years*, I saw fireflies in Princeton, New Jersey. It's as if, as Margaret Renki put it, "In a Brutal Summer, Miracles Still Bloom."⁶¹ And all this time, "tiny prairies" (strips planted with native flowering plants and grasses) have been rewilding the American Midwest, reintroducing it to microbe-rich soil and offsetting some of the hazards of aging agribusinesses.⁶² All this may be dismissed as mere band-aid measures, as some argue. Acknowledging this sentiment while fighting the defeatism that it embodies, the following chapters move from the surface into deeper layers and textures of societies, early and late, in order to appraise opportunities for substantive structural change. Those opportunities exist, but only if we move together.

---

declared that the climate crisis is a human rights emergency that triggers human rights obligations for nations and businesses, most especially in the fossil fuel industry. And on July 23, 2025, the International Court of Justice ruled that states and corporations may be held liable for policies that contradict climate science.

⁶⁰ BBC (America), on PBS, Sept. 5, 2024.
⁶¹ *The New York Times*, Sept. 2, 2024, A18.
⁶² *The New York Times*, Oct. 7, 2024, A10 (by-line Cara Buckley). Further good news: Australia decided to protect 52 percent of its territorial waters; see https://www.goodnewsnetwork.org/huge-environmental-win-australia-to-protect-52-of-its-oceans-more-than-any-other-country/?link_id=31&can_id=9e4bef2acfb380819208b57fce1cc45e&source. And, more than twenty museums, including the Getty and the Hammer Museum in Los Angeles, are participating in a project called "Art and Science Collide," which is about the climate crisis, as reported in the PBS "News Hour" for Oct. 10, 2024.

1

The Recalcitrance of Anglo-American Law

It is disgraceful to be unable to use our good things.
—Aristotle, *Politics*

Without delving into too many technicalities or tossing off too many acronyms, this chapter aims to review the multiple legal barriers that now impede serious action to minimize the effects of climate change.[1] Its central argument is this: nearly all of those legal barriers today can readily be traced back to a single pernicious and predominantly Anglo-American two-part legal fiction associated with John Locke (1632–1704), the English philosopher.[2] This fiction portrays actors on the world stage as essentially individual, rational, and autonomous human males, and then concludes that special weight should be given to the potential infringement of these actors' rights, rather than to the duties and obligations to which these same actors are bound concurrently in law. (The Supreme Court of the United States, and other judicial bodies gradually extended Locke's notion of individual actors to agents of any size and inherent complexity, including

---

[1] Some important information, including dates and acronyms, can be found in the Appendix on Chronology.
[2] Among Locke's political works, he is most famous for *The Second Treatise of Government*, in which he argues that sovereignty resides in the people and derives his notion of legitimate government from "natural rights" and the social contract (borrowed from Hobbes). See https://plato.stanford.edu/entries/locke/

multinational corporations.)[3] By Locke's vision, which saw both nature and humans as "physical objects of knowledge," the human body was converted into a unit of property and thus for him a unit of value, whose inherent integrity, by law, must not be violated. By Locke's *Second Treatise* a person's rights, as well as his labor and the products of his labor, were his property also: "Though the earth, and all inferior creatures, be common to all men, yet every man has a property in his own person: this no body has any right to but himself."[4] The expectation—reasonable enough in the seventeenth century—was that, with any damage to a person's bodily property, the perpetrator(s) in all likelihood would be immediately identifiable, since malefactors typically used such weapons as fists or knives or poisons to attack the intended victim.[5]

Locke's equation of the body with property fit well with the theories of monetary value advanced by Adam Smith, roughly a century later. For this principal reason, the levers of justice do not move in the right direction when it comes to environmental issues. As American historian Jill Lepore opines, "to be a human being held as property is to be a person without *any* rights."[6] Furthermore, contract theory in Locke (borrowing from Thomas Hobbes) is premised on four conditions: that the signatories to the contract always (a) are equal; (b) engage in informed consent; and (c) cooperate, because (d) the contract is deemed to benefit to both parties. In other words, traditional Anglo-American contract theory is single-generational; it was not designed for parties who are unequal in any way; and it construes breaches of contract largely as damage done by one or more of the signatories to another of the signatories, damage that is

---

[3] Both powers and privileges are attached to the sovereignty of the body, body politic, and para-body (corporate entity). See Grote Stoutenburg 2013.
[4] *Second Treatise*, section 27.
[5] See Sivin 1995, 6, for the "physical objects of knowledge."
[6] Lepore, cited in Greene 2021 (Foreword).

immediately palpable to the injured party. Needless to say, none of the presumptions a-d are true of most environmental harms.

In international law, history accounts for the dominance of this Lockean fiction today, well over three centuries after Locke.[7] In the late nineteenth century, Britain was undoubtedly the most powerful among the European colonizing powers. Then, in the wake of the First World War, the United States sought superpower status, on the grounds that "old Europe" had shown itself to be militarily weak and worse, intellectually and morally exhausted. By the end of the Second World War, the United States, which had escaped the devastation on its shores wrought by the war waged across Europe, Great Britain, and Asia, rose to become one of two main superpowers, the other being its former ally, the Soviet Union, which quickly positioned itself as the chief rival to the United States—a rival the US presidents were determined to thwart. Not coincidentally, in the postwar "West,"[8] the United States was the main impetus behind the development of the international criminal adjudication procedures, providing funding and expertise during the International Military Tribunals at Nürnberg (1945–46) and at Tokyo (1946–48), and later also in the prosecutions of war criminals from the former Yugoslavia (1993–2017) and Rwanda (1994–2015).[9] The American Relief Administration (1920–23), the Marshall Plan (1948–1949) and programs run by the Rockefeller Foundation (1913-present), were but three of the most prestigious avenues through which American ideas on international policies and practices flowed to areas well beyond the United States

---

[7] As Morgan Cloud put it, "We face different practical problems today, but concepts of liberty embedded in the phrase "persons, houses, papers, and effects" persist." See John Locke, "The Second Treatise of Government" (1690).
[8] For the shifting referents for this designation, see Lewis and Wigen 1997.
[9] Judges and prosecutors from the United States worked alongside their counterparts from other countries, and money from the United States helped to support many international organizations.

(in particular, Europe and China).¹⁰ Radio Free Europe (founded 1950), lavishly funded by the United States,¹¹ lent crucial support to the American endeavors.¹² De-colonizers were alarmed at the specific legal provisions in interstate and global affairs foisted on other peoples whose traditional worldviews did not match the Anglo-American "universal" legal vision, with its Lockean construction of mankind—note the intentional use here of the gendered noun—a legacy of the imperialist and Cold War eras.¹³ Yet, as Fredric Jameson said, "It is easier to imagine the end of the world than it is to imagine the end of capitalism."¹⁴

To understand the glacial pace at which climate change legal action has proceeded to date,¹⁵ one needs first to tackle such basic legal concepts as "governance," "sovereignty," and "standing." Yet no legal scholars, let alone academics working in their discrete disciplinary silos,

---

[10] The list of ways that the United States sought to influence world politics would include Radio Free Europe (founded in 1958), the Luce Foundation (founded in 1936), and many other units besides the CIA.

[11] In 2021, they reported a budget of 123 million dollars/per year. Radio Free Europe/Radio Liberty (RFE/RL) was funded by the American government as an international media organization that broadcasts news, information, and analysis to Eastern Europe, Central Asia, the Caucasus, and the Middle East. Nonetheless, RFE/RL was nominally a private 501(c)(3) corporation supervised by US Agency for Global Media, an independent government agency overseeing all international broadcasting services that received US-government support. For the agency's fate under Trump, see below.

[12] Note that Trump abolished Radio Free Europe and Radio Free Asia in one of his first acts as president (on March 15, 2025). That act is currently being challenged in the US courts, since it is Congress that set up these media.

[13] For example, the French, working in a different legal tradition, have been far readier at many points than the Americans to consider environmental harm within the definitions of harm-to-persons. Some Catholic thinkers (again, equipped with a different legal tradition) contributed to Liberation Theology (1950s-1960s) in Latin America and to the United Farm Workers' Movement of the 1960s in the United States, both of which fought Lockean notions, but these Latin American and American movements soon became targets of FBI and CIA reprisals, with both condemned as "socialist" and "Communist."

[14] Jameson 1994, xii. This quote is also attributed to Slavoj Žižek, who paraphrased Jameson, with whom he was in conversation. This quotation was then borrowed in Mark Fisher's *Capitalist Realism: Is There No Alternative?* (2009), 2, 13, 21.

[15] Solnit and Lutunatabua 2023 think it's important to focus on the accelerating pace of climate change action, lest we succumb to despair and are immobilized.

have been able to settle upon one concept of sovereignty,[16] let alone the far murkier (because more expansive) notion of governance. Attempts to define "sovereignty" and "governance" are of surprisingly recent origin, leaving the most fundamental issues to be worked-out, despite their earth-shattering dimensions,[17] in an era when time for action is running out. Furthermore, definitions of sovereignty and governance tend to be circular. As a result, at present, international law generally extrapolates the conditions of nation-state sovereignty from Lockean notions of personal "integrity" or "sovereignty."[18] Under the Vienna Convention (1969), the treaty on treaties that binds current

---

[16] In their influential *Sovereignty in Fragments*, editors Quentin Skinner and Hent Kalmo decided that sovereignty is and must be an early modern construction. The more revisionist Z. Ben-dor Benite et al. 2021 concurs. So, the term's recent origin is not under debate; just its definition. See Fowler and Bunck 1996, 4–8, for a sampling of definitions attached to the concept. While some prefer to trace this concept back to the Treaty of Westphalia in 1648, or to the "Social Contract" theory of Hobbes and Rousseau, it is more accurate, historically speaking, to trace it back to principles articulated by the colonial powers against the colonized, rather than to treaties forged by ostensibly equal countries or to the 1950s' pushback against the colonizers' claims during the process of de-colonization. Immanuel Kant is much to blame for the over-reaching quality of the concept in philosophy, which became dominant in American philosophical circles through the work of John Rawls, who imagined, despite all evidence to the contrary, that people could operate most fairly by imposing on themselves a "veil of ignorance" and thus attain perfect or near-perfect objectivity. The notion that objectivity is possible was thoroughly debunked by Hayden White (1928–2018), in his *Metahistory* (1973). The problem with Kantian analysis: "As soon as a person's ability to make self-determining choices is questioned, the person's dignity falls on shaky ground," as Ni Peimin 2014 notes.

[17] The case law for bilateral treaty infringements was established in 1917, with Trail Smelter (U.S. v. Canada), which concerned transboundary air pollution caused by a Canadian smelting plant whose toxic sulfur dioxide fumes created damage in the United States.

[18] International law mandates that a nation state be defined by four distinct and interlocking characteristics: (1) a clearly defined territory; (2) a permanent population; (3) a functioning government; and (4) independence of action. See Grote Stoutenburg 2013. While there are numerous examples of "failed states" that continue to be supported with the help of international law, cases are far more clear-cut when their sovereignty status is not at issue.

Recently, Marxine Burkett has suggested that international law should recognize "de-territorialized states" (aka "ex-situ governments") based on trustee status, but to date few international organizations have embraced that idea, which was generated with a view to the twenty-two island nations whose territories may soon be under water, despite recent UN backing. On Aug. 27, 2024, UN Secretary-General Antonio Guterres issued a global SOS (for "Save Our Seas") with a plea to the world to "massively increase finance and support for vulnerable countries" in grave danger from the human-caused climate crisis. "The ocean is overflowing," Guterres said, "and island nations are in grave danger of being submerged by rising sea levels."

international law in most instances, a nation-state is legally injured only if the breached obligation was owed to it *individually*.[19] Then, by law, the injury should occur in such a manner as to "*distinguish it from the generality of other States*" to which treaty obligations may be owed.[20] Obviously, contract law works best between two parties, and breaches of bilateral agreements are child's play to adjudicate when compared with breaches of multilateral agreements. Unsurprisingly, then, long-term environmental equity is hard to conceive within the framework of the two-party contract whenever largely invisible pollutants drift across national, state, and community boundaries. Note that, in consequence, in an unprecedented ruling preempting the normal judicial process, the Supreme Court of the United States in June 2024 blocked the Environmental Protection Agency's (EPA) Good Neighbor Plan designed to limit nitrogen oxide emissions from power plants and other industrial sources in twenty-three states, to prevent upwind polluting states from harming downwind states and their residents.[21] Less than two months later, a judge in the federal US District Court for the Western District of Louisiana ruled that the Biden-era EPA could not use civil rights law to prohibit states from locating polluting industries disproportionately in non-white neighborhoods.[22]

One group thinks to resolve the issue by inserting into international law a new type of state, an "environmental state," which by the group's definition exercises authority to "protect the environment" (air, water, land, species, ecosystems, landscapes, etc.) because "these are understood

---

[19] Italics mine. The Convention went through multiple drafts during the years from 1949 to 1969, when it was worked on by a group of distinguished jurists (all of them English or American). As of January 2018, 118 nation-states have ratified the Convention, meaning, they at least claim to abide by its provisions. James Brierly, Hersch Lauterpacht, Gerald Fitzmaurice, and Humphrey Waldock (all English) spoke of crimes against humanity.

[20] Articles 42, 48, principally.

[21] The ruling was issued on June 27, 2024. Also known as the Federal Implementation Plan (FIP). See https://supremecourt.gov>opinions.

[22] In April, for example, the Biden administration E.P.A. issued a brand-new rule requiring more than 200 chemical plants across the country to reduce the toxic pollutants they release into the air. See "Judge Blocks E.P.A.," *The New York Times*, Aug. 23, 2024.

as critical to individual and collective welfare, public health, economic activities, collective values and identity, and to the long-term good of the political community." But such a theoretical insertion only generates a new problem as new language necessarily entails a host of "changes to established property rights: for example, the conditions of land tenure or the rules under which businesses conduct their activities,"[23] all of which will be litigated. An additional complaint: the Anglo-American "world order" is the product of interstate interactions, and in turn is constructed to preserve the primacy of *states*—not civilizations, not empires, not commonwealths, and not tribes or clans."[24]

"Standing" is the third fundamental legal concept much debated in complex cases, particularly those involving several generations. By a 1992 decision by the Supreme Court of the United States, standing in a legal case may not be granted unless the party claiming an injury ("the plaintiff") has first demonstrated a sufficient connection to and harm from the law or action being challenged in the court—and that may take years or decades. Today, most courts use some minor variation on the Supreme Court's three-part test to determine whether a party has the requisite standing to sue the defendant:[25]

- *Injury in Fact*: The plaintiff must have suffered an "injury in fact," meaning that the injury is of a legally protected interest which is (a) concrete and particularized and (b) actual or imminent.
- *Causal Connection*: There must be a causal connection between the injury and the conduct brought before the court.
- *Redressability*: It must be likely, rather than speculative, that a favorable decision by the court will redress the injury.[26]

---

[23] Andreas Duit, et al. 2016, 11, citing Feindt 2013.
[24] Bajpai and Laksmana 2023, 1373.
[25] The Supreme Court of the United States formulated this three-part test in its decision on standing in *Lujan v. Defenders of Wildlife* (90–1424), 504 US 555 (June 12, 1992).
[26] This three-part test has unduly complicated the resolution of cases involving religious icons and ideals. See Mullick v. Mullick 1925, for example, or Hou v. Bd. of

If the plaintiff lacks standing, it is easy to throw out a case before it is even adjudicated. Unfortunately, the Supreme Court and the International Court of Justice enjoy considerable latitude in choosing the type of cases that will come before it on their dockets.[27] And one can readily see why these three tests which comport with Locke are poorly suited to environmental damage cases. First, the damage, while concrete, may not have been obvious to potential plaintiffs, their families, or their community until long periods of sustained exposure to environmental hazards have resulted in serious illnesses or deaths. Second, it is hard to establish a causal connection between an environmental exposure—potentially the "injurious conduct"—and the injury, if resources do not exist to elicit truthful evidence from a broad range of sources, as all too frequently happens when prior court cases based on scientific studies have been settled out of court for undisclosed sums in non-disclosure agreements.[28] The issue of redressability is no less fraught: is the primary duty of the judge and/or jury to forestall future harm or to compensate current victims?

Land & Natural Res. 2015, involving (and later revoking) a land-use permit to build an astronomical observatory on the summit of Mauna Kea and implicating the constitutionally guaranteed right of Native Hawaiians to exercise traditional customary practices. Stone 1972 was one of the first essays to argue "standing" for "natural objects" (non-human), such as trees. Miller 2017 writes, "In this modern imagination, the realms of the supernatural, the natural, and the human are fundamentally distinct from one another, and the three disciplines of religion, science, and philosophy focus on each of these three realms respectively" (12).

[27] In the interests of time, we co-authors do not explore a related complication: that protests, criticisms, or calls for other states to abide by an obligation cannot qualify as "invoking the responsibility of a state" when plaintiffs come before a Supreme Court or International Court of Justice. See ILC, for confirmation.

[28] Usually settlements out of court do not require an admission of guilt by the responsible party. One recent case demonstrates how easily evidence is squashed: Dominion Voting Systems Corporation's case against Newsmax (parent company of Fox News). Fox News agreed to pay Dominion $787.5 million and acknowledged the court's earlier ruling that Fox had broadcast false statements about Dominion. The settlement did not require Fox News to apologize, however, and striking the deal meant that key aspects of Dominion's defamation case were never publicly aired before the charges against Newsmax were dropped. Of course, there are other reasons why it has become so hard to ascertain the real costs and prices of exploiting certain valuable resources.

In uncharted territory like this, it should be obvious that seniors have a lifetime of experience from which to witness the injurious impacts of current and past practices and attitudes on their own health and that of their communities; also, that children, too, might have real complaints to lodge about the world that they are inheriting. Indeed, children often they have a greater awareness about climate change than do their parents, thanks to school programs and field trips, and some young people (Greta Thunberg and Ou Hongyi, among others) have advertised that the threat to their future well-being is truly existential.[29]

As if much of the foregoing were not discouraging enough, history has added yet another obstacle to justice. For once the chief activity of the modern nation-state came to be to legitimize the market and to make property rights the supreme consideration (during the Cold War, in the 1960s), it became dramatically harder to imagine that the exercise of authority by any governmental entity of any size might need, in today's world, other points of reference or sanctions.[30] Appeals to morality were widely held to be outdated and hopelessly partial, quite conveniently for big businesses. Equally, attempts to reference modern science or ethics, to diagnose problems and offer viable paths forward—attempts that made "ecological sense,"[31] in other words—

---

[29] Also romanized as Howey Ou 欧泓奕/欧泓奕. Little known outside the PRC, Ou is a celebrity inside the PRC. See her Wikipedia page: https://en.wikipedia.org/wiki/Howey_Ou

[30] The neoliberals often invoke Adam Smith, but their guiding "principles" are actually in defiance of that wary philosopher's precepts. Still, as one commentator observes, "the substantial divisions and tensions of capitalist society render the notion of a 'common good' for all individuals, groups, and classes elusive"; see Schumpeter 1950, 256; see Schnaiberg et al. 2002. Nussbaum 2017, 2024, offer a corrective. As early as the early 1970s, the OECD (Office of Economic Co-operation and Development), with 38 member countries worried mightily that environmental regulation could act as a restraint on trade, so it actively promoted "regulatory harmonization," to level the playing field for developed and developing countries, putting the latter at a disadvantage, many would argue.

[31] Some speak of "ecological rationality" (i.e., calculating the personal and societal value of ecosystems and their protections), but as "rationality" has so often been hijacked by those who would advance a short-term cost-benefit analysis, we prefer "ecological sense."

ran directly counter to neoliberal claims touting the deregulated market, whose infinite "wisdom" was now taken for granted by a surprising slice of the public. The rights of corporations to attend solely to their stockholders' profits gradually became enshrined in many peoples' *habitus*. At least that yielded a "clear" standard, whereas wading into an emerging environmental science did not seem to, due to the fabricated misinformation published by pseudo-scientific experts for hire.[32] In this context, egregious abuses of the environment were often celebrated as management "advances"[33] and costly environmental clean-ups were deemed "economic activities" contributing to higher GDPs.

Meanwhile, the current patchwork of human rights protections has centered around three basic obligations: (1) to respect the integrity of other nations and their people's human rights; (2) to protect nations and people from violations of human rights that might be perpetrated by outside ("third") parties; and (3) to act to fulfill human rights and their enjoyment, without interference, in other countries.[34] Theoretical agreement on these obligations can in no way obviate the messiness of implementing the theory, because the "development of natural resources finally is a political and not a legal

---

[32] Oreskes and Conway 2012. The inability of Neil Gorsuch, the US Supreme Court Justice, to distinguish laughing gas (nitrous oxide) from the air pollutant nitrogen oxide illustrates how poorly many "well-educated" judges understand the science. See *Forbes*, June 28, 2024 (byline Allison Durkee), reporting on Ohio v. Environmental Protection Agency.

Three movies that illuminate the problem are: "Erin Brockovich" (2000), unfolds the narrative of a determined single mother (Julia Roberts) challenging a power company accused of contaminating a city's water supply, revealing the profound impact of pollution on communities; "Blade Runner 2049"(2017), the sequel to the classic "Blade Runner" (1972), immerses viewers in a planet grappling with extreme climate change and turmoil; and "Dark Waters" (2019) follows the story of a corporate defense attorney facing an environmental lawsuit against a chemical company. Big polluters have imitated Big Tobacco, whose corruption and coercion Russell Crowe's character in "The Insider" (1999) experiences.

[33] For one good example, see *The New York Times*, Sept. 15/17, 2023, A1 (by-line Claire Cameron).

[34] See McInerney-Lankford 2013.

problem."[35] Moreover, the vague injunction to "do no harm" may be construed quite narrowly as "do nothing that will inflict immediate, visible, and irremediable harm" or, more broadly, as "do nothing that will predictably inflict harm over time." How narrowly to construe a court decision is always open for debate.[36] Up to now, legal precedents have generally favored the former construal, perhaps because it tallies nicely with the idea of sudden bodily harm inflicted by violent persons envisioned in Locke's early modern world. Common law nuisance liability, which holds defendants liable only for "unreasonable interference" with enjoyment of the land, only further hamstrings the equitable administration of the law. As no one has ever decided how to define rationality, a concept that remains firmly in the eyes of the beholder,[37] different people, states, corporations, and transnational organizations cannot agree upon basic standards for what constitutes "unreasonable" acts by one party, especially when corporate profits are involved. Put another way, this necessity to determine what constitutes "unreasonable" interference weakens other important principles of law, insofar as it deems some intrusions "reasonable," and therefore perfectly legal, especially if such intrusions are profitable, while leaving open the question of what constitutes "significant" harm to parties under the law.

Only very recently have certain legal scholars begun to argue that environmental protection is *erga omnes* (here, "the concern of all"), and thus *may* supersede other sovereign rights, most importantly, the rights of sovereign nations and corporations to exploit their own

---

[35] Perrez 1996, 1192.
[36] Let us take Citizen's United as a case in point. What could have been interpreted as a narrow finding soon became a guarantee for all corporations that they could enjoy legal immunity for many of their actions.
[37] For the first salvos against rationality, see the so-called "Oxford" philosophers (Iris Murdoch, Elizabeth Anscombe, Philippa Foot, and Mary Midgley), as analyzed in Lipscomb 2021; Mac Cumhaill and Wiseman 2022. Rosemont's *Against Individualism* (2016) and Fingarette's *Self-deception* (1969/2000) were two other important contributions to the philosophical literature on rationality, as commonly (mis)understood.

resources, as they see fit, within their own boundaries, regardless of the harm done to the local or global environment.[38] How resistant courts are to recognizing that environmental protection may supersede other rights is suggested by this timeline: the 2010 *Pulp Mills* case decided that "it may now be considered a requirement under general international law to undertake an environmental impact assessment where there is a risk that the proposed industrial activity may have a significant adverse impact in a transboundary context, in particular, on a shared resource." However, it was only in 2024 that the high court in Great Britain agreed that this was so, when it came to calculating the environmental impact of new exploration and exploitation of the North Sea oil deposits.[39]

For the foregoing reasons, we concur with the philosopher Mary Midgley's argument: that while this specific Lockean construction of human beings may have been exceedingly helpful in an earlier era when the prime concern of the bourgeoisie was to present legal challenges to the autocratic monarchs of the early modern period, this particular legal construction has long outlived its utility to humankind, and indeed now threatens humans' very survival.[40] Meanwhile, international norms for illegality are, by careful design, "fundamentally unenforceable,"[41] for at least one simple reason, besides the default protections for the status quo: demanding long-term protection and respect for actors in communities or societies or leagues has been far more difficult to *specify* in law than envisioning the violation of individual bodies and the larger entities modeled

---

[38] Brown Weiss 2020, passim.
[39] For the court case decision announced on June 20, 2024, see https://www.euronews.com/business/2024/06/21/future-of-north-sea-oil-drilling-in-doubt-after-supreme-court-ruling. Predictably, in rapid response, on Sept. 5, 2024, Shell and Equinor announced that they will defend the Jackdaw and Rosebank plans after Labour withdrew its government support for additional drilling.
[40] Midgley 2011.
[41] Wannier and Gerrard 2013, 638.

legally on those bodies, even when "increased risk can be foreseen."[42] Some "respectable" academics argue against the formulations of any new rules, protocols, conventions, or laws, on the specious grounds that such rules, protocols, conventions, and laws cannot possibly address the full range of issues that would need to be addressed in an ideal world.[43] That no law ever passed has addressed the *full range* of issues to which it conceivably applies, and all laws require interpretation and elaboration over time, seems to have escaped the notice of these adept contortionists.

As current trade agreements and interstate treaties and protocols, as well as international and national laws, do not question the long-standing inequalities of the status quo, they virtually ensure the rights of privileged people, nation-states, and corporate entities to act independently and with impunity, as autonomous and rational agents[44]—even when their actions defy the spirit of many legal norms. And, through the steady build-up of case law precedents, they concomitantly diminish the legally defensible grounds for upholding such basic personal human rights as the right to clean air and clean water, rights supposedly already "guaranteed" under the "Universal Declaration of Human Rights" (1948) and reaffirmed and clarified under the UN Guiding Principles on Business and Human Rights (2011/2012).[45] Therefore, during the four stages under UN "guidance"

---

[42] Biermann and Boas 2007 (Plan 25).
[43] Jane McAdam is among the most prominent of these academics arguing against the formulation of new provisions to protect vulnerable populations and regions. That protracted and inconclusive negotiations may "serve as an excuse for [further] inaction and distract from current needs" is an argument made by Klein, Solomon, & Warner 2013.
[44] "Independently," means here, "without considering the rights of others, whether those rights are personal, national, federal, or global."
[45] Bridle 2022, 8–9, notes that "growth and profitability" as the single corporate goal has led to a situation where corporations (now conceived on the model of individual human beings) have rights to exploit so extreme that they appear to be alien invaders in many landscapes. While many states have seen fit to embrace the Uniform Commercial Code,

since 1945,[46] strong nations have acted with impunity with respect to international law, in defiance of the international courts of justice. Two prime examples concern the United States and China: In 1998, the United States refused to ratify the establishment of the International Court of Justice, reasoning that certain provisions of international law were in conflict with provisions of the US Constitution, which meant that the United States could not be bound by the Court's decisions.[47] And on July 12, 2016, the Arbitral Tribunal, convened under the 1982 UN Convention of Law of the Sea to consider the case of Philippines v. China (aka the South China Sea Arbitration), ruled against the People's Republic China, citing its persistent incursions into Philippines' territorial waters. As it happens, both the Philippines and China had ratified the convention, in 1984 and 1996 respectively, but to date China has ignored the ruling, claiming an "optional" exemption (in other words, "try and make us!").[48]

and lots of states have enacted codes in whole or in part in various domains, in the main laws at the state level remain simply a loose collection of statutes that don't form an internally, intentionally coherent whole.

[46] Those four stages are said to be (1) pre-1945, and the founding of the United Nations; (2) 19,45–1962, with the period ending with the Stockholm Declaration, which provided for the creation of international organizations with competence in environmental matters and the adoption of legal instruments (albeit limited ones) to address environmental problems; (3) 1972–1992 Rio Conference on Environment and Development; and (4) post-Rio, a period in which the relevant environmental bodes have sought to integrate environmental concerns into all international activities.

[47] Amann 2002. Also, the United States was officially miffed that a writ against Henry Kissinger as "war criminal" had been issued by the EU authorities. Agents of the United States of America spirited Kissinger out of his Paris hotel when he was about to be served a summons to answer "war criminal" charges before the ICC, following Pinochet's arrest. This was widely reported in the European press (e.g., *Le Monde*), but not in the United States. For details, see Hitchens 2001.

[48] For the ruling, see https://en.wikipedia.org/wiki/Philippines_v._China. In an interesting twist, Taiwan has also rejected the Tribunal ruling. Eight nation-states have called on China to respect the Tribunal's decision, in vain. Sadly, Article 298 of Section 3 in Part XV of the Convention provides "optional" exceptions to the applicability of compulsory procedures provided in Section 2. China made a declaration in 2006 that it would not accept any of the procedures provided for in Section 2 of Part XV of the convention. Many countries including the United Kingdom, Australia, Italy, France, Canada, and Spain had already made similar declarations. Bajpai and Laksmana 2023 are inaccurate when they claim, "All Asian states, including China, understand that some states are

Frighteningly, the one aspect of Anglo-American common law traditions to which some parties looked for occasional relief—the doctrine of precedents (or *stare decisis*),[49] suggesting that most if not all judicial decisions are as much about the future as they are about the past[50]— is itself increasingly in doubt in both the higher and lower courts, just at the point when twenty-first century nation-states seem simultaneously to be fragmenting and hardening their internal and external boundaries, in response to thousands of explicitly transnational, international, and nongovernmental groups (licit and not) that have forged supranational loyalties.[51]

Some optimists nonetheless believe that neoliberal Anglo-American legal norms may be on the cusp of a revolution if a series of lawsuits is allowed to proceed and the ensuing legal judgments survive further reviews.[52] One case that has inspired local environmentalists with hope is Held v. Montana, filed in 2020 and tried in June 2023, where

---

more powerful than others, . . . [but] as most Asian states suffered under colonialism, it is not surprising that they do not hanker for hierarchy."

[49] In all legal systems where custom, predictability, stability, and coherence are valued—in the common law system especially—the doctrine of precedent (*stare decisis*) has been controlling. But things are changing.

[50] Weston 2008.

[51] The Yearbook of International Organizations reports in 2000 that there were 922 international intergovernmental organizations and 9,988 international nongovernmental organizations; this is surely an undercount, as it tallies only legally registered organizations. Nearly 30,000 organizations participated in bilateral or multilateral agreements, according to Weiss 2002, 798. The fragmentation of and challenges to state orders is undeniable. Therefore, we find Duit, et al. 2016 almost pleading others to restore the "rationale for the state as an analytical perspective in environmental policy and politics," against "the declining relevance of the state, not just as an international actor, but also as an organization that wields political authority within its own borders and acts as a meaningful social force" (2). That essay tries to argue the enduring relevance of the state in light of concerns . . . "not being addressed adequately by markets, voluntary action, or local government" (9).

[52] One might also mention these extra-environmental causes of hope that take the form of punishing egregious miscarriages of justice ("crimes against humanity"), despite claims of national sovereignty. On Oct. 16, 1998, Pinochet was arrested while in London at the request of a Spanish judge, Dr. Baltasar Garzon, who sought his extradition to Spain to face charges of genocide, terrorism, and torture. Pinochet was subsequently tried and found guilty. On the other hand, Kissinger was never tried for his war crimes, despite being served a writ in Paris.

the youngest plaintiff was but two years old, and whose final outcome remains still unresolved at the time of writing, since the preliminary judgment rendered on August 23, 2023 in favor of the plaintiffs is now being challenged in a higher court by the state's fossil-fuel-loving administration.[53] According to the complaint in Held v. Montana, Montana's extensive support for fossil fuel industries has been, in effect, creating pollution that is depriving the plaintiffs and future generations equal access to healthy lives and sustainable livelihoods. (Montana is one of the nation's largest coal-producing states.) Note that this was hardly the first lawsuit to be filed on behalf of climate change, but it is the first to grant the plaintiffs legal "standing" in an American state, in large part due to the specific language enshrined in a 1972 provision in the Montana state Constitution that explicitly guarantees "the right to a clean and healthful environment," and equally charges both the state itself and the individuals representing the state with the responsibility to maintain and improve the environment "for present and future generations."[54]

The sixteen plaintiffs in the lawsuit—most of them too young to vote and certainly not yet strongly affiliated with a single political party—were young Montana residents who had witnessed the environmental destruction that reckless acts by the Montana Legislature were wreaking on their communities and, most importantly, on their own families' landholdings.[55] Predictably, the state countered by speaking in vague terms of the economic benefits that corporate "innovation

---

[53] To clarify: two years old at the time the brief was first filed.
[54] "There have been almost no trials on climate change," said Michael Gerrard, director of the Sabin Center for Climate Change Law at Columbia Law School, in *The New York Times* essay dated March 20, 2023, A1.
[55] The right to a "clean and healthful environment in Montana for present and future generations" is guaranteed by Art. IX, § 1, in the Constitution of Montana (1972). The defendants, initially denied standing, were heard for the first time on June 12, 2023, in the first Judicial District Court in Helena, Montana, with First District Judge Kathy Seeley presiding. The sixteen young defendants were advised by lawyers hired by Our Children's Trust, a nonprofit organization. The state of Montana is fighting Seeley's decision in the higher courts.

and ingenuity" brings Montana residents, now and in the future. By the state's claim, these benefits satisfy the duty, under the state's Constitution to continue business-as-usual. In addition, the state tried to play up the enormous cost to current Montana residents that would be involved in implementing environmental regulations.[56] In her ruling against Montana, Judge Seeley remained unconvinced, mainly because the state's presentation ignored the enormous costs that the present laissez-faire practices entail for future generations. (Recently, upwards of one trillion dollars is the estimated annual cost of FEMA [federal emergency assistance] programs to disaster areas in the United States.)[57] Closely watched by environmentalists and their opponents, this lawsuit, more than a decade in the making, provides a suitable model for the other forty-nine states in the Union,[58] as well as federal court.

Why did it take so long for this case to come to trial? As yet, children have no generalized legal *rights* to a future environment of a specified quality, and the older generation has no legal *obligation* to help them,

---

[56] A change to the state's energy policy in 2011 effectively barred the state's administrators from considering climate change when reviewing applications for new permits for fossil fuel projects. Earlier, in 2023, in a thinly veiled attempt to prevent a trial, the state lawmakers repealed the state's own energy policy, but in May, the presiding judge, Kathy Seeley, ruled that the trial could nonetheless proceed. An effort by the state's lead attorney to delay the trial on other grounds also failed.

[57] In January 2023, Daniel Kaniewski, for the National Institute of Building Sciences, estimated that FEMA would pay out one trillion dollars in federal disaster aid to climate-change victims (https://www.nibs.org/blog/disaster-resilience-trillion-dollar-challenge-heres-what-fema-can-do-help). Public Television (PBS) in the United States confirmed those figures for the 123 storms in 2023–2024, as Hurricane Helene swept through the southeast coastal regions. The second Trump administration has instructed the states to absorb those costs, which they cannot do.

Meanwhile, internationally, the ICC said that already an estimated 2 trillion dollars had been paid out for past events in the last decade and the costs are rising. See https://iccwbo.org/news-publications/policies-reports/new-report-extreme-weather-events-cost-economy-2-trillion-over-the-last-decade/. Add to that the cost of inaction on health issues: In the United States alone, the health costs of air pollution and climate change far exceed USD 800 billion/ per year (NRDC, 2021). See Alberti 2024.

[58] At the time of writing, similar lawsuits are before the state courts in four additional states (Florida, Hawaii, Utah, and Virginia). In federal court, the first case in which plaintiffs were granted standing is Juliana v. U.S.

by Anglo-American legal traditions.[59] Up to now, American law does not compel action to assist another, even if some special relationships (such as caregiver/care receiver or parent/child) are thought by most to create some ill-defined sort of legal obligation. With this trial, we have witnessed an interesting phenomenon: most typically, when global entities and states review their regulations concerning environmental law, they do so because of strong pressure from groups arguing for families, for children, and for intergenerational equity. Within entire populations who are at risk, children and the elderly are often singled out as particularly "worthy of care" in public pronouncements by civilized nations, despite the fact that they are not typically high wage-earners. Something interesting may be going on (see below).

A Brief History of Revisionist Environmental Law

Behind such lawsuits today lies hard thinking that has been decades, if not centuries, in the making. While it would be impossible in a short book to detail all efforts made to develop a positive interventionist legal role on behalf of the environment, the names of two legal scholars stand out in shaping legal thinking among environmentalists: that of Edith Brown Weiss (whose work has been translated into Chinese) and Burns H. Weston (whose work has not).[60] The legal arguments advanced by these two thinkers will be treated as one, since Weston saw his main task as advancing those of Brown. Together, the two

---

[59] E.g., Weston 2008, 377.
[60] Weston died in 2015; Brown Weiss is still alive and publishing at the time of writing. Robert Solow, an economist, is also an important contributor to debates on intergenerational equity. For Solow, sustainability requires future generations to have the means to be as well off as their predecessors. He therefore proposes a modification of Gross Domestic Product (GDP), whereby the value of expended non-renewable resources, such as clean air and water, would be subtracted from fixed capital assets and products figured in GDP.

legal scholars have premised their arguments, quite unexceptionally, on the standard view that all complex civilizations are predicated on a social contract (implicit or explicit), wherein duties are balanced with rights or privileges in the name of "justice."[61] Where they have parted company with many legal experts is the conclusion they have drawn based on the preceding: that it is only logical to demand that the current generation has a duty to bequeath to future generations a livable environment, since the entire human family in the aggregate (including future generations), constitutes, as it were, the lessor of the global commons that is owned by no one but belongs to everyone.[62] Brown Weiss's *In Fairness to Future Generations* (1988) was among the first major pieces of legal scholarship to argue that we, the human species, hold the planet's environmental health in common with all members of the planet, past, present, and future. There Brown Weiss sought to remind us of two interdependent relations that are not grounded in Anglo-American law: humans' intergenerational dependencies and humans' complete dependence on the health of the biosphere, in which they constitute but a small, if incredibly destructive part.[63] Importantly, Brown insisted that each generation is equally trustee and beneficiary, steward and tenant, in an ongoing multigenerational process.[64] As she observed, were we to establish a realistic theory and implementing strategy predicated on the identification of present generations as "lessees of Planet Earth" legally accountable to the entire human family (including future generations), which would be appropriately recast as the "lessor of

---

[61] Often, Chinese scholars say that there is no word for justice in classical Chinese, and so no notion thereof. In fact, there are many words for justice, depending upon context, and all conduce to the same end of binding the living to the dead and to future generations.

[62] Weston 2008, 378. Cf. Brown 1988, 200. "Free will" and "agency" are thrilling concepts, but what do these even mean when to live one's life entails so many interdependencies?

[63] The environment, responding to human actions, appears by turns to be toxic and benign. See Brown 1990, esp. 199.

[64] Brown 1998, 200.

the global commons" (i.e., what belongs to everyone), we might just manage on behalf of Earth "to ensure its continued vitality, diversity, and sustainability for eons to come."[65]

In multiple publications, Brown Weiss has proposed three basic intertwined principles to guide environmental policies, each foregrounding "conservation": (1) the conservation of **options**, that is, to conserve on behalf of future generations equal options, when it comes to all forms of non-renewable capital (natural, man-made, financial, social, cultural, and human) in their manifest diversity;[66] (2) relatedly, the conservation of **quality**, meaning that no irreparable harm to the quality of the environment would be permitted, ideally; and (3) the conservation of **access**, ensuring that all people within a given community have roughly equal access to the goods associated with the local environment, with the ultimate aim of sustaining or improving that environment.[67] With access, Brown Weiss evokes two legal principles simultaneously: equal treatment under the law (meaning, that the law shouldn't discriminate between different people, due to their genders, races, ethnic origins, economic statuses, or other factors, including time) and equal access to the law (meaning, that every person should be able to appear in court as plaintiff to argue on behalf of their own interests). And whenever one speaks of "conserving options," one must be especially careful to conserve resources for which there is, apparently, no known substitute, as is true, for example, with helium, rare earth metals, and most aquifers and seabeds.

---

[65] Weston 2008, 378.
[66] "Natural capital" refers to natural resources; "manmade" capital, to material products and sociopolitical institutions; "social" capital, to solidarity within groups (i.e., communities); and human capital, primarily to people's level of education, health, skills, and knowledge. Some of this language follows that of Edith Brown Weiss, who speaks of conservation in numerous publications, including Brown Weiss 2002.
[67] Weiss 1990, 202.

As Brown cheerfully admits, adherence to her three principles in combination cannot but constrain present generations. At the same time, she was careful to note that they do not dictate the specific *forms* those constraints might take within individual cultures and communities. In the best of all possible worlds, pluralism in values could be preserved and local knowledge accommodated as a result. For instance, one generation living in community might choose to meet its obligations to curtail their present exploitation of the environment by vigorously cutting down on consumption, or by limiting population growth, insofar as pursuit of either or both of these approaches would likely conduce to a healthier environment, even if the pursuit of more than one approach would be optimal. (As we will see in Part II, the early empires in China used a multipronged approach.)

Planetary rights and duties would then be construed on an analogy with group rights (e.g., those of the federally recognized Native American sovereign nations), as opposed to individual rights.[68] As is well documented, poverty and neglect of the poor have long been considered the most pressing causes and most plausible justifications for environmental degradation. Arguably, today, however, the expansive rights claimed by nations and corporations on behalf of their citizens and stockholders, as justified by neoliberal doctrines supposedly rooted in Anglo-American traditions, pose bigger threats to the environment, insofar as they represent, essentially, rights without corresponding duties. For instance, Brazil under the Bolsonaro regime (2019–2022), claimed the absolute right to destroy the Amazonian rainforest (and the indigenous communities who resided therein), on the grounds of national sovereignty, despite the undeniable threat such destruction represented for the entire

---

[68] The concept of group rights is hardly new; Islamic law, for example, recognizes them, in addition to individual rights, when it discusses the "community of believers as a whole."

planet, not to mention the minority groups living at the margin of subsistence in those rainforests. Similarly, modern-day corporations have been empowered, legally and practically, to displace whole populations or to ruin their livelihoods and well-being, not just to coopt them temporarily in their profitmaking schemes, in the name of stockholders' "rights" to maximize profits.[69] In my own state of Kentucky (not to mention nearby West Virginia), strip mines were routinely praised for generating "jobs." In the past few years, however, because the mining companies no longer find the mines to be profitable, these same companies move their resources out of the town, without cleaning up the work sites.[70] By such means, potable water and unpolluted air become scarce commodities for poorer communities reduced to making environmental exploitation a short-term survival strategy, with many of them schooled to regard "the right-to-work laws" as "free" expressions of their sovereign rights to agency, instead of slogans cunningly designed to infringe upon their human right to have unpolluted air and soil.

Obviously enough, to implement strategies to ameliorate global warming, we must hold present generations on planet Earth legally and administratively accountable to the entire human family, including future generations.[71] Still, it is undeniably tough to accept that present generations and wealthier nations will have to pay more for earlier abuses, and downright antithetical to Anglo-American conservative strains of legal thinking and legal practice.[72] That explains

---

[69] Stockholders, needless to say, have no such legal rights, as when they buy stocks they buy risk. Nonetheless, this claim has been pervasive since Morton Friedman and Gordon Gekko.

[70] From the climate perspective, that Mitch McConnell in Kentucky and Joe Manchin in West Virginia, as two ardent defenders of the mining companies who have made millions off of poor people, continue to be seen as "reasonable" guardians of Republican economic rights is outrageous. On their way out, both still hold too much power over their constituents and their parties.

[71] Weston 2008, 378.

[72] In defense of more complex views, one might cite the views of Adam Smith and Edmund Burke, as summarized in the *Stanford Encyclopedia of Philosophy* (online).

why "conflict over distributive acts" characterizes the politics of climate change, and "collective action" has been the exception, rather than the rule.[73] Even so, common but differentiated responsibilities (CDR) must become the reality in which the world's nations, some 190 in number, operate, and this imperative is all the more obvious with environmental harms, whose cumulative impact recognizes no national or state boundary lines.[74] Logically speaking, those who have inflicted the worst harm to the planet must pay proportionately more, especially when, as it happens, their GDP is appreciably higher than those of the developing countries. At the same time, one cannot allow states such as China, the second largest economy in the world today, to exempt themselves from any responsibility to help clean up the environment, simply because the PRC unilaterally announces that it will "always" be developing, rather than developed, and thus is exempt from sensible rules.[75] ("Developing" status confers upon states the right to do relatively little to ameliorate transnational problems; worse, "developing nations" may apply to multiple international organizations for special work-arounds and dedicated funds.)

Burke celebrated careful stewardship of the family property, and, "as the ends of such a partnership cannot be obtained in many generations, it becomes a partnership not only between those who are living but between those who are living, those who are dead, and those who are to be born." Smith assumes the state would regulate trade and production.

[73] See Aklin and Mildenberger 2020.

[74] Brown Weiss 2002. CDR (nonbinding but already influential in trade law) reflects the "common partnership among states in pursuing agreed norms" [i.e., goals], "the differences among states in their ability to implement them," and "the historical differences in states' contributions to specific problems." Jeffrey Rothenberg has suggested a theory of intergenerational equity based on the present generation's acknowledgments and gratitude for what it has received, such that countries with fewer resources have lighter obligations. See Weiss 368n7. The status of India and China is fraught, as both countries present themselves, by turns, as developed superpowers and as historically disadvantaged developing nations. Meanwhile both countries are major contributors to environmental destruction.

[75] See *The Global Times* (Sept. 15, 2023). This claim was lodged by Li Xi, as "special representative" of Xi Jinping at a recent meeting of the Global South countries. Li Xi also claimed for China, no less improbably, a "Global South" country status. Both claims built upon claims registered at the BRICS Summit in Johannesburg, South Africa, earlier in the year.

What is to be done, then, when every nation-state today contains a multitude of people—anarchists, libertarians, neoliberals, Social Darwinists, "patriots"—who feel no obligation to anything but their own perceived well-being, sanctioned as they are by Anglo-American rhetoric of such long-standing?[76]

The bottom line: one cannot expect people to live in dignity if the conditions for a dignified existence no longer exist. To ignore this basic principle is shortsighted at best and murderous at worst,[77] for we humans have but three options before us: to act now, to remediate later, or to do nothing and die. One need not require whole populations to embrace altruism to lodge better arguments for action now. At no time in modern history has it not been true that the central function of leaders and leading institutions, *in theory*, is to *plan for the future*, not cower and wait for the polls and pols.[78] It is hardly radical, then, to contend that "the central function of the principle of sustainable development is to guide intergenerational allocation."[79]

---

[76] One has come to fear most acutely the dramatic rise of libertarians and a certain brand of Christian evangelicals looking to hasten the Second Coming. Social Darwinism ("survival of the fittest") has provided a strong justification for capitalism that supplies, sometimes in disguise, the ideological underpinnings for the neoliberal global order and the far-right political parties down to today.

[77] The philosopher Whitehead 1933, no. 34, held that failures to comprehend human society as a web of interdependent relations with the past, present, and future is "without any validity for modern civilization."

[78] Prior to the early modern period, past, present, and future were deemed to be essentially the same. Note that Americans are well aware of how cowardly their representatives are. If they needed reminding, Senator Lisa Murkowski of Alaska has reminded them; see https://www.youtube.com/watch?v=lvheGKFIHYQ;watch?v=KNil8fbEme8.

[79] Revesz, 1009. These are the futurists, many of whom welcome AI taking over. See Kirsch 2023, arguing this type of thinking is driven by two antithetical ways of thought, the first being "Anthropocene anti-humanism, inspired by revulsion at humanity's destruction of the natural environment" and a rejection of humanity's insistence on dominating the scene; and secondly, "transhumanism," which glorifies nearly all the things the first group movement rejects (e.g., scientific and technological progress, the supremacy of [male] reason.) Transhumanists fervently hope that genetic engineering and nanotechnology will allow humans (mainly male) to "transcend" such human limitations as mortality and confinement to a single physical body. A small subset imagines a cosmic data-processing system, something like God, which "will be everywhere and will control everything," according to Israeli futurist Yuval Noah Harari, in his book (2016) *Homo Deus*. Harari described "dataism" as a new form of religion that celebrates the growing importance of

Still, we would be foolhardy to discount the conceptual difficulties that beset long-term visions of a sustainable future even in the eyes of well-meaning people.[80] A broad consensus holds that all theories and practices must be grounded in a plausible notion(s) of "justice,"[81] but such terms as "justice" remain ill-defined and are subject to local interpretations, both genuine and disingenuous, as the early Greek playwrights told us millennia ago. Indeed, many current constructions of justice in developed and developing countries reduce "human life" to "earning power today." And even those experts who in theory support full, undiscounted compensation to address the latent consequences of past harms often see this principle quite differently, just as they usually disagree about how quickly entities by rights must move to stem irreparable environmental damage. Moreover, there is no settled consensus approving engagement in pre-emptive acts (including pre-emptive spending) as part of the solution to obviate or minimize the problems of compensating future generations,[82] even when science, journalistic reporting, and pop fiction alike reveal that the costs of later remediation are exponentially higher than the costs of present action to reduce or forestall harm, calling into serious question the routine methods of calculating costs vs. benefits.[83] (One

big data, believing that a greater reliance on science and technology can "save" us from the age-old human problems.

[80] By focusing on the well-meaning, we do not discount the dearth of wily manipulators on the scene. Barbara Ehrenreich's classic *Bright-Sided* (2009) alerted us to the huge investments US corporations designedly poured into the project of skewing our perceptions of "the good life." At the same time, inaction and bad actions cannot all be put down to free riders. See Aklin and Mildenberger 2020. "Unconditional non-cooperators," they argue, are relatively few, if hardly inconsequential (18).

[81] Weston 2008, 380.

[82] Logically, two aspects must be separated: (1) cases where there initially are only benefits from a given environmental action, and harms appear down the line due to the latency period; and (2) cases where the benefits of environmental controls appear only in the future, as is the case with climate change.

[83] For bogus bureaucratic claims, nothing beats "Under the Dome," the self-financed documentary about pollution in China (2015). For novelistic and sci-fi takes on environmental issues, we recommend Jake Bittle's *The Great Displacement* (2023) and Kim Stanley Robinson's *The Ministry for the Future* (2020).

need but recall that American GNP soared with the Exxon Valdez oil spill in Alaska in 1989, since the effort to clean-up Prince William Sound was counted as "economic activity.")

At the same time, attempts to claim past precedents for the unprecedented existential threats that we now face are equally untenable, as "bad faith."[84] Too often, cost-benefit calculations are made from the perspective of a single point in time, but it is scarcely feasible to tabulate on any single day the "total environmental harm." Not only do the costs of all actions and inactions accrue over time, but it may also take decades to register the negative impacts on the afflicted generations, including hazardous waste disposal, the loss of biodiversity, and biochemical contamination.[85] However, until very recently, regulatory bodies empowered to act have tended to focus on cases of instantaneous death or injury in workplace settings in their valuations of human life and to discount latent, incipient, or potential harms.[86] Therefore, until quite recently, "practically **no** expenditure for the benefit of relatively distant generations could be justified (i.e., quantified) within a cost-benefit framework."[87] As Michael Gerrard, director of the Sabin Center for Climate Change Law at Columbia Law

---

[84] Weiss 1990, 200, for example, claims that intergenerational rights and obligations are enshrined in the Preamble to the UN's Universal Declaration of Human Rights, but historians today agree that the "economic rights" of human beings (the right to livelihoods, shelter, and food) have never been a prime concern in the international order, as defined by Anglo-Americans, with the political rights being thought of as the best guarantors of economic rights (and thus primary).

[85] The co-authors think of "Under the Dome," the self-financed documentary about pollution in China made in 2015 by the former CCTV (China Central Television) journalist Chai Jing 柴静 (b. 197b), which purportedly garnered over 150 million viewings before its removal by the Party.

[86] Revesz 1999, esp. 941. In the late 1980s, in the case of asbestos, the EPA was urged to figure saving a life at the discount rate of $22,000; see Revesz, 946. Derek Parfit 1984, 357, seemed to oppose such discounting, on the grounds that the discount is far too deep.

[87] Revesz 1999, 987 (with the bolds mine). Revesz deems "unpersuasive" (988) many of the objections put forward by those who want to steeply discount the human lives of future generations. As a low discount rate makes expenditure seem more desirable, "Environmentalists have traditionally favored low discount rates because the costs of environmental protection generally must be borne well before the benefits begin to accrue" (989). It is also not easy to shift tactics *after* recalculations.

School, remarked in astonishment at the Montana v. Held outcome: "There have been almost no trials on climate change (before this)."[88]

Already in 1966, Michel Foucault opined that "Man is an invention of recent date. And one perhaps nearing its end."[89] Still, very few people living today would likely celebrate the imminent demise of humanity, which has wreaked so much damage on other species, on planet Earth, and even on the stratosphere.[90] Only a small fraction still accepts the claim that "we are post-humans or soon will be,"[91] obviating any need to care today about the Anthropocene. As it turns out, most people can rally around one basic idea: that the day when humanity disappears should be postponed as long as possible. Nonetheless, many express considerable discomfort when tasked to consider who should serve as ultimate arbiter charged with the task of devising a calculus for ecological cost-benefits designed to aid future generations living in communities, states, and transnational organizations.[92] (Perhaps this is akin to people's disinclination to confront their individual deaths. As a species, "homo sapiens" seems to be strangely "addicted to irreality.")[93] Some object that the thought of applying any cost-benefit exercises to living and breathing human beings is itself overly reductive and mechanical, if not repulsive or fantastical, but how are we to punish transgressors, if we refuse to calculate harm? Many simply give up, knowing that any re-orientation towards our living space requires profound re-orientation of the taxonomies and values that nearly all of us have been taught to revere. But how is it that it still seems wildly "radical" in the Western context to argue, as legal

---

[88] *The New York Times* essay dated March 20, 2023, A1. Cf. https://www.nytimes.com/2023/08/28/climate/ united-nations-children-climate-lawsuit.html
[89] Foucault 1966.
[90] David Benatar: "The concern that humans will not exist at some future time is either a symptom of human arrogance . . . or is some misplaced sentimentalism."
[91] Derek Parfit was one of the people who began to argue this in some of his work.
[92] Revesz 1999, 997.
[93] The phrase is James Baldwin's, during his 1965 Cambridge Union debate with William F. Buckley. It has wide applicability to subjects outside of race relations.

scholar Jebediah Purdy does, that "the familiar divide between people and the natural world is no longer useful or accurate"? After all, "we [humans] shape everything, from the upper atmosphere to the deep seas, there is no more nature that stands apart from human beings."[94]

Some New Developments: Three cases

Lest the foregoing leave readers with an indelible impression that climate laws in nation-states and in international organizations are too resistant to update and improve, below we offer three recent case studies to supplement the earlier account of Held v. Montana, as these may be harbingers of substantive changes to the default legal framework around the world. Note that each case foregrounds older people and young people, partly because these two groups have been qualified to enter complaints in a court of law, by virtue of their standing. Note, meanwhile, that the time frame the courts in each case have mandated for correctives represents a maddeningly slow pace of change, with the judges ever-anxious not to upset the present-day apple cart.

Case no. 1. In 2020, a group that calls itself Klima Seniorinnen Schweiz (aka Senior Women for Climate Protection, Switzerland), composed of Swiss women over the age of sixty-four, took their grievances to the European Court for Human Rights (ECHR), a Division of the Council of Europe, accusing their own government of violating their fundamental rights as Swiss citizens, due to its sustained inaction in the face of dramatic climate changes.[95] One member, who grew up on a farm, has watched a nearby glacier

---

[94] Both statements are in his *After Nature* 2015.
[95] Article 2 of the Convention says, "Everyone's right to life shall be protected by law. No one shall be deprived of his life intentionally save in the execution of a sentence of a court following his conviction of a crime for which this penalty is provided by law."

disappear. The Senior Women group state correctly that the elderly are the most vulnerable when it comes to heat-related deaths, and the four leading litigants in the Swiss case are women with heart and respiratory diseases that put them at particular risk among the aging population. But, as one of their lawyers said, the litigants felt a moral obligation to pursue the case, since if Switzerland, one of the richest and most technologically advanced countries in the world, failed to tackle climate change, what hope would there be that the poorer countries in the world would grapple with the issue? Notably, as one member remarked, "Statistically speaking in ten years, I'm gone. So whatever I fight for now, I am not going to be the benefactor. It'll be for the next generation."[96]

As background, note that the ECHR began to hear arguments on September 27, 2023, in a Grand Chamber hearing, the climate case of "Duarte Agostinho and Others v. Portugal and 32 Others," where the "thirty-two" refers to thirty-two other countries who accuse their countries of failing to curb emissions, despite the existential threat.[97] However, the case of Switzerland is particularly interesting because Swiss voters have tended to be ahead of Swiss politicians when it comes to climate change. In June of 2023, Swiss voters, by referendum, required the state to reach a "net zero" emissions target by 2050, perhaps because climate has been in the conversation for several decades by now. A Swiss governmental report produced in 2007, *Intergenerationelle Gerechtigkeit—Die Bedeutung von zukünftigen Klimaschäden für die heutige Klimapolitik* (English: *Intergenerational justice: the significance of future climate damage for today's climate policy*), was one of the furthest-thinking reports to have appeared in recent decades, albeit its conclusions were overly optimistic, as was not

---

[96] Ms. Elizabeth Stern, aged seventy-five, quoted in *The New York Times*, August 7, 2023, International, sec. A13.
[97] https://www.echr.coe.int. A French citizen has brought a similar case against the French government.

unusual two decades ago. Commissioned by the Environmental Ministry, the report looked at the impact of climate-change related damages to one of the most efficient and affluent economies in the world.[98]

While conceding that great uncertainties attend any of the present models predicting the impact of climate change on the country of Switzerland itself (which has a very complex topography to boot), two issues stand out in the report. First, no great change (impact damage) is expected until 2050; therefore, one may deduce, the obligation toward the immediately following generation is so minimal as to be negligible. Second, it is nonetheless recognized that Switzerland does not exist in a vacuum, and therefore must plan for different energy security scenarios, as well as for more robust logistical infrastructure planning post-2050. A recurrent subtheme informing the deliberations on obligations owed to future generations is the implausibly high living standard of Switzerland today, which led the commission to adopt the principle of equivalence, i.e., the current generation should ensure that the future generation has a similar, if not equally high, standard of living.[99] Note, in this connection, that the projections of intergenerational justice of developing nations differ from those in developed nations: while the former most certainly hope for a better life for the following generations, nearly all of them hold that nation-building and economic prosperity comes first.[100] In April 2024, Europe's top human rights court ruled that the Swiss government had violated the human rights of its citizens by failing to

---

[98] Meyer and Roser 2007.
[99] ". . . jeglichen plausiblen Schwellenwert eines minimal akzeptablen Lebensstandards überschritten hat." English: [Switzerland] has surpassed any plausible threshold of a minimally acceptable living standard. Meyer-Roser 2007, 18.
[100] As the world's first carbon-negative country, Bhutan is an exception, as it embraces a green standard for development ("gross national happiness" or GNP). Bhutan is a global leader in forest and biodiversity conservation, with 70 percent of its area covered by forests. Noam Chomsky, Henry Rosemont, Jr., among others, with the backing of Bhutan's own enlightened royal family, worked together to devise a truly effective path to lasting sustainability.

do enough to combat climate change. As the ECHR court oversees the actions of the forty-six member countries of the European Union,[101] the favorable ruling will likely have two multiplier effects: to multiply the impact of such lawsuits, and to multiply the number of similar cases in the pipeline for adjudication by the courts.

Case no. 2: In the late summer of 2024, a new legal victory came in South Korea. (The South Korean case was the first to be won in an Asian country.) By South Korea's Carbon Neutral Act of 2018, the South Korean legislature said that the country should cut carbon emissions by 40 percent from 2018 levels. In the recent court case, 250 defendants (1/3 of them young children or teenagers) replied that this pace of change was not going to be fast enough to ensure safe levels of emissions in their own lifetimes. (One testified, "Grown-ups . . . don't listen to our voice on matters of important responsibility.") The court gave the National Assembly until Feb. 2026 to come up with a plan, reasoning that, "Future generations will be more exposed to the impact of climate change, but their participation in today's democratic political process is limited . . . . So the legislators have the duty and responsibility to make concrete laws for mid- and long-term greenhouse gas reduction plans." This ruling in South Korea, it should be noted, came on the heels of the German Federal Constitutional Court's 2021 landmark ruling, which mandated stronger action on climate to protect the rights of future generations.[102]

In case no. 3, we see litigation unfolding in Hawai'i, where the state, on June 22, 2024, announced that it had reached a settlement, out of court, with a young plaintiffs' group led by Navahine F., by which the state's Department of Transportation would reduce its reliance on fossil fuels, to which Governor Josh Green assented. The plaintiffs, as in Held

---

[101] *The New York Times*, August 7, 2023.
[102] See "South Korean Court Orders Country," *The New York Times*, Aug. 29, 2024 (byline Choe Sang-Hun).

v. Montana, were organized by Our Children's Trust and Earthjustice, another environmental law group, but the breakthrough almost certainly occurred because Hawaii's state constitution guarantees its residents the "right to a clean and healthful environment." The state's plans are to fully decarbonize its transportation system within twenty years, and much sooner than that to work on expanding bicycle lanes and installing electric vehicle chargers. (Airports and airplanes are much harder to decarbonize, as are the many cruise ships that hop the islands.) Meanwhile, Honolulu became the plaintiff in yet another high-profile climate case. In 2020, the city sued Sunoco and other big oil companies, accusing them of misleading the public about the risks of climate change. Almost certainly, this court case will make its way slowly to the state and federal Supreme Courts.

Progress has been made, yes, but all is not rosy, as many famous legal disputes are in limbo as this book goes to press. Here are two further examples of pending cases whose final outcomes are bound to be consequential:

"Greenpeace Tries New Tactic in Dakota Pipeline Suit"[103]

The energy company ("Energy Transfer") that backed the North Dakota pipeline has filed suit in federal court, 2017, alleging that Greenpeace incited the protests in North Dakota in 2016 and 2017, whereas Greenpeace says it was only lending support, via an *amicus* brief, to the plaintiffs in the case, the Standing Rock Sioux, a legally constituted sovereign nation. The Sioux were suing Energy Transfer because the pipeline would have run through their reservation, and

---

[103] *The New York Times*, Business, Wed. Aug. 23, 2024, B3.

any oil spill would have irreparably damaged their water supply and cultural resources. Moreover, the construction of the pipeline indisputably violates Article II of the Fort Laramie Treaty (1868), which guarantees the *"undisturbed* use and occupation" of the reservation lands surrounding the proposed location of the pipeline.[104] Lawyers for Energy Transfer wanted to charge Greenpeace under the RICO laws (Racketeer Influence and Corrupt Organizations), initially designed to stop organized crime. The federal judge dismissed the claim, but sent the case on to state court. North Dakota jurors there, in March of 2025, held Greenpeace liable for damages exceeding $660 million in Energy Transfer's SLAPP lawsuit. Greenpeace has announced its intention to appeal the verdict, since it would otherwise be bankrupted and unable to pursue its mission as a NGO.

As of March and April 2024, the European Union adopted a law to protect persons (and by extension, others) who speak out on matters of public interest against abusive lawsuits meant to silence them. Journalists, marginalized groups, and NGOs in the EU should benefit from this "Anti-SLAPP" law, but no comparable federal law exists in the United States, although thirty-four states have enacted such laws (but not North Dakota).[105] Basically, the anti-SLAPP provisions in the law recognize that big corporations have always had ways to make NGOs go silent, chiefly by bankrupting them with legal fees. Still, anti-SLAPP statutes remain a highly litigated type of legislation over constitutional and procedural concerns, primarily because while it is easy to say a SLAPP suit should be prevented, it can be hard to determine what constitutes a SLAPP suit.[106] If the conservative

---

[104] For details, see McKibben 2016; Miller 2016; https://americanindian.si.edu/nk360/plains-treaties/dapl
[105] Directive (EU) 2024/1069 on protecting persons who engage in public participation from manifestly unfounded claims or abusive court proceedings ("Strategic lawsuits against public participation" or SLAPP).
[106] "State Anti-SLAPP statutes differ greatly in scope and requirements as states try to balance the above concerns. In federal courts, the circuits remain split on whether state

commentator Anne Applebaum is correct, one way out of many of today's seemingly insurmountable dilemmas is first, through regulatory legislation backed up by enforcement mechanisms, and second, by making global corporations identify the true identities of their owners and major stakeholders. This latter provision would remove the shield that predatory companies have used and abused and open these companies up to paying their fair share of taxes (as is already being done in the EU).[107]

The End of Impunity for Tech Giants?

As we put this book to bed, Telegram, X (formerly Twitter), and TikTok are beginning to face legal pushback that may "signal a new era of accountability."[108] Small wonder that the Tech giants strongly backed Donald Trump in the 2024 election, with Elon Musk reporting that he had spent more than $290 million to get Trump elected.[109] A recent whistle-blower case at Mark Zuckerberg's Meta (formerly Facebook) suggests how comfortable the Tech giant CEOs are with

---

Anti-SLAPP laws are substantive or procedural and thus whether they can be applied in federal court." As of July 2024, thirty-four states and the District of Columbia have anti-SLAPP laws, including Arizona, Arkansas, California, Colorado, Connecticut, Delaware, Florida, Georgia, Hawaii, Illinois, Indiana, Kansas, Kentucky, Louisiana, Maine, Maryland, Massachusetts, Minnesota, Missouri, Nebraska, Nevada, New Jersey, New Mexico, New York, Oklahoma, Oregon, Pennsylvania, Rhode Island, Tennessee, Texas, Utah, Vermont, Virginia, and Washington. For SLAPP suits, see https://www.law.cornell.edu/wex/slapp_suit; https://www.rcfp.org/anti-slapp (several entries).

[107] For details, see https://www.europeansources.info/record/directive-eu-2024-1069. The Cornell Law website says of the United States, "SLAPP suits and Anti-SLAPP statutes pose multiple challenges" to all parties. The first test of the new anti-SLAPP laws brought a directive instructing EU member states to not recognize judgments in foreign SLAPP suits, and to allow counter-suits. Deepa Padmanabha, acting director of Greenpeace, USA, said she saw the case to be particularly concerning, given a rise in anti-protest laws in many states since 2017. "Freedom of speech and freedom of assembly are what this case is about." See also Applebaum 2024.

[108] "Has the Tide Turned for TikTok, Telegram, and X?", *The New York Times*, Sept. 11, 2024.

[109] https://www.cnn.com/2025/02/01/politics/elon-musk-2024-election-spending-millions/index.html

lying under oath at Congressional hearings on their national and international activities.¹¹⁰ But let us backtrack a bit, to a time shortly before the 2024 election.

Three similar cases, all in late August and early September of 2024, suggest that legal authorities are beginning to push back against certain kinds of misinformation, disinformation, and criminal activity on social media, some relating to climate change and some to social cohesion and social equity. First, French authorities have detained Pavel Durov, the billionaire backer behind Telegram, for allowing illegal transactions to populate Telegram's site. By the writ issued to Durov, Telegram's failure to oversee its customers has been instrumental in enabling fraud, selling drugs, and organizing child sex rings. Adding insult to the injury stemming from its policy of "virtually no content monitoring," Telegram has consistently refused to reveal the names of its customers, despite national and EU laws

---

[110] The whistleblower is Sarah Wynn-Williams, a former New Zealand diplomat and Zuckerberg's aide. Her allegations in *Careless People* (by late March, 2025, no. 1 on the Times best-seller list) include the charge that Meta executives, working under explicit orders from Mark Zuckerberg, worked "hand in glove" with the PRC government to allow Beijing to censor and control content in Hong Kong and Taiwan in exchange for access to the lucrative China market. That Meta's lawyers won a temporary injunction against the book is obviously a Pyrrhic victory, as the arbitrator's ruling doesn't apply to Macmillan, which published the book on March 11 and now can sit back and watch as the book has shot up to No. 1 in the politics and social sciences section of Amazon's website without further PR outreach. By the way, the arbitrator didn't address the veracity of the book's content—only that its publication breached the non-disparagement terms of Wynn-Williams' severance agreement. For details, see the LA Times account, by https://www.latimes.com/business/story/2025-03-20/inside-the-tell-all-book-that-mark-zuckerberg-is-trying-to-suppress (now itself suppressed by Zuckerberg, so "no longer available" precisely a month later). But information is available elsewhere on the Web. On April 20, 2025, the best is on Youtube (showing her sworn testimony, as reported by CNN on a Congressional hearing) https://www.google.com/search?q=Sarah+Wynn-Williams&newwindow=1&sca_esv=0583650a8b1bb9c0&rlz=1C1GCEA_enUS1093US1093&ei=4WUFaJzUMNvJ0PEP7dfFgA4&ved=0ahUKEwjcyOLuxeeMAxXbJDQIHe1rEeAQ4dUDCBA&uact=5&oq=Sarah+Wynn-Williams&gs_lp=Egxnd3Mtd2l6LXNlcnAiE1NhcmFoIFd5bm4tV2lsbGlhbXMyBRAAGIAEMgsQABiABBixAxiDATIFEAAYgAQyBRAAGIAEMgUQABiABDIFEAAYgAQyBRAAGIAEMgUQABiABDIFEAAYgAQyBRAAGIAESLgHUABYAHAAeACQAQCYAW6gAW6qAQMwLjG4AQPIAQD4AQGYAgGgAgnKAgYYABgHGB6YAwCIBgGQBgjSBwMwLjGgB7MFsgcDMC4xuAcA&sclient=gws-wiz-serp#fpstate=ive&vld=cid:c89fb602,vid:WbuBdHqYENM,st:0

requiring that it do so. Meanwhile a Brazilian Supreme Court judge, Alexandre de Moraes, suspended the microblogging service X (formerly Twitter) on two main counts: issuing misinformation knowingly and intentional wrongdoing in the form of interference in local elections.[111] And a federal appeals court in Pennsylvania ruled that the mother of a ten-year-old child who died copying a TikTok self-asphyxiation video can sue the service, circumventing the near-blanket immunity the company has long claimed.[112] The outcomes in these three cases may tell us much about the state of our civilization.

Interim Conclusion

Locke and his early modern companions brilliantly articulated the notion of "bodily integrity," but, from today's perspective, they signally failed to reckon with what we might call "subsistence rights": what it takes, at a minimum, to live a life of dignity. That goes some way to explain why efforts to apply subsistence rights in legal terms to nation-states, multinationals, and corporations have proven so far to be an unmitigated disaster. Nothing has so clearly brought home to me the fact that contract law inherited from Hobbes or from Locke must be rethought from the ground up, being premised on the four beliefs that signatories to the contract always (a) are equal; (b) engage in informed consent; (c) cooperate, because (d) the contract is deemed to be of benefit to both parties. Moreover, traditional contract theory is single-generational and requires palpable and immediate damage.

Carlo Rovelli, the physicist, observed in a recent book, "If we discover a bomb that has remained buried beneath what is now a children's playground, we do not leave it there because 'it might not

---

[111] Jon Lee Anderson, "Letter from Brazil," *The New York Times* (April 7, 2025).
[112] *The New York Times*, Sept. 11, 2024.

explode'" . . . Whoever says, 'But there is no certainty . . . [so] let's calmly carry on' is a cretin. And yet this is precisely the attitude taken by those who argue that the [global warming] problem is not serious, because we have no certainty regarding the climate."[113] All kinds of excuses are being deployed to do nothing, though what is at stake is the future of our children and the world we inhabit. But let us be frank: such excuses can be maintained in the face of undeniable, mounting evidence because the greatest and most imminent harm happens to the "wrong" people (mainly the poor), or to people far away, or to people we are willing to let see die, the people whose lives can be somehow "discounted" in our minds.[114] So perhaps the only summation to be registered is that made by the prosecutor at the Nürnberg trials: "Civilization asks whether law is so laggard as to be utterly helpless to deal with crimes of this magnitude by criminals of this order of importance."[115]

Cognizant of all the impediments to clear thinking, we co-authors recall that to see humans as part and parcel of the myriad things comprising the cosmos is an age-old Chinese insight.[116] The recognition of the special needs of children and the elderly did not need to wait for modern feminist care ethics (undeniably "Western" in origin).[117] And since we think the traditional framework for "rights" talk is really code championing the rights of privileged individuals, construed as rational and self-interested actors in eras when Social Darwinist "survival of the fittest" theories have reigned supreme, we suggest that

---

[113] Rovelli 2018, 197.
[114] Eerily, as noted above, several countries' leaders now speak cheerily of acceptable "casualty tolerance thresholds," with regard to their own citizens.
[115] This was the question the Chief Prosecutor Robert H. Jackson posed in his opening statement at the trial (Nov. 22, 1945), as cited by Attorney General Merrick B. Garland in "Remarks at the American Bar Association, 2023."
[116] See Nylan 2019, on humans as animals. How much of this insight contradicts Christian notions is the subject of the oft-debated Lynn White essay of 1967.
[117] See Spakowski 2021.

hard thinking about workable solutions for the environment[118] should entail consideration of the case of China, past and present. Mindful that the rhetoric of most revolutions hearkens back to "returns," we will travel first back to antiquity in China, while on the lookout for exemplary models for more recent pasts,[119] in the firm belief that appeals to progress are but a popular form of hucksterism that will almost certainly doom us to awful outcomes.

Perhaps it is good to remember that there are three main impediments to rational discussions that might lead to better outcomes for many: one or more of the parties intentionally lies; one or more of the parties prevents meaningful discussions from happening by resorting to bureaucratization, that is, excessively complicated administrative procedures, for example, Robert's Rules of Order or arcane provisions of the law; or one or more of the parties engages in elaborate circumlocution after circumlocution, in order to evade substantive discussions of real problems. Today, we see all three types of shenanigans on display, often in tandem, under the direction of highly skilled operatives.

---

[118] See, e.g., Heather and Rapley 2023, particularly 66–72, 134–64.
[119] Here Wendell Berry may be our guide.

2

Intergenerational Equity during the Early Empires in China

Showing courtesy to guests and taking pity on those in dire straits are the sacred origins of ritual propriety. 禮賓矜窮，禮之宗也.

—*Guoyu*, "Jinyu" 4

To honor the bright sacrifices [to the ancestors] and to protect the small and the weak is the very definition of ritual propriety in Zhou. 崇明祀，保小寡，周禮也.

—*Zuo*, Lord Xi, Year 21

Four centuries after Darwin, most people still resist the notion taken for granted by the early writers of classical Chinese: that humans are part of the animal world, with no more than one or two distinctive traits that set them apart in any way.[1] To re-orient our habitual ways of thinking (pun intended), let us begin by conceding, along with the French sociologist Michel Maffesoli, our general reluctance to rethink our relationship to the "universalism" promised by the Western tradition and the particularism more favored in early China:

> The human species needs a new episteme and we lack the word that would correspond to this need to overcome a universalism

---

[1] See Nylan 2015, 2019.

which is already showing signs of wear. It may be time to overcome this "essentially Western" universal quest, . . . and to replace it with an "Oriental" notion of the cultural terrain, the place where diverse new ways of living together come into being, which is instead loco-centered, rooted in the locus, the local. . . . This is not a form of . . . relativism—unless we mean it in the sense of Simmel, for whom relativism is the putting into relation of different cultures—nor a reduction to unity.[2]

For the trained historian, the local—that is, references to specific times and places—is fundamental to any critical analysis of the tensions between rhetoric and realities, impeded as we always are by an inability to see beyond our own island, and that helps to explain why this chapter, largely penned by Nylan, insists upon the salience of the antique Chinese model to reconceiving today's world, whether it's East or West.[3]

The early empires in China are highly relevant to today's world for several reasons. First, classical-era thinkers and statesmen represent a vast non-Western resource of smart thinking about healthy environments. Second, thinking about healthy environments in early China is tied inextricably to governmental concerns for disadvantaged

---

[2] Maffesoli 2005. The original has been necessarily emended, changing a "neither" to a "not" (in "not a form of relativism") since our book does not quote the rest of Maffesoli's paragraph.

[3] Talk of our own "island" draws upon E.M. Forster's *Howard's End* (1910), where the Schlegel sisters debate the practicalities of socialism and the difficulty to leaving their own economic island (the comfortable bourgeoisie) to understand the plight of the truly poor, try as they might. Since today's "know-nothings" in the PRC (many of them highly educated) purport to be unable to distinguish or prefer not to distinguish "empires" from "imperialism," it is best to reiterate that "empire" is a fairly neutral term, insofar as empires can be relatively good or relatively bad in their treatment of their subjects or citizens. Contra some recent blogs generated in the PRC, empires from early times have existed in the territory we know today as China, as well as in Europe, America, and Japan, and both the United States and the PRC are empires in the usual sense of the word ("dominance over different ethnic groups and kingdoms by a single supreme power"). One may speak of the *pax Romana* as one benefit of empire, though the "peace" (i.e., freedom from war) has probably been over-played, due to external invasions and internal civil wars. Ditto for the *pax Sinica*.

populations and the equitable, but not equal, treatment of all.[4] In consequence, patriotic citizens of the PRC can justifiably take pride in their own traditions, and neither they nor the Party need dismiss all talk of human rights and the rights of the planet as "Western" and thus antithetical to "socialism with Chinese characteristics." (In these two regards, there is no question that the Chinese "got there first," while radical EuroAmerican thinkers and *avant garde* contemporary artists have been left to play "catch-up," but should such considerations count in the present crisis, or is this discourse left over from outworn Social Darwinist theories?)[5] Third, the early empires in China offer a good test case for today's political realists from which to consider the human condition, insofar as they show us what has been possible for real human beings who were socialized to think differently than we moderns. Judging from the early empires in China, people have it well within their power to operate in less shortsighted ways and in ways more focused on achieving communal equity than are seen in the developed countries of today, especially the United States and the People's Republic of China.[6] As the classical "Pan Geng" chapter from the *Documents* phrases it,

---

[4] There are three kinds of distributive mechanisms, whose aims differ: (1) those aiming for perfect equality among community members (a state that has never yet been achieved); (2) those aiming for equitable treatment for community members, usually based on their contributions to the community, as valued by the community; and (3) those aiming for what philosophers today called "decent-share" of the common goods (whose proponents are called "sufficientarians"). None of these three is the same. The classical thinkers and statesmen all aimed for no. 2, equity.

[5] Take, for example, the Parliament of Bodies on June 15, 2019, in Bergen, Norway. It named as its chief goal figuring out "how to redefine our alliances with those who are not presently living... [and take] responsibility for those who are no longer, or not yet, here." It called for an anti-fascist, transfeminist, and anti-racist coalition and the celebration of many voices fighting against the techno-patriarchal and colonial regime worldwide, arguing that "Actually, the dead are not dead."

[6] The Gini coefficients for both the United States and China have been worsening, although Biden's infrastructure bill may help to reverse some of this in the United States. See https://worldpopulationreview.com/country-rankings/gini-coefficient-by-country.

> If you do not plan for the long-term, or consider the disasters that will befall you, you continually encourage such troubles. If you care only about the present and not the future, what possible life will be granted you by or among the powers above?![7]

Therefore, what constitutes a "life worth living" for people in different situations (a lively debate these days) is the perennial question raised by authors in China during the early empires and long past that time.[8] The conclusions advanced in this chapter depend on recent research on the pre-Han *Guoyu*, *Guanzi*, and *Xunzi*, as well as the Han-era *Documents* classic, also by a firm belief, derived from *Xunzi* and *Zhuangzi*, that it is simply not possible for people to continue in the way they have been doing.[9]

To delve more deeply into these topics, it may be wise to first draw a contrast between some modern narratives contrasting compassion and altruism with "selfish" and "self-interested actions," if only because in some circles these days it has become fairly common to discount compassion as "natural" to the human psyche. The naturalist E.O. Wilson insisted that compassion is selective and often self-serving; "it conforms to the best interests of self, family, and allies of the moment."[10] More dismissively still, Richard Dawkins described human beings as "survival machines, robot *vehicles* blindly programmed to preserve the selfish molecules known as genes."[11] In stark contrast to Wilson

---

[7] *Shangshu/Documents*, "Pan Geng, B." The Chinese reads: 汝不謀長。以思乃災。汝永勸憂。今其有今罔後。汝何生在上.

[8] Nylan's *Pleasure Book* (2018) shows this. For today's debate, see, e.g., Fumagalli 2024.

[9] For this sentiment, see, e.g., *Zhuangzi*, *juan* 2 ("Qi wu lun" 齊物論 chap.); *juan* 4 ("Renjian shi" 人間世 chap.); *juan* 11 ("Zai you" 在宥 chap.), for the inevitable entanglements that come with the human condition (有為而累者, 人道也); *Xunzi*, *juan* 18 ("Zheng lun" 政論 chap.); *juan* 10 ("Fu guo" 富國 chap.), etc.

[10] Wilson 1974, chap. 7 (esp. 155): "Compassion is flexible and eminently adaptable to political reality; that is to say it conforms to the best interests of self, family, and allies of the moment."

[11] Dawkins, of course, posited the existence of *memes*, constituent parts of culture that function like genes. Many ground their findings in Nietzsche, who wrote, "The world is the will to power and nothing besides.... Life itself is essentially appropriation, injury,

and Dawkins, Mary Midgley notes that modern science finds, inside and outside the human body, patterns of movement and mutual resonance, currents of connection and flow, which seem to match more closely the early Chinese belief in circulating *qi* flows.[12] Through the continual exchanges of *qi* that takes place through the senses, all sentient beings are bound together, profoundly interdependent within a tightly knit web of social and cosmic relations.[13] One may debate the degree to which that symmetry is significant in the end, but what is indisputable is this: if we take the Chinese patterns seriously, we must conclude that acting on one's own behalf more often than not means acting on behalf of others, insofar as the quality of our interactions with all others, by the early cosmic resonance theories, affect, for good or for ill, our potentials to lead healthy and productive lives.[14]

By the antique theories, all perceptual understanding—what we see, hear, smell, feel, and sense—results from the complex exchanges of *qi* that occur during each and every encounter the person experiences: I see you, the person, and some of my basic stuff in the form of invisible *qi* travels out to meet you while some of you then travels from you in the form of invisible *qi* to become a part of me.[15] (The same palpable *qi* exchange happens if I see a painting or a tree, instead of a person, or hear a piece of music or smell a ripe peach.) In consequence, no experience leaves me unchanged, an idea that happens to tally with the idea of carving neuropathways today. And so my successive experiences over time constitute a substantial part of the entire body, including its surface and the invisible organs that nestle within the empty, fathomless cavity formed by the rib-

---

subjugation of the strange and the weaker, suppression, severity . . . " *Han Feizi* would do as well.

[12] Nylan's conclusion, not Midgley's.
[13] See Midgley 2011, 44, 48, 57, contra Wilson and Dawkins.
[14] See Kuriyama 1999.
[15] For more on resonance theories, one may consult Nylan 1992, 2010, 2018 (esp. chap. 1), 2021.

cage, among them the heart organ system that processes emotions and intellectual responses.[16] And it is the *quality* of those interactions that either sustains and amplifies[17] or depletes and exhausts us, so that when bad interactions pile up, our *qi* is exhausted and we sicken and die. I think of this portrait of *qi* exchanges as instilling a simple lesson: the quality of our social relations is, essentially, the very air we breathe, no less important than oxygen, when it comes to human flourishing.

It follows, then, that during the early empires in the area we now call "China" the sources attest to a consciousness that the boundaries we moderns have tended to view as discrete and fixed were instead blurry and porous in all bodies, including the body politic, since the component parts, seen and unseen, of such bodies were in continual communication and deeply intertwined, even if only a small portion of the continual *qi* exchanges were captured and identified by the human senses as "significant." In a culture where "the only constant is change,"[18] statesmen and thinkers alike were intent upon devising suitable answers for how best to honor and acknowledge that ever-changing mutual reliance, rather than mandating fixed autonomy. The key question was, then, How best to formulate, revise, and implement new policies to fully address the changing conditions on the ground? For the early thinkers in China, the purest expression of one's consistent reverence for the "constant values" or *jing* 經 was to apply them appropriately in the arena of shifting contexts or *quan* 權.[19] And

---

[16] Much space is wasted on Daoist constructions of "emptiness" and "quietude." Suffice it to say that these tend to be Buddhist-inflected and may refer to nothing more than that we are mysteries to ourselves, and unaware of what is happening in that cavity.

[17] After all, *Analects* 6/30 and 14/29 advise that it is human beings who enlarge the Dao and not the reverse.

[18] This sort of thinking is laid out in the *Changes* classic, Hexagram 1, esp. 9/yang in the fourth line.

[19] When today's philosophers and historians see *jing* and *quan* as opposed, they fail to read their early sources carefully. Liu Ming 2022, chap. 1, shows that the relevant corpus of writings on such matters has been dubbed Yinyang, Confucian, Daoist, "daily life," or administrative or legalist in content. Wang Lihua 2014 argues that care for the natural

for thinkers and statesman in the early empires, it mattered, hugely, how they conceptualized the world, since the imagination shapes, if not determines "what we find to be important, what we select for our attention among the welter of facts that constantly flood in upon us,"[20] and only the most capacious of imaginations can counter the physical propensity to narrow its perspectives and to dichotomize aspects of the world,[21] a propensity especially marked in times of rapid change when people grow fearful.

Possibly, the thinkers in early China were able to think "outside the box" of perceived necessity to pose larger questions about human existence because the early empires were unusually rich, densely staffed at all administrative levels, with governing elites that were, for their time, comparatively of one mind when identifying the most pressing problems of the day, if far less rich, well-staffed, and equipped than any developed countries today. (Developed countries today have stunningly dense transportation, communication, and surveillance capacities, plus "invented traditions" designed expressly to encourage cohesion across disparate groups, which are continually reinforced in schools and in all types of social media.)[22] Thanks mainly to the production and circulation of silk, lacquer, and eventually paper; to the abundant crops grown from loess soil; and to the rich mineral and

---

world and its rhythms is a form of technical know-how familiar to nearly all in an agrarian-based society. Perhaps. In any case, it is best to register my doubts that the "Yueling"/ Monthly Ordinances literature became more influential in Eastern Han, as we have so many instances of alluding to it in late Zhanguo or Qin texts. Note, however, that it is difficult to posit trends when we lack the vast majority of texts from the early period.

[20] Midgley 2011, 2.
[21] For our brain's physical preference for reductionism, due to its unwieldy architecture, see Kahneman 2011. Human beings are not machines; they react in various ways, depending on the beliefs they hold and the assertions they have been fed. Lies told repeatedly quickly become beliefs. Recent studies also show that people who identify a story as "unlikely to be true" are often willing to circulate those false or misleading stories in order to reaffirm their belonging to the social group with whom they identify.
[22] Hirase 2005 refutes modern patriots who presume greater unity of thinking in pre-unification China.

timber resources,[23] the early empires in China were also remarkably urbanized for the antique world and thus enjoyed, in all likelihood, the highest literacy rates and the highest rates of social mobility.[24]

Underlying Theories of the Body and Body Politic

One might begin with a legend, as legends and myths serve as reliable "mirrors" conveying the probable spectrum of imagined human potentials for members of the literate elite during the early empires in the area we know today as "China." The legend concerns Old Duke Danfu, a petty ruler in the far northwest who founded the Zhou dynastic fortunes that would come to fruition four generations after Danfu.[25] Once upon a time, the good duke saw that his fertile fields were the envy of all his neighbors, and thus an invitation to repeated incursions by rival powers. He knew that his family members and nobles would willingly fight to save their homelands, but he knew equally well that there was no good reason to ask them to endanger

---

[23] Until the fourth century AD, how to manufacture silk was unknown outside China. Paper was invented ca. AD 100 although proto-paper exists earlier. By the fourth-century AD, paper produced in Sichuan was inexpensive and of excellent quality. Lacquer performed many of the tasks that plastic does today.

[24] These are large and complex claims, but we know that the immense administration of the early empires required roughly 30–40 percent of "new men" for its employ; the high rates of urbanization also encouraged some level of literacy. The highest guesstimate for urbanization in the Roman Empire is roughly 14 percent, according to Carlos Norena, my Berkeley colleague, whereas the figures for the taxpaying population in Han come to roughly 27 percent, or nearly twice as much.

[25] See Nylan 2001. By the legends, King Wu, the Zhou dynastic founder, was the great-grandson of Danfu. Similar themes occur throughout the classics and masterworks, e.g., in the *Mencius* (Book 1), *Guoyu* ("Zhou yu," Book 1.07), and in the Pan Geng legend. These multiple sources advise rulers, for both pragmatic and moral reasons, to share their goods with their subjects, and such advice cannot be attributed solely to dedicated ethical followers of Confucius, or even to the Ru (classicists, as experts in the past), as this theme is found everywhere in discussions on legitimate rule. (On the Pan Geng legend, I respectfully disagree with Tan Sor-Hoon's 2014 analysis, believing it not to reflect Pan Geng's "autocratic threats," by the early commentaries, but rather the difficulties of leading a recalcitrant population to recognize its own best interests.)

their own lives and livelihoods for his own sake. As "the people enthrone a ruler in order to benefit from him," he knew he ought to think of his subjects' welfare before that of his ruling line. After consulting with his ministers, who advised him to stay and fight, he hit upon a far better solution: he would simply move his family base some sixty miles west to the less fertile lands in the foothills of the mountains that were less liable to invasions. Then, he reckoned, he and his former subjects could live in greater peace, even if they occasionally encountered a hostile force. To his utter astonishment, "the entire populace of Bin, bearing their old on their backs and their children in their arms," followed him to the new location on foot, in a spectacular demonstration of loyalty that many neighboring polities took note of, and sought to capitalize upon by forging alliances with Danfu.[26]

What this legend was meant to instill is plain enough, especially as the same message is reiterated in so many texts, oral and written, received and excavated, from the antique past: geographic boundaries are permeable and liable to change (here in size, location, allegiance, and authority), with the ultimate health of the body politic depending rather on flow and change than upon defined territories or small privileged groups.[27] Neither a person nor a realm is ever truly the "possession of one man." Instead, both entities are held in trust, they being in effect "works in progress" extending over time and space. The *White Tiger Discussions* (*Bohu tong* 白虎通) of AD 79 go so far as to insist that even children are not in all senses solely the product of their birth mothers and fathers, since heaven-and-earth (i.e., the cosmos), as well as the imperial court and local community, have contributed to the child's coming into the world, being reared, and

---

[26] See *Shiji* 4.113–14.
[27] This same story is repeated in the *Documents* classic, in "Pan Geng," Part II.

acquiring the potential to become a fully mature human being.[28] Ergo, the benefits associated with bodies or terrain should be spread as widely as possible within the community: in the case of the family, with its members living and dead, and, in the case of the polity, with all residents past, present, and future.[29] Supreme power, then as now, rested on a leader's ability to call upon others' aid in a crisis, an expectation whose reliability was confirmed through long-term, often multigenerational relations of personal trust.[30]

Such obvious facts attesting to the blurry boundaries of the body and body politic by no means precluded order, since order, by the early traditions, emanates from a stable center—stable not because it is rigidly placed, but because it is exquisitely attuned to the ever-shifting social and cosmic patterns. In the body, the center is the heart's organ system mysteriously housed in an empty cavity or void, the locus of the thinking and feeling that spurs motivations.[31] In the body politic, the legitimate ruler or the powerful court,[32] as

---

[28] Explaining why a father may not kill his own son, the *Bohu tong* (Zhufa 誅伐 section) reads, "People are all are born of heaven-and-earth, which avails itself of the *qi* of the father and mother to bring the child to life. Because the true king nourishes the child to maturity and instructs the child, the father may not claim the child is exclusively his" 人皆天所生也，託父母氣而生耳。王者以養長而教之，故父不得專也. For the early empires' notion of filial duty (less absolutist than that known from late imperial China), see Nylan 1996.

[29] The idea of a self-made man or of self-made, one-man autocratic dynastic rule would have struck members of the governing elite as ludicrous. Benefits to the dead included regular sacrifices.

[30] Obviously enough, the early empires in China were not unique in having registered this thought early on, a thought reiterated in the *Rites Record* (*Liji* 禮記) 9.1 ("Li yun" 禮運 chap.). Compare Sennett's view of earned authority in his 2012 classic, *Together*, esp. chap. five, outlining the "social triangle." Khayutina 2010 confirms this picture, tracing it back to Western Zhou, when royal receptions and feasts served to cement relations that are used in war (esp. 27).

[31] I suspect the physical fact of the cavity explains the origin of much talk of "emptiness" and the "void." Cf. the work of Brooke Holmes positing such connections for classical Greece.

[32] What becomes clearer after living with the *Xunzi* and the *Documents* classic, the two chief repositories of political thought in the early empires, is that the reference to the "ruler" often is shorthand for either the ruler and his advisors or the ruler and his court. Indeed, in stark contrast to the Roman Empire, the figure of the ruler during the early empires in China was neither highly gendered nor inherently commanding or militaristic. I have dealt with this in numerous publications, so I do not repeat the evidence here.

theoretical center, was to help direct and facilitate flows of people and goods by various means, while taking those living in the very lowliest conditions as a constant concern.[33] To act in this way was to shine on all equally with a life-giving face, akin to that of the beneficent sun or Dao or Heaven, for people who looked upon "food as Heaven."[34] Pulling together as one to achieve long-term goals,[35] and thereby realizing the most elevated of all human potentials, human communities could achieve what no one single person, family, or clan could possibly manage. That said, to act constructively in concert for a common goal (*qun* 群)—identified by Xunzi as the only distinctly human capacity in the animal kingdom—required purposeful activities by leaders and led alike,[36] and acting in concert was feasible and productive only when individuals' distinctive talents and training were appreciated and well-coordinated, as the proverb *he er bu tong* 和而不同 intimated. After all, a sublime musical effect

---

[33] "Facilitating flows" meant planning and executing initiatives as disparate as building roads and canals to enhance transportation, or "employing the worthy" to improve the quality of the administration or offering cult to bind the living and the dead in constructive communities. The famous story of Chancellor Bing Ji speaks volumes, as the emperor's chief advisor exhibits a preoccupation not with petty thievery, but with an ox panting, a sign of yin and yang imbalance (*Hanshu* 74.3147). As I wrote earlier, the king is "center" because he, by virtue of his position, has the potential to spur the greatest number of effective acts in all directions. His beneficent powers flow out from his capital, which need not be placed at the geographic center of the realm. What made a city a king's capital was the erection of ritual halls, where the classical Way of the Ancients—both the practice and theory of it—could be transmitted to successive generations. See Wheatley 1971; Nylan, 2005; Feng Wenwen 2016; Nylan 2026; also, the *Shangshu/Documents* translation for the University of Washington Press (2026?).

[34] E.g., *Shiji* 97.2694; *Hanshu* 43.2108.

[35] Cf. Charles Taylor (1991), who wrote that the chief malaise in modern life is "not actual despotic control but *fragmentation*—that is, a people increasingly less capable of forming a common purpose and carrying it out" [italics mine]. As Williams 1991, 68, notes, "Epistemic distraction can make it harder to ... detect common structures across associations ... and hence [destroy] the capacity to effectively plan one's own projects and goals." Roethke wrote, "A mind too active is no mind at all."

[36] According to Xunzi, the human potential to *qun* 群 is the chief capacity that distinguishes humans from animals and makes them more effective in long-term initiatives. Acting upon this potential is the precondition for all civilized life lived within the community. See *Xunzi, juan* 8 ("Wang zhi" 王制 chap.).

depends upon the interplay of different instruments.³⁷ Establishing a strong sense of community in this way obviated the chief problems that beset dysfunctional communities: it worked against a "we" vs. "them" mentality, so it did not create scapegoats, and discouraged the creation of rivals engaged in fierce competition with one another. Neither did "unity" require the person's submersion or dissolution in a collective identity, be it that of the clan, the ethnic group, or the nation-state, contra the canards.³⁸ By establishing guideposts but few hard-and-fast rules, both the body and body politic could in real-time adapt actions to the precise exigencies of the situation, with experts and generalists alike seeking the best possible actions after multiple factors were weighed.³⁹ Small wonder, then, that children, regents, and women could wield supreme power, and even in the early empires, the king's capital was but one of several major metropolitan areas, with primary and secondary capitals the norm.⁴⁰

Chinese medical theories underscored this picture of health reliant upon flows among constituent parts of the well-functioning whole.⁴¹ Most to be feared was prolonged somatic statis, that is, blockage of the circulatory flows, which gave rise to "a hundred pathologies . . . in concert, and a myriad catastrophes," reverberating on several resonating planes. For "if one thing is harmed, then no living thing remains unharmed."⁴² People, in company with all the myriad things,

---

[37] Fingarette 1983.
[38] Lü Simian rpt. 2005, 650; Loewe 2011, 177–83, is adamant that talk of "unity" expressed a desire for more ideological consensus at court, not among the general populace.
[39] See the first half of Nylan and Yin, "Consequential Voting" (forthcoming for CUP) on majority rule voting. This way of acting has nothing to do with "relativism."
[40] That Western Zhou had multiple capitals, each serving its own functions, is the thesis of Khayutina 2010. Contrast this with Rome, where Rome far outshone other cities, by design.
[41] Three classic modern studies outline the microcosmic-macrocosmic continuum: Sommer 2008, 294; Kuriyama 1999; and Csikszentmihalyi 2004.
[42] Lüshi chunqiu 12.10a-b, describing stasis in the realm: "Countries, too, have their stases. When the ruler's virtue does not flow freely [i.e., when he is out of touch with his subjects], and the wishes of his people do not reach him, this is that type of stasis." The idea continues in Ibid., "Ben sheng" 本生 chap.: 以害一生，生無不傷.

are wondrous yet highly vulnerable. Appropriate intra-actions meanwhile could marshal a host of regenerative energies.[43] Or, as a second early text put it, "Now, as we all know, to join hearts (with others) is to renew oneself" 夫同心自新.[44] The authoritative *Inner Canon of the Yellow Emperor* (probably the first century AD) is explicit in its analysis: "The subject of discourse, briefly put, is the free travel and inward and outward movement of the divine *qi*," with the result that "the body was defined not by what sets it apart but by its intimate, dynamic relation with its environment."[45] As the philosophers Jane Geaney and Li Zehou have remarked, the division between inner and outer, subject and object, was far less important in the classical traditions than we have made them out to be, given our EuroAmerican models.[46] Indeed, so interdependent were the body, body politic, and cosmos that they "are best considered a single complex," with even talk of interconnectedness profoundly "misleading."[47]

Crucially, throughout antiquity, in the competing resonance theories that were elaborated over the centuries, human beings at once enjoyed the "most honorable" (*zui gui* 最貴) status and an unexceptional position as but one of the myriad things, and hardly the swiftest, smartest, or most dexterous of things at that.[48] Exceptional and unexceptional—these two narratives remained in productive tension in a wide range of sources,[49] moving the human story out of

---

[43] "Surplus energies" could refer to population, to energetic *qi* flows, or to a surplus production of material goods. "Intra-actions" (and not "interactions" between discrete entities) is the preferred term used in Neimanis and Walker 2014.

[44] Observation ascribed to the third Eastern Han emperor, Zhangdi, on his Eastern Tour of Inspection, in *Quan Hou Hanwen*, volume 5.

[45] Sivin 1995, 14.

[46] Geaney 2002; Li Zehou 1999, esp. 174.

[47] Sivin, 1995, 5; cf. Stein 1990. As English language conventions don't make it easy to talk about this oneness, I borrow the clunky term "intra-actions," for lack of more felicitous phrasings.

[48] See, e.g., *Xunzi* ("Wang zhi" 王制 chap.): 力不若牛，走不若馬，而牛馬為用，何也？曰：人能群. Cf. *Lunheng* ("Shi chong" 適蟲 chap.) for the second view. Nylan has discussed this in detail in Nylan 2019.

[49] Nylan 2019.

the absolutist binaries of good/evil, Man/Nature, inherently valuable/ exploitable that Lynn White, Jr. believed undermined care for the environment in the lands adhering to the major Mediterranean religions.[50] Instead, by the classical Chinese accounts, the human potential for constructive action is immense, yet far too few people learn to develop their inherent potentials. Sentiments preserved in the *Annals of Mr. Lü* (*Lüshi chunqiu*) thread through many early writings: "Good learning and emulation, by definition, mean doing whatever one must do to keep what one receives from heaven whole and intact, without doing it harm,"[51] and this general principle pertained, no matter which aspect of the body or body politic was under consideration.

Equally crucially, family rituals, like those at court, tended to mark weddings, births, and mourning, advertising the close bonds that persisted over multiple generations.[52] Fundamental to all rituals were two notions: first, the notion of *bao* 報, usually translated as "reciprocity" but more precisely as "just requital," which the eminent social historian Yang Lien-sheng took to be the basis of all Chinese morality,[53] and second, the notion that all ordering activities, of which formal rituals form but a part, somehow reflect and instantiate the "great basis" of all living things, an entity that has existed from time immemorial and will endure forever.[54] Building upon those insights,

---

[50] White 1967. However, it must be said that most of our languages and even our brain structure predispose us to think, speak, and write in binaries. More holistic visions sound "whiffy" to the uninitiated, whereas they are better thought of as being "as precise as possible, " which is vastly better than being "precisely wrong," in John Maynard Keynes' famous formulation.

[51] *Lüshi Chunqiu* ("Zun shi" 尊師 chap.): 能全天之所生而勿敗之，是謂善學.

[52] Early theories of disease show that the dead ancestors, if they do not receive their due portion, can and will harm future generations, especially the vulnerable bodies residing in the womb. Families were intergenerational in the additional sense that the same elite families intermarried with each other over successive generations, as shown by Liu Tseng-kuei, cited in Figure 10.3 in Nylan and Loewe 2010, 273–74.

[53] Yang 1957.

[54] *Xunzi* ("Wang zhi" chap.) says this of the endless cycles: 始則終，終則始，與天地同理，與萬世同久，夫是之謂大本.

as one early ritual text avers, one may add a third: that husband and wife are one body, parent and child are one body, siblings are one body, friends are one body, and those who identify with their superiors likewise form a single body with them.[55] In rituals of sacrifice, we find the commensal consumption of grain and animal victims whose *qi* (perceived by the senses and vital organs) participates in, invigorates, and sustains the living and the dead, strengthening the ties generation after generation, forming one living body with the dead. For by the cosmogonic sequence, people somehow emerge from that mysterious numinous repository to become fully individuated selves, only to return to it in the fullness of time.[56] For this reason, Xunzi identified acknowledgment of the distinctions to be made between young and old, the worthy and debased, the living and the dead, to ground the stable exercise of good governance. As he puts it in his "Way of the Ruler" chapter,

> The sage kings' abundant wealth is used to make clear the distinctions and differences. Above [i.e., at court], they use it to adorn the worthy and good, and mark out the noble versus the debased persons. Below [i.e., in the lower offices and in the provinces], they use it to distinguish the elders from juniors, the closer or more distant . . . . Everyone under Heaven [i.e., in the realm] realizes that their motivations in making such distinctions reflects their intention to make clear social divisions and achieve good rule, in order to protect the ten thousand generations.[57]

---

[55] *Yili, juan* 11 ("Sang fu" 喪服 chap.), a "tradition" associated with Zixia 子夏.
[56] The phrase is *lingfu* 靈府, cited in several early sources, including *Zhuangzi* 5 ("De chongfu" 德充符).
[57] *Xunzi* 12 ("Jun dao" 君道 chap.): 天下曉然皆知其所以為異也，將以明分达治而保万世也. The passage continues, "Therefore, it is said, "With good rule, the embellishments flow down to the Hundred Families, whereas with bad rule, they do not even reach kings and dukes" (故曰。治則衍及百姓，亂則不足及王公。此之謂也). My translation modifies that of Hutton 2014, 124.

Another foundational text, the *Gongyang Tradition*, tersely asserts that "the realm and the ruler are one body," then asks rhetorically, "How are the realm and ruler one body? It is because the ruler considers (all residing in) the realm to be a single body."[58] Not to consult one's subjects or citizens is for the one body part, say the head, to ignore the condition of the fingers or nose. Certainly, pictures of good governance in the early empires are premised on the beneficial flows, including informational flows, that stem from the cycle of blessings conferred and blessings received.[59] This is far more than a "happy symmetry," surely, however difficult it is to articulate in modern languages.[60] (Raymond Williams and Greg Anderson, among others, have reminded us how ill-suited our current vocabulary is to capture past realities, relying as it does on a host of abstractions that were not yet imagined in the distant past.)[61]

The idea that, according to early theories, mother, father, and child are at once visibly autonomous yet consubstantial units, has immense consequences,[62] for by those theories, the child is but "the bequeathed body" (*yi ti* 遺體) of the parents.[63] As we are all bequeathed bodies held in trust, by the antique views expressed in classical Chinese, none of us can escape our interdependencies, nor would we be wise

---

[58] *Gongyang*, Lord Zhuang, Year 4: 國君一體. Cf. *Zhuangzi* 25 ("Zeyang" 則陽): 周盡一體; cf. *Zhuangzi jishi* ("Tianxia" 天下 chap.), 1102.
[59] See, e.g., *Shuoyuan*, 1.14 ("Jun dao"), which conceives of the *enliu qunsheng* 恩流群生 (beneficial flows, powered by a sense of mutual obligation) moving "all living things," from ruler down to the very vegetation: 潤澤草木.
[60] "Happy symmetry" is the term used by Ivanhoe 1991; cf. Tu Wei-ming's "anthropocosmic" term (borrowed from Mircea Eliade).
[61] Williams 1976; Anderson 2018.
[62] Fetal training (*tai jiao* 胎教), mentioned in not a few Han texts including the *Da Dai Liji*, complicates the story even further. Here I respectfully part company with Anne Behnke Kinney's otherwise thoughtful works, "Dyed Silk" and *Representations of Childhood*, where she pits "Confucian" against "Daoist" views of child development, when the two views frequently appear in the same sources. For a convincing analysis, see Despeux 2003.
[63] This sentiment is echoed in no fewer than twelve Han texts, including *Liji*, 25.35 ("Ji yi" 祭義 chap.), where Zengzi, one of the supreme exemplars of filial piety, articulates this principle. The text there continues, "When putting this bequeathed body into action, does one ever dare to be irreverent?"

to seek to do so. They are a basic fact of life, and one that requires us to consult widely with others, before proceeding to act in ways that may well affect others.

Seasonality for the Body Politic, as for the Body

During the early empires in China, members of the governing elite took it for granted that care of the body must be adjusted by hours, days, months, and seasons, in light of the body's complex biorhythms, and that the same necessity for continual adjustments, by extension, was needed in the body politic and, ultimately, the cosmos itself. By legend, the ancient sage-ruler Yao paid equal attention to calendrics and to farming, establishing the correct model for all legitimate rulers, and Han emperors publicly performed their commitment to strengthen the ties that bound heaven, earth, and human by engaging in the spring ritual ploughing in the capital.[64] From its inception, we are told, the Han powers-that-be recognized that the ruling house must "conform to the four seasons" and to the movements of the stars, if it hoped to retain legitimacy.[65] Certainly, the Han thinkers and statesmen were ready to invoke the "Pan Geng" chapter of the *Documents* classic on this topic; it states,

---

[64] See *Shiji* 1.16, 1.16n7: 敬道出日，平均次序東作之事，以務農也. The best account of the imperial ploughing rite, paired with the autumn hunts, remains Bodde 1975, chap. 9 (223–42).

[65] See Wei Xiang, advising Xuandi, in *Hanshu* 74.3140. Wei Xiang explains the necessity for the emperor to wear seasonal robes during court rituals, which is item no. 8 on Wei's agenda. The seasonal robes are to advertise and exemplify the emperor's care for seasonal policies. As the proverb goes, "Conformity with the four seasons cannot be neglected" 四時之大順，不可失也, cited in *Shiji* 130.3995. We know that the annual "sent-up accounts" rendered to the central court were to report on local environmental conditions. See *Shuihudi Qinmu zhujian*, 33, the "Explanatory" section; also Zhu Kezhen 1926.

Of old, Our previous rulers to a man always thought only of the people's protection. The rulers all had such care and grace that they did not dare disturb the sacred seasonal round.[66]

The most effective rulers down through the ages evinced their reverence for the hallowed orders by strict observance of the "Monthly Ordinances" ("Yue ling" 月令), and we find Qin's First Emperor celebrating these in the Langya stele inscription that he commissioned, as did the Han emperors and advisers who succeeded him.[67] During the early empires, multiple texts, including the *Guanzi* 管子 and the standard histories, enjoined this way of thinking until, by late Eastern Han, there appeared an agricultural estate manual entitled *Four Occupations' Monthly Ordinances* (*Simin Yueling* 四民月令), compiled by one Cui Shi 崔寔 (d. 170), to great acclaim.[68] Two antique budgets (one pre-imperial and one imperial) have long commanded the attention of serious historians, because they were designed to persuade pampered rulers how precarious was the life of the average farming family.[69] But far less attention has gone to the real policies, from late Zhanguo on, that successful administrations felt they must deploy to aid their farmers, for moral and pragmatic reasons, not only in times of natural disasters, but also during years with average yields.[70] Indeed, until quite recently, modern historians have paid scant attention to the importance of timely action to good

---

[66] *Documents/Shangshu*, 6B ("Pan Geng," second speech).
[67] *Hanshu* 75.3188: Thus, the ancient kings revered Heaven and Earth; cf. Zhangdi's edicts on timing in AD 76, 85. In the *Huainanzi*, reference to technical matters (including timing) in relation to agriculture appear in the chapter entitled "Explication of the Ruler's Techniques" ("Zhushu xun" 主術訓).
[68] Not coincidentally, Cui Shi was trained by his father, an astronomer. His text describes many plants and planting methods, methods to cultivate land and process field crops, how to raise cattle, and how to organize a large estate in all its aspects, including provisions for ritual sacrifices (*jisi* 祭祀), family rituals (*jiali* 家礼), and instruction (*jiaoyu* 教育), suggesting the degree to which the large manorial estates had become self-sufficient by his time.
[69] For the first budget, see Li Kui (ca. 387 BC), cited in *Hanshu* 24A.1124; for the second, see Chao Cuo 晁錯 (200–154 BC), cited in *Shiji* 101.2749; *Hanshu* 24A.1130.
[70] One could consult the *Xunzi*, *Guanzi*, or *Qimin yaoshu*, for example.

rule, thinking discussions of cosmological and human time to be abstract theories having little relevance to sociopolitical realities, despite repeated stress on this topic in the received texts and in the excavated manuscripts found in tomb sites.[71]

That comparative neglect was bound to end after the publication of two pieces of evidence excavated and published in the first two decades of the new millennium.[72] First, in 2001, came the publication of the first complete Han imperial edict ever seen, in a report on an archaeological excavation carried out in August-December 1992, in Xuanquan, on the outskirts of Dunhuang.[73] This Han edict issued in AD 5 (unknown from other sources) proved just how determined the Han throne was to convey to even the peripheral areas in the empire the latest scientific advances in the care of the material environment.[74]

---

[71] Elsewhere, Nylan has identified timing as a chief preoccupation of Han thinkers and statesmen. For twenty years and more, we have had multiple copies of the Monthly Ordinances in circulation; see Liu Ming 2021, 104, 124. If the Yuelu Academy manuscripts of the Qin laws are genuine, they offer additional support, as mentioned in ibid., 126–28, which tallies with Liye (excavated) strips J1(16)5, J1 (16)6.

[72] We forget how often important manuscripts languish in the PRC storerooms, unpublished for years, for decades, or even not at all, as happened with most of the Fuyang cache. This can happen for many reasons, including inexpert storage (as at Fuyang), the death or incapacity of lead excavators, or the decision by the CCP to withhold publication.

[73] Other tombs contain related evidence. For example, a Linyi, Yinqueshan tomb had part of an edict discussing the yin/yang seasons and a second manuscript, the "Four Seasons Ordinance," 四时令). For those tomb finds, see the archaeological report *Yinqueshan Han mu jujian* 银雀山汉墓竹简. Chen Mengjia thought the *Annals of Mr. Lü* represented, in one part, a Qin-era "Yueling."

[74] See *Dunhuang Xuanquan*, "Zhaoshu sishi yueling wushitiao" 詔書四時月令五十條. Often called the "Fifty Articles," the AD 5 edict has been the subject of intensive study ever since it was published. The site from which it derived was in continuous use from 111 BCE until the third century CE, when a tower was constructed over it, as it had fallen into gradual disuse over the course of Eastern Han. The "Fifty Articles" was found in Room 26 (F26), written on the collapsed wall there. The black-bordered, two-part inscription [main contents plus label], as reconstructed, consists of 101 lines (81 representing the "Yue ling") having roughly 13,000 logographs. Measuring roughly 2.2 meters high and 38 cm. long, it is now held by the Wenwu kaogu yanjiu suo, in Lanzhou, Gansu province. NB: Dunhuang was an important trading post for the early empires and Central Asia, and Xuanquan, a nearby fort. In English, the single best study and translation of the edict remains Sanft 2008/9.

Second, in 2014, came the publication of wooden boards excavated in Qingchuan 青川 county, Sichuan province, showing that, as early as 309 or 307 BC (if not earlier) attempts were being made to affix the seasonal activities to the progress of the months throughout the lunar calendar year, attempts said to exemplify good governance.[75] In addition to these two spectacular finds, multiple examples of scientifically-excavated local registries for taxpaying households further underscore the courts' interest in upholding the seasonal order, as local officials were forbidden to levy their labor during the farming seasons.[76]

To illustrate the throne's preoccupation with timely action on behalf of the intergenerational common good, this section highlights the lengthy Xuanquan edict, known as the "Four Seasons, Monthly Ordinances Edict, in Fifty Articles,"[77] whose sole purpose was to mandate that local officials pay due attention to training the local farmers, shepherds, and hunter-gatherers in their charge to discriminate timely versus untimely actions, lest temporary or lasting harm be done to the environment, which in turn would wreck the locals' livelihoods and ritual lives. As part of a popular "seasonal and monthly" writing genre,[78] the Fifty Articles attests the early empires' preoccupation with alerting local officials to the need to conserve local resources, lest impoverished local communities become unsustainable, for themselves and for the Han administration,[79] which

---

[75] See *Qin jiandu heji*.
[76] Mencius has much to say on the same topic, as in *Mengzi* 1.3.
[77] Note that the title is given by the modern editors; for details, see note 7 above.
[78] Modern secondary scholarship is not in complete agreement on the question of how the seasonal (*si shi* 四時) literature relates to the "Monthly Ordinances" or "Yueling" 月令 materials, as some materials seem to distinguish them while others do not. Plainly, however, they are closely related, as per Xue 2014.
[79] Contra Sanft (2008/9), Nylan believes, with Liu Ming 2022, that the edict is undoubtedly addressed to local officials, not to commoners, which would mean emending some of Sanft's translations (for instance, changing "Do not do X" to "Do not let X be done." Unlike many scholars, Nylan dates the Monthly Ordinances genre to Zhanguo and leaves the question of origins to would-be metaphysicians, unlike Sanft's summary, 156–68.

depended upon dependable revenue flows. (The next section in this chapter will describe the early empires' efforts to further care for the welfare of the local population—efforts for which we now have ample proof and that went far beyond what most scholars had previously imagined, stipulating the care of the aged, the disadvantaged, and the disabled, as instances of environmental concerns subject to the court's "instructions.")[80]

Meanwhile, the classical sources registered continual complaints equating bad governance with interference with the farmers' seasonal round of activities, there being time enough after the harvest, in late fall and winter, to attend to other tasks such as infrastructure repair and worship of the household gods.[81] Then, as now, there were officious bureaucrats sticking to the letter, not the spirit of the laws, and local administrators who clearly liked to bully. Then, as now, there were debates over the degree to which the cumulative effects of human conduct upon the environment prompted natural disasters with the consequent loss of life. Some officials noted the plausible, if not certain links,[82] while others traced disasters to eccentric *qi* movements in specific times and places generated by conjunctions

---

That said, we in the scholarly world are deeply indebted to Sanft's painstaking work on this topic.

[80] Two exceptions must be mentioned, both of whom suggested the scope of the imperial efforts: Lü Simian and Hulsewé. See Lü 2005, e.g., 600, on Han officials' making loans (sometimes interest-free) to farmers; also Hulsewé 1987. The association made between *jiaoling* 教令 and the "Yueling" genre is clear in multiple sources, such as *Shiji* 130.3995; *Hanshu* 24A.1124.

[81] Section 3 of Part II will show many associations with seasonality we moderns might not make, but Han officials did. These associations included adjudicating lawsuits, going to war, and nominating candidates for court office. From this basic prohibition was extrapolated, I suspect, the multiple cautions against interfering with other officers as they attended to their various duties, whether playing elevated roles at court or carrying out more humble tasks in village hamlets.

[82] *Hanshu* 83.3386, citing Gu Yong: "They [the natural disasters] are not necessarily not occasioned by this" 未必不由此. *Hanshu* 10.312, for 23 BC, during the reign of Chengdi, provides a clear statement that many high-ranking officials of the time preferred to ignore the possible connection or profess skepticism so that they might continue along their customary ways (多違時政), extracting more from the land and its people than was warranted. See also Liu Ming 2022, esp. 25–26.

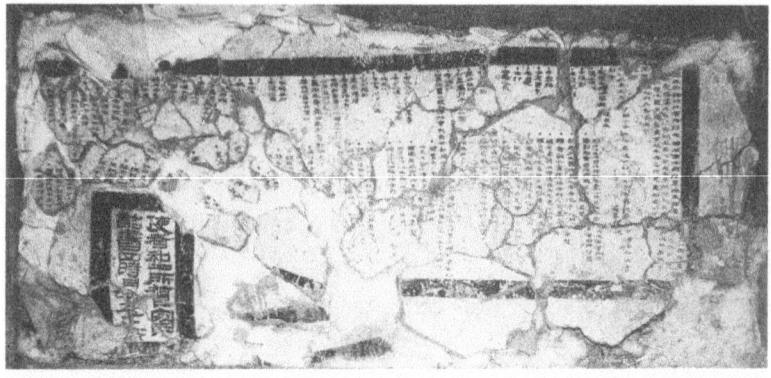

Figure 1 The Xuanquan edict.

of multiple factors too complicated and unpredictable for human policies to forestall.[83]

Case Study: The Xuanquan Edict of AD 5

Claiming ancient authority for its decrees,[84] the Xuanquan edict of AD 5 consists of three parts: (1) the prohibitions and stipulations that the local officials are to impart to those in their charge; (2) an expanded explication and rephrasing of the initial passage in the edict, to obviate mistakes in transmission of the court's will; and (3) more specific instructions delimiting proper timing, sometimes expressed in terms of months and sometimes in terms of changes in the natural world (e.g., "Only after the leaves have fallen . . . " and

---

[83] See, e.g., *Hanshu* 75.3188.
[84] Edicts carried the force of law during the early empires. Like other pieces of writing in this genre, the edict explicitly and implicitly alludes to ancient authorities while diverging in its wording, judging from the present evidence at hand. For example, some edicts in this vein (e.g., *Hanshu* 43.1343) cite the "Hong fan" chapter of the *Documents* classic to justify prescriptions and proscriptions regarding timber.

"It applies until the end of the ninth month"). A sample of the fifty articles, representing the first seven of the fifty, appears below.

- "Assiduously order the people's time."[85] • Tell them to sow grain, and have everyone hurry to the fields.
- It is forbidden to cut down trees. • This means that neither large nor small trees may be cut down, and it applies until the end of the eighth month. Only after the leaves have fallen from plants and trees may one cut down those trees that should be cut.
- Do not gather birds' nests. • This means that neither occupied nor unoccupied nests may be gathered. It applies to empty nests until the end of summer. [Gathering] occupied nests is constantly forbidden in all four seasons.
- Do not kill young insects. • This refers to immature insects that do not harm people. It applies until the end of the ninth month.
- Do not kill fetuses. • This refers to wild and domestic animals that are pregnant and bearing fetuses. [Killing them is] constantly forbidden until the end of the twelfth month.
- Do not take young birds. • This refers to killing young birds so they do not get to grow up. It is constantly forbidden until the end of the twelfth month.
- Do not take fawns. • This refers to four-legged ... and domesticated animals that are young and not yet steady, and it applies until the end of the ninth month ... .[86]

And so the edict continues, with all fifty articles tying the latest calendrical knowledge closely to the court's concerns to make its subjects' household production sustainable for many generations, the better to ensure community stability and resilience for the long term.

---

[85] This injunction cites the "Great Plan" chapter of the *Documents* classic, as does another injunction below.
[86] These translations are slightly modified from those given in Sanft (2008/9).

To this end, local officials are to "with all due reverence, follow yin and yang, and 'assiduously confer [as a gift] the proper timing upon the people'" (欽順陰陽, 敬授民時).⁸⁷ They accomplished this charge, presumably, by having the edict publicized in comparatively out-of-the-way places like Xuanquan, a frontier outpost near an agricultural colony in the inhospitable northwest. By the edict, during high summer, the officials were to assign only one task to the local farmers, a reduced burden that seems more realistic than the tasks listed for the same period in summer in the *Annals of Mr. Lü*, whose wording is loosely similar to that in this edict.⁸⁸ Several articles, particularly Articles 37 and 38, specifically forbade the local officials to interfere with the planting, weeding, and harvesting activities. To ensure the correct timing for the prescriptions and prohibitions, the court's minister in charge of agriculture was to work closely with the court's calendrical masters.⁸⁹

However, the edict concerns matters beyond agricultural life, because the administrators of the early empires saw their oversight duties in more capacious terms, even if the edict makes no explicit provision for sacrifices and only the most rudimentary references to astronomy. The text says in Article 19, for instance, "to bury the flesh of the sick and disabled [animals?]" (*yi ge li ci* 瘞骼貍骴)⁹⁰ and Article 21 contains the injunction, "See to it that all the solitaries are maintained" (*cun zhu gu* 存諸孤), accompanied by the explication, "This refers to the very young [orphans]."⁹¹ In addition, the edict mentions activities said to establish or reestablish the crucial corridors

---

⁸⁷ Sanft 2008/9, 178, translates instead as "assiduously ordered the people's time," probably following Legge.
⁸⁸ See *Lüshi chunqiu xin jiaoshi*, 31,4–15. See also Liu Ming 2022, 89–90.
⁸⁹ See, e.g., *Hanshu* 19.731, 858.
⁹⁰ Translation very tentative. Unlike Sanft 2008/9, 180, I take the line to mean that diseased carcasses should be buried.
⁹¹ The term "solitaries" does in other texts apply to larger groups of people living alone.

of communication, in order to "convenience the people" (以 . . . 便民), as in Article 31.

During the early empires, two of the chief metaphors for good rule were (1) an admixture of allusions to the shepherding and farming ways of life (with shepherding the older metaphor, perhaps);[92] and (2) the ruler as "father and mother" for the people, a Zhanguo-period metaphor popularized in the Qin and Han dynasties.[93] Both imply a degree of pastoral care and foreplanning, for shepherds do not merely protect their flocks; they move them to greener pastures to ensure the health of the flock, like good parents seeing to their children's present and future developmental needs. To much the same end, the ubiquitous plant metaphors bespoke personal and social cultivation under the court's guidance, with the propagation and nurturing of seeds, their rootedness below the earth's surface, and their flourishing life cycles all suggesting a "material continuity of identity from one life form to the next,"[94] while hinting at the slow pace of cultivation.

Evidence attesting to the Han preoccupation with environmental conservation in relation to timing, both theoretical and highly practical, abounds.[95] As has been noted,

> Orientation to seasonal change involves dense and complicated cultural practices, which we pick up less through explicit teachings than by accommodating ourselves to certain rhythms of society. Xunzi pointed out, however, that orientation to unexpected natural

---

[92] The metaphor of the pastor appears in the *Documents* in a few late chapters, and the *Odes* classic also alludes to it (Mao ode no. 42: 自牧歸荑).
[93] Dating is fraught for most pre-Han and Han texts before the Eastern Han; linguists often fail to consult historians and vice versa, making for considerable confusion.
[94] Sommer 2008, 296 and note 8, where Sommer asks, "how a personal identity associated with a particular person's body persists over time."
[95] For example, *Shangshu dazhuan, juan* 1, remarks that there is a proper time to plant each and every crop; Yu therefore "gave it [the knowledge of proper timing] to the people" (*Tianzi fu zhi min* 天子賦之民), in the sense of teaching them. One interesting writer on timeliness and the "Yueling" is Baba Rieko, whose work emphasizes the legal thinking enjoining timeliness for farmers within the context of the environmental understanding of the antique eras.

disasters and the sudden appearances of barbarians requires high culture, a government capable of thinking ahead, laying plans, and commanding the cooperation of vast numbers of people. Societies without good governments cannot find an adequate orientation to these surprises and are usually overwhelmed by water or warriors.[96]

In this connection, one may note the ritual importance of the Mingtang built in Chang'an, in AD 5 (the same year as the edict was promulgated),[97] as well as solemn ceremonies performed at the sites of the local community god, or *tudi gong* 土地公. In the localities, the local officials were to "meet the spring," and "welcome all the four seasons," performing these ceremonies in the emperor's stead.[98] Moderns may scoff at such constructions,[99] even if one of the most solemn duties of the emperor was to foster the seasonal turn in the calendar year through his ritual circumambulation inside the Mingtang worship hall, and solemn worship was duly replicated on the local scene to the community god(s), as services paid to one's own ancestors.[100] But even hardened skeptics among us may find it difficult to ignore the numerous Daybook tomb finds that evince the early elites' preoccupation with timing; these Daybooks specify the lucky

---

[96] Neville 1998, 267.
[97] Nylan and Constantino 2022, section 2. Cf. Corradini 1995. Usually called the "Hall of Light," the *ming* in Mingtang almost certainly refers to the unseen powers, the gods of heaven and earth, who help to ensure that the seasonal round proceeds.
[98] Xue Mengxiao 2014, chapter 4, says that there is now no doubt that these ceremonies were performed at the local levels on behalf of the Tianzi, given the multiple excavated strips describing them (e.g., Yinqueshan, strips 1880–1886). In Eastern Han, under Mingdi, in AD 59, the "Welcome the Seasons" rites were "first held" in Luoyang, at the five suburban altar sites, according to *Hou Hanshu* 2.104: 是歲, 始迎氣五郊. By edict, these ceremonies were to be conducted in the commanderies and kingdoms as well (郡縣也有迎气活动). Zhangdi then performed another, related "first": he had special music performed to welcome the seasons, by the Monthly Ordinances 始行月令迎氣樂.
[99] Madame Pirazzoli-t'Serstevens, one of the gods in my academic pantheon, once dubbed the Mingtang a "cream puff," i.e., a confection that is all air and no substance. In retrospect, I realize she was probably talking about the "substanceless" scholarly papers rather than the archaic site.
[100] A good account is provided in Xue Mingxiao 2014b, 124ff. NB: most secondary studies still presume the early empires operated on the same model as the early modern states in EuroAmerica, which is plainly ludicrous. See Crone 1989.

and lucky days for all types of ordinary activities, such as planting crops, traveling from home, burying the dead, and even dying, replete with remedies for ill-luck.[101] The excavated Yinwan finds include one diary of a functionary, Shi Rao 師饒, dated to 11 BC, which makes it easy to track how closely his travels (often on tours of inspection in the county) were timed to the seasonal work in his locality.[102]

To some degree, the foregoing, knowingly, poses a strong challenge to Mark Elvin's pathbreaking *The Retreat of the Elephants* (2006), not because Elvin's *Retreat* is not a good book (it emphatically is), but because Elvin's narrative (a) tells only one side of the story; and (b) was compiled nearly two decades before we had better data on environmental changes in early China. By Elvin's account, the Chinese story is one of steady expansion and environmental destruction:

> The basic social story of "China" is the four-thousand year expansion of "Han" or "Chinese" population, political power, and culture from their birthplace in the Northwest and Northeast, with secondary centers in the West and Center, into all the other areas shown [of the Nine Provinces], and indeed beyond them ... into what is now Vietnam and Korea. Overall, ... the picture is one of Han Chinese expansion up to natural limits—coasts, steppes, deserts, mountains, and jungles. It was a multi-millennial transformation of a variety of habitats by some version of the *Chinese style of settlement.*[103]

Importantly for our purposes, Elvin said this "Chinese style of settlement" was ruinous for the natural environment, regardless of the local topography, north or south, for all of imperial and post-imperial

---

[101] The most famous of these maps are from Fangmatan (two examples), from Shuihudi, from Jiangling Fenghuan shan, no 168 M5, and from Kongjiapo. See Poo Mu-chou 1995; Liu Tseng-kuei 2013; Michelle Wang 2023; Olberding 2023.

[102] See *Yinwan Hanmu*, Forward. Li Ling believes several references to *zhi ri* signify dates of inspection (*shi ri* 視日), but no established consensus exists on this point. See Liu Ming 2022, 16,7–71.

[103] Elvin 2006, chap. 1 (italics mine).

history. Elvin outlined three successive stages of the destruction: in Stage 1, farmers clear-cut or set land alight to make it possible for them to easily lay out their croplands, even if such activities lead to erosion (especially in the loess soil of North China) and to the destruction of animal habitats; in Stage 2, farmers, in defending their farm plots from the wild animals in the area, exterminate them individually and sometimes collectively in mass hunts; and in Stage 3, farmers hunt down the animals in their remaining but evermore circumscribed habitats, since such animals represent valuable products, including animal skins, tusks, and meat. Colder weather tends to exacerbate stages 2–3, by Elvin's account, as farmers are driven to hunt more animals, whenever their grain harvests are diminished. Overall, the picture is grim: short-terms gains in economic and psychological security inevitably led to a panoply of long-term losses, among them losses in environmental diversity and sustainability, "rural involution," flooding, and soil erosion.

But is Elvin's story, adopted by nearly all secondary sources today, the whole story of "Chinese style" settlement, or is it merely one undeniable facet of it? Accustomed to considering "dual-use" technologies (use for good or for destruction) when it comes to new technologies, scholars would be wise to apply that consideration to the age-old Chinese farming techniques as well. Surely, it was mainly the poorest farmers and landless emigrants who were forced to resort to such shortsighted farming methods, when so much of Chinese tradition deplored such practices. After all, as Elvin's book shows, Chinese households facing stable economic situations tended to opt for conservation over "efficient" exploitation of the land;[104] then, too, Craig Clunas pictures the allure of "fruitful sites" for Chinese elites,

---

[104] Elvin, meanwhile, shows that the worst environmental destruction took place in the Ming and Qing, Ming because of the colder conditions that exacerbated poverty, and Qing, due to exponential population growth.

fruitful because properties were replanted with trees, whenever feasible, for household consumption, for market, and for ritual gifts.[105] Quite often, the population could be supported by more advanced (and not more exploitative) techniques, including the introduction of new seed strains through selection, the introduction of new crops (in Han times, sesame and alfalfa, for example), the expansion of fallow-fielding, the development of better tools, and the provision of more draft animals (valued for their manure, as well as their ability to pull a plough).[106] Study of the latest manuals on environmentally-friendly agriculture today—George Monbiot's *Regenesis* comes to mind—suggests that the typical small scale of Han farms was more likely to foster an acute sensitivity to the peculiarities of the terroir,[107] along with an inherently conservative and intergenerational consciousness towards land use, which minimizes disturbances and maximizes biodiversity. Planted today, a fruit tree might take a decade to bear a full crop; a timber stand was a much longer-term investment. Even Zhuangzi knew that.[108] For the foregoing reasons, resort to what Elvin calls "Chinese-style" agriculture (i.e., raping the land) was likely to happen only when populations were too hard-pressed at the moment to plan for their own long-term well-being.[109]

---

[105] Clunas 1996.
[106] Sala 2024 explains modern scientists' belated awareness of these desiderata. For example, we know from *Fan Sheng zhi shu*, a late Western Han technical farming manual, that double-cropping of wheat had become possible in North China, thanks to the careful selection of seeds over generations. The *Shuowen jiezi* shows us how many varieties of grains and pulses were known by mid-Eastern Han.
[107] *Terroir* is a French term that means more than "terrain"; it includes the soil, climate, topography, flora and fauna, and management practices.
[108] See *Zhuangzi, juan* 1: "He who goes out to the grassy suburbs, returning for the third meal [of the day], will have his belly as full as when he set out. He who goes a distance of 100 leagues will have to pound his grain where he stops for the night. He who goes a thousand leagues will have to carry with him provisions for three months." On the terroir in *Zhuangzi*: 果蓏有理，人倫雖難，所以相齒。聖人遭之而不違，過之而不守。
[109] If Elvin were right, we would have to assume steady changes to the environment over the empires, but what we discover instead is dramatic changes happening to the environment in Ming. This was true, apparently, in the Xi'an area, judging from the recent Wei River excavations. For details, see the multiple Wei River reports (2013) following the discovery of several new Wei River bridges.

There is an irony here: According to the famous State of Nature stories, East and West, extreme precarity leads people to see the advantages of cooperation and trust.[110] Yet over and over, most recently during the global pandemic, we saw precarity inducing people to feel greater mistrust. Are the State of Nature stories wrong? No, they are partial, just as Elvin is.

"Instructions" on Seasonal Disbursements

Humans are the single species of the animal kingdom that must learn to learn. This point is driven home in the early Guodian manuscripts (ca. 300 BC), which contrast the spontaneous and instinctual existences of non-human animals to the human reliance on others for the acquisition of speech, *habitus*, and other basic life-skills.[111] A similar point is made in Xunzi's famous opening essay which ties learning and emulation to "augmentation" and "borrowing" (both plausible renderings of Xunzi's *jia* 假).[112] Accordingly, this section treats the early empires' allied efforts to attend to the welfare of the local population, particularly care of the aged, the disadvantaged, and the disabled, with such care explicitly tied to environmental concerns and characterized as the court's civilizing "instructions" (*jiao* 教 and *jiaohua* 教化). Past scholarship has usually treated *jiao* 教 and

---

[110] Xunzi and Hobbes are comparable in this regard. For them, see Nylan 2026a; 2026b; Nylan 2025b.
[111] Nylan tried to drive this point home in a Zoom talk for the lecture series "Sihai wei xue" (organized by Paul d'Ambrosio) on Oct. 17, 2022; for Guodian, as per Trenton Wilson 2022, adapting Middendorf's translation, as here: 凡心有志也，無與不可。心之不可獨行，猶口之不可獨言也。牛生而長，雁生而伸，其性使然。人生而學，或使之也. "In general, that the mind has a destination without any guidance [from others] is [impossible. The mind cannot] engage independently in [cognitive and affective] activity, just as the mouth cannot say words independently [of another person]. Oxen are born and grow [fat], wild geese are born and stretch out [necks and wings], their [respective] natures [make it so. Human beings are born] and [must] learn, someone makes them do so."
[112] Rather than "falseness," as shown by Constantino 2021.

jiaohua 教化 either as dogma or as moral teachings,[113] but neither the received nor the newly excavated texts support these readings, which presuppose relatively advanced literacy and a pervasive Kantian sense of morality. Instead, the early sources have *jiao* and *jiaohua* referring to the most basic "instructions" deemed of use to the general populace, including commoners in the localities, as with the Xuanquan edict described above. For them, acting to ease others is the very foundation of the rites by which all communities, regardless of location, prominence, or wealth, can become well-governed, as stated in the epigrams to this chapter.[114] For instance, the Wei Zhao 韋昭 (204–273) commentary to the *Guoyu* 國語, defined the *jiao* of the former sage kings as "what is subsumed under the Monthly Ordinances genre," in a dialogue on the right time of the year to repair dikes, bridges, and roads.[115] Moreover, at least since Kongzi and Mencius (and not just for Confucians),[116] the general understanding was that all but the most exceptional people needed a secure standard of living before they could ever heed ethical teachings or suasive examples.[117] Ergo, by theory and practice, what should follow the initial imposition of peace and order in the empire (*ping ding sihai* 評定四海) was the establishment of ritual centers (*xiangxu* 庠序) based in the localities, where the "nourishing the aged" ceremonies were to be held for the edification of the locals.[118] As one fairly typical

---

[113] Contra Brindley 2021, for example.
[114] See the epigraphs for this chapter.
[115] In Chinese: 教謂月令之屬. See *Guoyu* ("Zhou yu" 周語 chap.), 單襄公論陳必亡 episode. The dialogue features Lord Xiang of Dan/Chan 單襄公 (r. ca 590 BC).
[116] The case of Wei Xiang, identified as a Ru, a classicist, if not a Confucian, shows how closely Wei's ideas match those identified with Qin and Qi in the early sources. See *Hanshu* 88.3617, analyzed in Chen Sudong 2018 and Xue Mengxiao 2014, 71ff.
[117] Some adduced rare cases of innately enlightened persons, such as Shun, the filial exemplar who went on to become sage-king.
[118] *Hanshu* 24A.1117n17. Cf. *Shuowen* 9B/5a: 禮官養老, which it relates to *xiang* 庠. *Xiang* and *xu* are usually construed as "schools" in the modern sense, devoted respectively to primary and secondary education. Instead, *xiang* and *xu* are ritual centers, where community members met to discuss events, practice some rituals, and perhaps, as local resources allowed, provide some type of minimum formal instruction, possibly including

statement put it, tying together legitimacy, appropriate growth of many types, and "comforting" the people:

> Speaking of the [wise] ruler's way of governing: . . . The people have their natures, their conditions, their gradual but profound transformations, their customs. The inclinations and natures concern the heart [seat of cognition and feelings], as that is the root. The transformation of customs is practice; it is secondary, in being born of the more basic. This is why the ruler above comforts and soothes (*fu* 撫) the aged, putting the basic first and later [achieving] the secondary [goal of transforming the people], thereby making their hearts concordant [with his], and ordering their conduct. Surely, so long as the heart's core is upright, treachery will not arise nor will bad intentions find any support.[119]

Today, our evidence for what A.F.P. Hulsewé dubbed "proto-welfare" institutions and policies comes from the standard histories, the Classics, and masterworks, whose remarks are given flesh in the wooden boards and bamboo strips recently excavated from an array of sites scattered across the lands of the Qin and Han empires.[120] In the received texts, one of the first extended discussions occurs in the "Basic Annals" of Wendi for the year 179 BC in the standard histories. Wendi's court discussed care of the aged and seasonal loans to farmers in spring in one and the same breath. Gifts of food and brew

---

teaching the young the rudimentary skills of reading, writing, and calculating. Dong Zhongshu imagined that these institutions in antiquity were located in the major cities or settlements (*Hanshu* 56.2503). Under Han Pingdi (r. 1 BC-AD 6), Wang Mang submitted a memorial urging the establishment of schools (*xue* 學, *xiao* 校) in the commanderies and counties, but *Hanshu* 12.355 leaves readers in doubt as to whether the edict was ever acted upon.

[119] Wang Fu 王符, *Qianfu lun* 潛夫論, *pian* 33 ("Ben de" 本德). Cf. *Hanshu* 56.2499–2512, where Dong Zhongshu in memorials insists that all wise kings in antiquity attended first to the transformation of their subjects' hearts (*jiaohua* 教化), regarding this as the dynasty's most pressing task.

[120] Wang Wentao 2007 deserves credit for being one of the first secondary sources to utilize all the newly excavated sources relating to imperial relief measures following natural disasters. Lü Simian 2005 explored these issues at the beginning of the twentieth century, though without the benefit of recent excavations.

would attest the emperor's basic humanity (and hence basic decency and sense of fairness) toward the aged, winning over his subjects. Members of the court suggested that monthly stipends for the aged be established, and calls were made for the 2,000-bushel officers at the apex of government to take personal responsibility for teaching their subordinates to proffer these disbursements respectfully.[121] Subsequent policy discussions, often framed in the same language, named six precise groups (expanding upon Xunzi's list of five) who merited special consideration: "widowers and widows, orphans and those who lived alone, the aged, and the poor" 鰥寡孤獨高年貧困.[122] What compels interest here is how closely social welfare conferrals were tied to concerns about the seasonal round. For this reason, throughout the two Han dynasties, awards and gifts were conferred mainly in spring and fall, to herald new life and celebrate great maturity respectively, with the young receiving greater attention early on in the lunar year and the old, as the year drew to a close. The population registries found in disparate sites (Shuihudi, Zhangjiashan, Yinwan,

---

[121] *Hanshu* 4.113. *Hanshu* 8.248 (two-thousand bushel officers); *Hanshu* 9.279 (speaking of those who have lost their professions (*shi ye* 失業), presumably farmers). Earlier, ca. 238 BC, the compilers of the LSCQ called for emptying the granaries for such purposes, as needed, so that" the Son of Heaven would distribute his favors and carry out his liberality" 天子布德行惠 [here *de* must mean "favors"].

[122] See, e.g., *Hanshu* 8.248, 258. Xunzi had written casually of the "Five Afflicted Groups" (*wu ji* 五疾) in several chapters, including his "Cultivating One's Person" (Xiu shen 修身) and "Kingly Regulations" (Wang zhi 王制) chapters, which term referred to widowers and widows, the aged and orphaned, plus the disabled. In some rituals, the court's deference to the collective aged is represented by the service of the court-appointed *sanlao* 三老 and *wugeng* 五更, but in many instances, disbursements were to be made on a much wider scale. See Watson 2019; Feng Wenwen, 2016. Ideally, the disabled were to be employed in special jobs (e.g., gate-tending) or in less onerous or shorter (half-time) labor service, as noted in Feng Wenwen 2016, 2. See, e.g., the "Nanjun baliu bu" 南郡罷癃簿 from Songbai, showing that local administrations worked hard to find the disabled suitable employment. As for the aged, a Yinqueshan ms. states that those who are sixty or between fourteen and sixteen *sui* perform half the labor service. Registries mention, in connection with seizing human labor and material resources, that some people are *da* 大 or *xiao* 小 (big or small); *lao* 老 (aged); *mian* 免 (excused from labor service); *shi* 使 (to be employed) and *weishi* 未使 (not yet employed). The Yinwan registry, for example, lists some males and females as *neng tian* 能田 (able-bodied farmers, liable for service). Yinwan also uses the phrase 春令成戶, which experts take to refer to establishing new households in the spring (again, a seasonal activity).

Wuyi guangchang, Mozuizi, Songbai, and Dongpailou, to name a few) confirm the courts' determination to see that social welfare measures were carried out in the localities, as per the theories, at least until late in Eastern Han, when the court's ability to dispense largesse to the provinces closely had collapsed.[123] (Note, meanwhile, that the local registries in Qin and Han were unparalleled in the antique world, both in their intent and in their complexity.)[124] The most detailed of the excavated examples of these registries lists by household (*hu* 戶) not only the head of household (male or female), but also the ages and sexes of the individual family members and live-in servants (as indentured?); the status assigned to the household head by the twenty orders of honor (*jue* 爵); the extent of their landholdings; plus any exemptions from corvée labor that persons in the household might enjoy, by virtue of their age or condition in life.[125] Usually (mis)characterized as merely "control mechanisms" imposed by a supposedly autocratic regime, these registries were no less crucial to the organisation of the local workforces by the seasonal round and

---

[123] On the relatively abrupt end to the Han disbursements for social welfare, see Loewe 2021, in *The Technical Arts in the Han Histories: Tables and Treatises*.

[124] While Rome provided bread and circuses to the citizens of the city of Rome to forestall rebellions in heavily populated areas, the Chinese disbursements were to be made throughout the empire, regardless of the size of the population, although one imagines them more likely happening near the county administrative seats. Roman law stipulated care for orphans, as producers and army men once they reached adulthood. But there were no disbursements towards the aged or the elderly, before Byzantine Christianity, so far as we know. Under the Roman empire, there were three main kinds of disbursements: essentially (a) grain to the Urban Plebs of Rome; (b) cash handouts (*sportulae*) to the same on special occasions; and (c) alimentary programs in some municipalities. On this, one may consult Beck and Vankeerbergen 2021; Noreña 2011. One other major difference: under Qin and Han law, parents did not have the right to kill their children or household members "in servile status," in contrast to Roman law.

Of the voluminous literature devoted to the population registries, three secondary sources stand out: Du Zhengsheng 2013; Hsing I-t'ien and Liu Tseng-kuei 2013; Wang Aiqing 2010.

[125] There is some dispute over whether the lands listed in such registries represent the household's entire holdings or the lands conferred on the household with one or more orders of honor (*jue* 爵). On this, see Wang Aiqing 2010, 153–55.

to the provisions of social welfare supports by season than would be Internal Revenue statistics today.

During the early empires in China, all improvements to local practices were premised on the empire's need to reverently uphold the farmers' seasonal round (敬授民時),[126] and secondarily to adjudicate lawsuits, going to war, and nominating candidates for court office. Whenever possible, then, civil lawsuits, penal cases, and army campaigns were to be put off until the fall and winter months, to allow the farmers to focus their energies upon planting, weeding, and harvesting the crops, while local elites after the harvest were to use some of their free time to deliberate the question of which candidates they should recommend to the court for its consideration. While it would be foolhardy to try to describe so many topics in a work of this size, the early empires' firm commitment to dispensing equitable treatment to its subjects, with the help of social welfare measures from the cradle to the grave, may be illustrated by two facets of the welfare system dating back to Wendi's court discussions in 179 BC: care of the aged and the forgiveness of farming loans.[127]

Exhibit A: Care of the Aged

Elder care was the most pervasive sign of the court's support for its subjects. "Yang lao" 養老 ("nourishing the aged") was deemed crucial to good governance, and via such standard phrases as "to revere the aged" (*jing lao* 敬老), "to render the aged secure" (*an lao* 安老), and "to honor the aged" (*zun lao* 尊老), the early sources show it in action, in the capital ceremonies in which the emperor

---

[126] *Shiji* 1.16n5 ties this to apocryphal texts commenting on the *Documents* classic.
[127] To beat an elderly person was adjudged "akin to great refractoriness and immorality" (*bi dani budao* 比大逆不道), with those terms describing treason against the imperial line (see below).

humbly served a representative of the elderly *sanlao* 三老 (Triply Aged) down to the county-level attention paid to the *fulao* 父老 (Fatherly Aged), who were employed as advisers to the local officials and negotiators in civil cases. Graded by the ages of the recipients (aged seventy, eighty, or ninenty and above), in this system, the exceptionally old—either those aged ninety or above or those seventy or above who enjoyed relatively high status for other reasons—were to be awarded turtledove staffs to advertise their unique standing as figures worthy of special veneration by the community who were blessed with extraordinary legal and administrative privileges.[128] As two highly influential works, *Xunzi* and *Xiaojing* (the latter, a Qin-era compilation),[129] traced the achievement of social order to finding the right balance between reciprocity/just requital and hierarchy, two main rationales underpinned provisions for the care of the aged: the first, that elder care represented a repayment for the seniors' earlier economic and social contributions to the empire, and the second, that elder care, which included deference to the aged, signaled the wise person's willingness to honor those having greater or different experiences. Additionally, the early texts insist that in general those qualified to receive turtledove staffs "have ceased to hold malice in their hearts," and since intentionality played such a large role in the trials of the early empires, beginning with age seventy the elderly were not to be prosecuted or sentenced for crimes, unless they "took the lead in murdering or assaulting someone."[130]

---

[128] In one set of tomb documents, the person who received a turtledove staff was just shy of aged seventy, but other documents seem to require the much higher bar of 90. Age, commendations for merit, and ranking in the orders of honor (*jue*) may all have been factored in when dispensing the turtledove staffs. At this point, we cannot be sure.
[129] See Hsiao 1973.
[130] This statement comes from the tomb of one You Bo, where not only a turtledove staff but also various documents roughly comprising a "user's manual" for the dove staff were found. See note 131 on the next page.

Repeated edicts express the crown's will to have local officials personally see to the care of the aged.[131] The extant statutes seem to posit four levels of support that were expected of legitimate government:

yuan lao 院老, house-bound elders (?)
mian lao 免老, excused from corvée service
ci zhang 赐杖, granted a staff
bing mi 禀米, conferrals of rice

To facilitate elder care within households, those who were the sole support of one or both aged parents were not to be summoned for army service or for corvée labor projects located far from home. The texts expressly forbid the local administrators from "sending them out on punitive campaigns,"[132] and court cases show that local administrators were heavily punished if they infringed on this type of rule.

With "nourishing the aged" believed to be one of the most powerful "civilizing projects" launched during the early empires, the material evidence for this practice has been turning up everywhere. "Nourishing the aged" is the principal subject of pictorial stones from Sichuan, Shandong, and Henan; of excavated manuscripts in sites as far distant as Gansu, Hubei, and Jiangsu; and of nearly forty pre-Han and Han received texts."[133]

In Donghai commandery (one of roughly one hundred administrative divisions of the empire at the time) alone, officials in c. 10 BCE counted no less than 2,823 staff holders, in a commandery

---

[131] Tomb 18, Wuwei, Mozuizi (Gansu), the tomb of one You Bo, speaks of the king's staffs, as do edicts in Eastern Han, under Zhangdi and Hedi, referring to earlier precedents. See, e.g., *Hou Hanshu* 2.102; 30A.3109; 30B.3124.
[132] See Feng Wenwen 2016, 37.
[133] The best accounts of these practices include Bodde 19,75, 34,1–48, 36,1–80); Hulsewé 1987; Zang Zhifei 2002, rich with references to specific archaeological reports from 1957–1994; Watson 2019, chap. 4 ("The Birth of Old Age"); Lu Xiqi 2021, esp. 1–217. For pictorial stones, see Shen Zhongchang 1979. One of the M18 turtledove staffs is published in Sun 2017, 131, plate 54.

Figure 2 A pictorial stone depicting an elderly man with a dovestaff.

that reportedly had 358,414 households around that time.[134] On the one hand, it is very hard to imagine that local officials had sufficient resources to provide all the very aged with a "monthly dole," yet that is precisely what some of the edicts, as reported, seem to call for. At the very least, household registration allowed the Han administrative officers to give special attention to aged persons, male and female, as "potential recipients of honors and rewards." The dove staff, per the edicts, was to be regarded as an "emblem of an official" and staff holders were legally treated as "equivalent to [officials of a] rank of 600 bushels," the bottom rung of the high-ranking court officers, corresponding to the rank of a county prefect or magistrate.[135] By law,

---

[134] *Hanshu* 28A.1588, the geographic tratise from which this data comes, date to AD 2, we think.

[135] For comparison, the magistrate (prefect) of a county with a population of 10,000 or more was ranked 600–1000 bushels; if the population was less than 10,000, the magistrate

anyone who "dared heedlessly to curse, revile or beat" a staff-holder was to be executed; so, too, officials who tried to levy staff holders for state service. To drive that point home, the Mozuizi finds include the summary of the case built against an unfortunate local official named Wu Shang from faraway Runan commandery (modern Anhui province) who had an altercation with a seventy-year-old named Xian; for this reason, the local official was sentenced to death "by analogy to the greatly immoral" 比大逆不道, i.e., the equivalent to personally insulting the emperor or the members of his ruling line.[136]

Exhibit B: Debt Relief for the Poor

Among the wide variety of activities that the *Hanshu* stipulates as the duties of the local administrators at the county, district, and hamlet levels are the duties to encourage agriculture, sericulture, and frugality; to instruct people how best to raise domesticated animals;[137] to set up local elders (*fulao*) to arbitrate civil disputes among the people; and to lend money to the poor on regular and on ad hoc bases, which loans are sometimes to be forgiven. Moderns may find debt relief most interesting, as it is currently under debate in developed and developing countries, such relief dubbed "handouts" being anathema to many mainstream economic traditions.[138] Of no less interest to

---

ranked 500–300 bushels. In theory, a septuagenarian might thus outrank even the county magistrate. See Bielenstein 1980, 100.

[136] See Shang Huan 2008, 173–78, marshals many court cases relating to the treatment of the aged, as does Watson 2019, chap. 4; Feng Wenwen 2016, 8. For a famous court case, in the reign of Chengdi, where an unnamed local minor official 某鄉史 who maltreated or berated someone who had a dove staff, see Liu Ming 2022, 109–110; Feng Wenwen 2016, 6.

[137] *Hanshu* 89.3635–37 (biog. of Zhu Yi, an exemplary official).

[138] See, for example, in the United States today, https://studentaid.gov/manage-loans/forgiveness-cancellation/debt-relief-info, where President Biden proposed a one-time student loan debt relief program for 260,000 students, which was promptly declared illegal by the US Supreme Court. The United States is also struggling with other ways to

moderns, given the current political climate, are reform proposals (some enacted in Han and some not) for the throne to give up massive tracts of land to benefit the farmers, as with Chancellor Xiao He's proposal to the Western Han founder to abandon his pleasure park[139] and, in one later case, an emperor abandoning an entire commandery.[140] Here, as multiple secondary studies show,[141] such initiatives were very much tied to the spring season, when the genial, life-giving face of imperial rule was especially felt, like the warmth of the sun. In times of good governance, the court or its emissaries were quick to "extend favors" 施惠, issue "liberal policies" 惠政, and make regular tours of inspection 巡守, to inquire about the local conditions and to pre-emptively distribute largesse, rather than merely wait to react to assorted crises post facto.[142] Granaries were to be opened to relieve any instance of severe distress, and this policy likewise was explicitly tied to the Monthly Ordinances.[143]

Indisputably, during the early empires there were deficiencies in the social welfare system, given the low literacy rates and severe constraints on the antique transportation and communication facilities, not to mention the limitations on the imperial finances

forgive debts that will pass muster not only with a fairly conservative fiscal Congress but with a far more radically conservative US Supreme Court.
   Today's China (i.e., "the Party," led by Xi Jinping), facing a continuing real estate crisis of mammoth proportions, struggles to find the right response to domestic debt relief, which has greatly complicated its impact under the Belt and Road Initiative. China spent $240bn (£195bn) bailing out countries struggling under their Belt-and-Road initiative debts between 2008 and 2021, new data shows. Research found that Chinese state-backed lenders released bailout funds to 22 countries, including Argentina, Pakistan, Sri Lanka and Ukraine. See Hawkins, reporting in *The Guardian* (March 28, 2023).
[139] For this, see *Shiji* 53.2018; *Hanshu* 39.2005–12 (上林中多空地，弃，願令民得入田 … 賤貫貸). A later Western Han emperor was induced to give up vast tracts in Shanglin Park to benefit the local farmers.
[140] Han Yuandi, a later Western Han emperor, abandoned Zhuya commandery, rather than hold onto territory at a great cost to the soldier-farmers. See *Hanshu* 9.283.
[141] Liu Ming 2022, 175, citing Qin and Han Tian Lü.
[142] One of the best studies of these tours of inspection is Sanderovitch 2017.
[143] E.g., *Han shu* 57A.2572.

and surveillance capabilities.¹⁴⁴ Still, imperial provisions focused on those populations deemed most vulnerable or most worthy of aid,¹⁴⁵ although, upon rarer occasions, general conferrals of "orders of honor" (*jue* 爵) went to every household, regardless of need, adding, in theory, to the landholdings some households could claim. Numerous sources trace the downfall of dynasties to their failures to curb land-grabs by the rich,¹⁴⁶ and certain offices and commissions were expressly charged to calculate discrepancies among the rich and poor in the localities.¹⁴⁷

As both dynastic legitimacy and the potential for moral suasion were thought to rest upon the self-sustaining character of local intergenerational orders, the scope of the early empires' ambitions to ensure the welfare of their most vulnerable subjects is best traced to motives that were neither wholly altruistic nor wholly self-interested, insofar as the very vigor of the ruling line and its courts depended directly upon the distribution of largesse to the needy. To claim legitimacy, the center (the ruler and his court) had to exemplify "having no selfish motives," which mature attitude promised longer life for the

---

¹⁴⁴ To give but a single example of such limitations, Wang Aiqing (2010) notes that the whole system of land conferrals meant to accompany the conferrals of *jue* depended upon two conditions, neither assured: first, a certain minimum level of capital accumulation in the realm; and second, the requisite deaths and births in the locale ensuring enough surplus land in the locality to facilitate a timely redistribution of fields in successive generations. By the Han statutes, newly established households were to receive a land grant of 100 *mu*, which was not always feasible, unless the households were dispatched to relatively depopulated areas (generally the frontiers) or to newly opened lands, including local marshlands.

¹⁴⁵ For example, with orphans, two categories tended to be especially privileged: the sons (children?) born posthumously, sons (children?) of heroes (often martial heroes). Often, these two categories were conflated, but not always, judging from the available evidence.

¹⁴⁶ See Cui Shi's *Zheng lun*, for the allegation (likely false) that the Qin fell because its failure to check land grabs resulted in a situation that virtually enslaved the poor. The story of Xiao He's own calculated land grabs (specifically designed to blacken his reputation) confirms this general picture.

¹⁴⁷ This was the case, for example, when Wudi set up the office of *cishi* 刺史 (*Hanshu* 6.197), and it was also the case with multiple envoys dispatched under multiple reigns on an ad hoc basis from the capital to oversee local conditions.

ruling house.¹⁴⁸ As Xunzi and then the compilers of the *Annals of Mr. Lü* averred, "reducing self-interested claims means the public-spirited model prevails [among the populace], which, in turn, means the courts' efforts become concentrated and unified."¹⁴⁹ In the same vein, Guo Xiang's commentary to the *Zhuangzi* notes that, while it is necessary for agriculturally-based empires to exploit the available labor and talent, if they are to survive, an empire may well fall, if it resorts to excessive exploitation of ordinary people and those in power pretend to greater talent and virtue than they have.¹⁵⁰ When a series of natural and man-made disasters beset the late Western Han courts, critics were quick to advise the emperor and his court to empty the granaries and introduce economies in the palace, with a view to restoring the balance between ruler and subjects, capital and provinces, yin and yang. Much the same happened in mid-Eastern Han.¹⁵¹ And when the customary conferrals of land grants, grains, and wine ended rather abruptly in Eastern Han in AD 147, reflecting the gross mismanagement of the administration's abundant resources,¹⁵² a chorus of thinkers predicted that it would only be a matter of time before the dynasty collapsed, insofar as it had failed to demonstrate its life-giving, beneficent face to the populace, and therefore did not merit its subjects' allegiance in return.¹⁵³

If we return to the basics, the goal of ritual and ritualized politics is to sustain mutual esteem among parties, as that prompts feelings of trust and dispositions to cooperate.¹⁵⁴ Consequently, at the core of this

---

[148] See, e.g., *Guanzi, juan* 40 ("Si shi" 四時/ Seasonality). The *Guanzi* text mentions seasonality hundreds of times, as does the *Guoyu*. To favor no one interest was to go a long way to secure everyone's allegiance.
[149] See *Lüshi chunqiu*, in Chen Qiyou, 1718–19: 土容論, 上農: 少私義則公法立, 力專一.
[150] See Chapman (forthcoming).
[151] See Nylan with Wilson, on Deng Sui (forthcoming).
[152] However, it is also true that a climatic pessimum (colder and drier weather) likely played a role, as that meant shorter growing seasons, smaller harvests, and more invasions from the semi-nomadic groups in the north.
[153] Loewe 2021. Other factors that are often adduced, despite firm evidence, include the growth of magnate estimates, more likely to be the result than the cause of dynastic collapse.
[154] Williams 1993, 113.

argument about the early empires in China lies the productive tension between "dependence" and "authority" that characterizes the discourse on two allied topics in early China, those of learning and legitimacy.[155] When misguided leaders today boast and bully, while exploiting their human and material resources, they forget many basic lessons that many antique officials and rulers once knew very well: to wit, that in policymaking taking the long-term, intergenerational view is almost always best and a lack of egotism smooths the path to building firm friends, allies, and alliances.[156] To project an "awe-inspiring" (*wei* 威) authority worthy of others' emulation often one needs to do less, consume less, be kinder and gentler, and "know what is enough."[157] As the Han-era *Documents* states, no less than three times, "Gentleness shown the distant will bring the able close."[158] Awareness of this might help to lead us out of the ceaseless Social Darwinist struggles between countries and people that have, disastrously for the planet, propelled us into multiple humanitarian and environmental crises.[159]

---

[155] "The dependence necessitating learning is not only the province of children learning to speak and act. Even the otherwise competent adult must maintain a willingness to inquire of others, as well as the humility to gather teachers around herself," as Wilson 2022 observes. As *Xunzi* says, "*Even when one is capable* of acting independently, the proper way to act is to move by relying on others." On this and allied statements, see *Documents/Shangshu*, "Introduction," discussing epistemological modesty at length. Wilson 2022, citing other examples adduced in Nylan 2022, highlights this image of sagely "epistemological modesty," which Nylan equates with a kind of "heroism in early China," to contrast this with the ethically and politically dangerous idea of the "omniscient sage" found in certain later depictions in Chinese thought. In Nylan 2022, many examples are cited: Kongzi inquiring of ritual in the ancestral temple (*Analects* 3.15), Xunzi's Son of Heaven, who must rely on his chancellors to move "even though he is capable of walking," the multiple ministers "facing south" (i.e., acting as rulers) in the *Yi Zhoushu*, and even the Zhuangzian swimmer who relies on the water rather than himself. All are images of a sagely practice that plays up the virtuosity of living dependently See Figure 3.

[156] See Nylan's Introduction to *The Art of War*. As Carl Schmitt, the famous Nazi and post-Nazi era philosopher, famously observed, the sole function of the nation-state is to determine who is a friend and who is a foe.

[157] The last phrase appears in multiple (no fewer than thirty) pre-Han and Han classics and masterworks, including the *Mencius* (twice), *Liji* (twice), *Laozi* (eleven times), and *Huainanzi* (eight times), based on the ICS/CHANT concordance indices.

[158] The Chinese reads *rou yuan neng er* 柔遠能邇.

[159] See Midgley 2011.

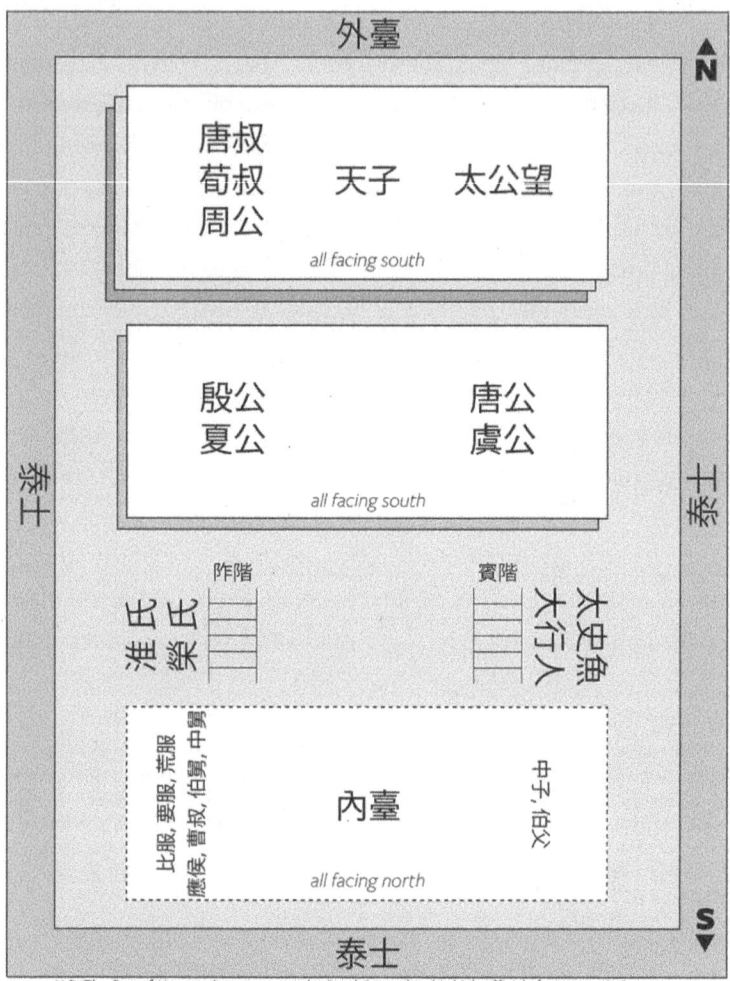

Figure 3 N.B. The Son of Heaven does not wear the Pearl Crown but his high officials facing south do. Source: Yi Zhoushu, "Wang hui jie" chapter.

By early resonance theories, as readers will recall, we flourish or not, depending on the long-term cumulative impacts of our decisions and habits, and the level of care we devote to intergenerational equity and balance in our daily lives.

3

The World We Want

There are a number of candidates when it comes to determining historical pivots or tipping points, although the process of singling out one admittedly does not reflect any form of scientific rigor. In the sphere of ecological thinking, the definition of sustainability formulated in the United Nations' 1987 landmark "Report of the World Commission on Environment and Development: Our Common Future" (also known as the Brundtland Report) comes to mind: "Sustainable development is development that meets the needs of the present without compromising the ability of future generations to meet their own needs." As Norway's former head of the Ministry of the Environment from 1974–1979, Brundtland, when tasked in 1983 with compiling this report, was uniquely qualified. That was before Norway started exploring for oil in the Norwegian or Barents Seas, which now is a major driver of the Norwegian economy, not to mention a major contributor to European pollution.

Another benchmark, one could argue, lies with Angela Merkel, Germany's chancellor from 2000 to 2016. Merkel had also served as Minister of Environment, between 1994 and 1998. Shortly after the start of Merkel"s tenure as minister, in October 1994, to be precise, the German constitution was amended by paragraph 20a: "Mindful also of its responsibility towards future generations, the state shall protect the natural foundations of life and animals by legislation and, in accordance with law and justice, by executive and judicial action, all within the framework of the constitutional order."¹ In short, the German state is henceforth constitutionally mandated to safeguard the nation's biosphere for future generations, and to protect animal rights. Man and beast, finally, would enjoy equal protection. Sort of.

Yet another date to single out is 2015. Mindful of the best-selling economist Robert Heilbroner's ambivalent verdict at the end of his study on "Visions of the Future" (The first [possible scenario that is of use] is effective global government; the second, . . . its abolition"),² I'd have us go back to 2015, when yet another United Nations report produced by the UN Millennium Development Goals Task Force ("A Million Voices: The World We Want") summarized a huge effort to engage with a great variety of groups and populations to produce a shared vision of a world which leaders and rank-and-file might deem desirable.³ Based on a "UN-led global survey of people's priorities for a better world," the results of the survey were "shared with international leaders in setting the next global development agenda."⁴ On September 25, 2015, the UN celebrated the outcomes of this unprecedented (in scale at least) survey in glowing terms: "World leaders today embraced a sweeping 15-year global plan of action to end poverty, reduce inequalities and protect the environment, known as the Sustainable Development Goals, at the opening of a United Nations special summit."⁵ Notably, among Asian nations, China, India, Vietnam, Thailand, Cambodia, and Pakistan undertook the momentous task of organizing a national consultative process devoted to the subject of "The World We Want."

---

[1] The German reads, "Der Staat schützt auch in Verantwortung für die künftigen Generationen die natürlichen Lebensgrundlagen und die Tiere im Rahmen der verfassungsmäßigen Ordnung durch die Gesetzgebung und nach Maßgabe von Gesetz und Recht durch die vollziehende Gewalt und die Rechtsprechung."
[2] Heilbroner 1996, 177.
[3] United Nations Millenium Development Goals Task Force 2015.
[4] Report, Preface, V.
[5] Gonsalves 2015.

Looking ahead towards 2030, when the seventeen goals and 169 targets in the Development Goals document are to be met in each country around the globe, the honorable Ralph E. Gonsalves, Prime Minister of Saint Vincent and the Grenadines, addressed the elephant in the room:

> Making Mother Earth a much better place for all required deeds that matched words. The current model of a "perverse" and environmentally-destructive global capitalism must be restructured in order to achieve the Sustainable Development Goals.[6]

One other major problem: the 169 targets could conceivably result in considerable "policy sprawl" in the form of confusion and redundancy of regulatory ambitions on behalf of the state, no matter where. Over-specificity is often the enemy of the good.

The relationship between the two systems of global capitalism and the natural and social environment it operates in is saddled with as many questions as with tentative answers. Let us tarry in the year 2015, before we wade into a discussion of a moral or ecological economy (two very different things—moral economy aims at fair and equitable exchange of commodities, while ecological economies include the health of earth systems in their planning approaches). Imagine the countryside of Wales, where pollsters and action committees had been working hard to engage the public in the question of "What World Do We Want?" With a population of roughly 3.1 million, in its latest census (2021), Wales counted 830,000 under the age of 25, and about 530,000 over the age of sixty-five. (Later, we will consider how age differentials can play a tremendous role in the transfer not only of knowledge, but also of decision-making power.) The result of this intensely explorative exercise was a rather unprecedented Act of the Assembly of Wales, entitled "Well-being of Future Generations

---

[6] United Nations, Plenary, Press Release, Sept. 14, 2023.

(Wales) Act 2015."[7] Probably the main outcome of this Act was the establishment of a so-called Future Generations Commissioner, whose office has wide-ranging duties and responsibilities cutting across all government departments and agencies, including the treasury, transportation, public health, forestry and natural resources, education and tourism. (Recall that Wales is a country known for mining.) The Well-being Act 2015 requires the ministers of these departments and agencies to deliver annual future trends reports.

In preparing a future trends report the Welsh Ministers must (a) take account of any action taken by the United Nations in relation to the UN Sustainable Development Goals; (b) assess the potential impact of that action on the economic, social, environmental and cultural well-being of Wales, and (c) take account of the report containing an assessment of the risks for the United Kingdom of the current and predicted impact of climate change most recently sent to the Welsh Ministers under section 56(6) of the Climate Change Act 2008 (c. 27).[8]

> The general duties of the Future Generations Commissioner are to promote the sustainable development principle [as defined in the Brundtland Report], in particular to
> act as a guardian of the ability of future generations to meet their needs; and
> encourage public bodies to take greater account of the long-term impact of the things that they do; and
> for that purpose to monitor and assess the extent to which well-being objectives set by public bodies are being met.[9]

The Welsh did not stop there. In addition to its auditing and assessment duties, the FG Commissioner functions as a passive clearinghouse for

---

[7] Well-being of Future Generations (Wales) Act 2015. Online at https://www.futuregenerations.wales/about-us/future-generations-act/ Accessed Sept. 5, 2023.
[8] Well-being Act 2015, 10.
[9] Well-being Act 2015, 13.

government projects that may have mid-to long-term impacts on the environment. In other words, the office of Commissioner and the agency itself have teeth. The Well-being Act 2015 explicitly states that the Commissioner may undertake research or other study into the following:

- the extent to which the well-being goals and national indicators are consistent with the sustainable development principle;
- the extent to which the sustainable development principle is taken into account in the national indicators;
- the sustainable development principle itself (including how it is applied to setting and meeting objectives); and
- anything related to any of those things that exerts impacts upon the economic, social, environmental and cultural well-being of Wales (or any part of Wales).

What logically follows from the combination of functions, duties, and rights is this: the Future Generations Commissioner has official whistle-blower status. Since the Commissioner receives annual progress reports from the major (and minor) ministries, a much greater degree of transparency is achieved. If something should prove to be going against the well-being / sustainability principles detailed in the 2015 Act, the Commissioner has the right, nay the duty, to conduct independent research into the matter and perhaps suggest a different course of action, always keeping in mind the mid- and long-term goals and values of Wales. When considering the Well-being goals as defined in the Wales 2015 Act, one has to keep in mind that these goals are closely aligned to the goals set forth by the United Nations Development Agenda (2015–30), on the one hand. On the other, they naturally surpass in scope and depth the one-line Brundtland definition of sustainability (see Table 1).

There is a lot to unpack here. One aspect that stands out immediately is the Act's "think large and small" principle: Wales, while being

Table 1 The Wales Act of 2015 (Summarized), pp. 3–4

Goal	Description of the goal
A prosperous Wales.	An innovative, productive and low-carbon society which recognizes the limits of the global environment and therefore uses resources efficiently and proportionately (including acting on climate change); and which develops a skilled and well-educated population in an economy which generates wealth and provides employment opportunities, allowing people to take advantage of the wealth generated through securing decent work.
A resilient Wales.	A nation which maintains and enhances a biodiverse natural environment with healthy functioning ecosystems that support social, economic and ecological resilience and the capacity to adapt to change (e.g., climate change).
A healthier Wales.	A society in which people's physical and mental well-being is maximized and in which choices and behaviors that benefit future health are understood.
A more equal Wales.	A society that enables people to fulfill their potential no matter what their background or circumstances (including their socioeconomic background and circumstances).
A Wales of cohesive communities.	Attractive, viable, safe, and well-connected communities.
A Wales of vibrant culture and thriving Welsh language.	A society that promotes and protects culture, heritage, and the Welsh language, and which encourages people to participate in the arts, and sports and recreation.
A globally responsible Wales.	A nation which, when doing anything to improve the economic, social, environmental, and cultural well-being of Wales, takes account of whether doing such a thing may make a positive contribution to global well-being.

protective of its culture, heritage, and environment (and perhaps actively promoting Nativism/Natalism to a degree), also recognizes certain global responsibilities. The social equity dimension is covered under the heading "A More Equal Wales," with people fulfilling their potential "no matter what their background or circumstances."

Likewise, the Act recognizes that resilience and adaptation have become increasingly critical survival strategies on both a regional and a national scale.

The one central future (and present) value missing from the Wales Well-being Act 2015, however, is *freedom*. No guarantees are made that a future Wales might be a *freer* Wales. One may speculate why that is the case, but other, similarly designed future generations agencies (or councils) in continental Europe insist upon what is called *intertemporal freedom securities* in their deliberations and reporting language, solidifying the foundations of constitutionally encoded freedoms. For example, according to the decision of the German Federal Constitutional Court of March 24, 2021 on the Federal Climate Change Act, "the legislator is obliged to distribute opportunities for freedom proportionately across the generations, i.e. to protect future freedom today."[10] The German Parliamentary Council for Sustainable Development, in its forty-third session (June 21, 2023), discussed just this subject: how it is incumbent on us today, in times of the corrosion of the private sphere and civil liberties, to securitize hard-won liberties for future generations. Christian Calliess, the invited speaker for this session, referred to the fact that there is a designated budget for climate change, and so logically, there should also be a budget for safeguarding current and future liberties. Ironically, the significance of Calliess's remarks was reduced by free market advocates to the statement that "Expert demands a higher degree of competency (i.e.,

---

[10] See Stephan Harbarth's discussion on the subject at the Leibniz Center for European Economic Research, online at https://www.zew.de/en/zew/news/climate-protection-is-intertemporal-protection-of-freedom. As backdrop, the Federal Constitutional Court of Germany (2021), Judgment, says, "... one generation must not be allowed to consume large portions of the CO2 budget while bearing a relatively minor share of the reduction effort if this would involve leaving subsequent generations with a drastic reduction burden and expose their lives to comprehensive losses of freedom. . . . The objective duty of protection arising from Art. 20a GG encompasses the necessity to treat the natural foundations of life with such care and to leave them in such condition that future generations who wish to continue preserving these foundations are not forced to engage in radical abstinence."

political integration) and stronger impact of the parliamentary council for sustainable development."[11] In actuality, Calliess admonished the political establishment for paying lip service to the recommendations of the council, while only pursuing sustainability goals on a symbolic level, with no regard for freedom.

The 2015 Wales Act has since served as a model for other countries, such as Canada, which in its first Session of the forty-second Parliament, in June 2016, discussed the inadequate tools the country's public bodies had devised to address the needs of future generations administratively. Using the United Nation's Sustainable Development 2015–2030 framework from September, 2015 as a guideline, Canada's parliament turned to the Welsh example.[12] Ottowa recognized that Canada's Federal Sustainable Development Act (SDO)—Canada's closest equivalent to the Welsh administrative act—fell far short of the scope and breadth of the Welsh example. For Wales, "by framing the legislation in terms of well-being, [. . .] incorporates health, free time, public space, equality, cultural heritage, and many other integral elements that are often overlooked . . . and engages across the policy-making sphere." Accordingly, the Welsh Future Generations Commissioner was invited to testify how and where the Welsh efforts had fallen short in institutionalizing an agency whose main functions were to create a shared vision for a future worth living and to design a set of pathways to get there. The failure to devise a creative anchor institution peopled by visionary experts (almost an oxymoron, that) within the policymaking structure of the Canadian government was freely acknowledged:

---

[11] "Experte fordert mehr Kompetenzen für Nachhaltigkeitsbeirat," https://www.bundestag.de/dokumente/textarchiv/2023/kw25-pa-nachhaltigkeitsbeirat-weiterentwicklung-952678. Source accessed August 31, 2023.
[12] NB: Canada could not cite the Paris Accord that followed two months later.

Which central body should be responsible for leading federal sustainable development was not conclusively determined during the study; however, it was noted that there are only certain agencies within government with the kind of mission to roam and the authority to be able *to compel*.[13]

The agencies under consideration for this task were the Prime Minister's Office, Privy Council Office, Treasury Board Secretariat and Department of Finance. The need for one of these organizations to be assigned overall responsibility for sustainable development—either solely or jointly with the SDO—was repeated in testimony from the invited third parties. The session ended with a recommendation to completely overhaul the Federal Sustainable Development Act, in the full knowledge it is no small feat to install an effective office within existing federal, democratic structures that had the "mission to roam and the authority to be able to compel" on behalf of future generations' well-being, no less. The Prime Minister's Office would perhaps be the natural home for such a forward-thinking body, but at the time of this writing, finding a secure institutional home for the office has still not yet come to pass.[14] One could argue that in a non-democratic system such an office might be easier to establish, by "imperial" or "authoritarian" fiat, but we co-authors have yet to see such an example of foresight and initiative in an authoritarian

---

[13] *Italics* are not in the original, but added by Hahn.
[14] The so-called *Century Initiative*, a registered charity, tries to fill this gap in Canada. Its mission statement promises to shape "a bigger, bolder Canada, [. . .] champion data-driven solutions for responsible population growth, advocate for long-term planning, and drive bold policies that secure Canada's future." The *Initiative*'s stated "vision is a Canada that thinks and plans not just for today, but for future generations." The *Initiative* announces its objective for "responsible population growth" is the astonishing target of adding to Canada's population one hundred million residents by 2100. For further details see https://www.centuryinitiative.ca/. Nylan adds: governments and businesses want young and cheap labor to support the aging population. Today, such calls for increased population are often hailed as the main "fix" for demographic imbalances in many countries, including Japan and the People's Republic of China. For the current PRC pressure on single women over thirty, see NZZ.

system we know. A counter-argument would suggest that such an office, equipped with veto powers and other legislative or executive tools, would be the last such agency for any totalitarian regime to put on its to-do list, since the (hopefully, supposedly) lawfully appointed commissioner of said office might function as the proverbial wrench in the nation-state's resource-hungry and ecologically destructive machinery. It might stall or even halt the social engineering projects of such regimes, especially in states that are still classified as "developing nations," with China advertising itself as such.[15]

*** Intermission ***

Staying in 2015, but pivoting into the much narrower context of the urban sphere, where, admittedly, most of society's forward-looking thinkers and policy makers now reside, the Chinese journal *Urban China* (*Chengshi Zhongguo* 城市中国)[16] included a small booklet edited by the Dynamic City Foundation (*Dongtai chengshi jijinhui* 动态城市基金会). After various short introductory essays on democratic design, modern cities and quality of life,[17] there appeared results of a Chinese survey on the global appeal of the notion of "well-being." Living in a mega-city by 2020 obviously had significant appeal, since 43 percent of survey respondents preferred this option to, say, living in a town ("less than 100,000 inhabitants"), which was the preference of only 8 percent of those surveyed. Of those surveyed, 26 percent thought there was not enough green space in the urban environment, however, while urban traffic and transportation were generally thought to be abysmal, no matter where one looked. Most of the respondents were under the age of 35, some of an optimistic disposition but others less so. In the

---

[15] Bandursky 2023. As we go to press, on Sept. 23, 2025 Vice-Premier Li Qiang announced that China is voluntarily giving up its status as a 'developing country,' with the implications of that move still to be seen.
[16] *Urban China* (Shanghai) 70 (2015).
[17] Mars and Hornsby 2008.

comments section, reprinted in the booklet, a small goldmine of public opinion unfolds. These are rare, personal insights into the mental state of a Chinese younger generation. Disillusionment appears to duel precariously with hope and optimism. One (translated) example of the former state of (un)well-being, years before the pandemic:

> My dream for 2020 is to have my own apartment in a tower, with western accommodations. I would like to fit it out with all western furniture. I tend to go for decadence, to state my financial position in life. As for life in the city, it will depend more on shopping public places and how to decorate your own apartment. Most of public city life will be replaced by fear of provincial unrest gone wild in our cities. And the pollution awaiting our weakened lungs outside. So, the interior of our buildings will be what remains of our city life, or how to fit out your apartment. Oops, that's my negativity creating a protective cocoon or just a nightmare.
>
> But my true dream is too idealistic and altruistic to be true, green spaces, lively public life, and environmental standards. But let's be honest, this capitalist/communist hybrid has yet to bring good things to the average Chinese citizen. Political unrest, an unhealthy environment, and rampant consumerism will only plague us Chinese citizens. So, all we have to dream for is a nice place to live in. Negative, yes, but honest. So, sell me your development with rendered comfort, traditional Chinese serenity, and a large fence to keep the negative energy outside.

It should be noted that during Covid, China locked down tens of millions of its citizens, sometimes for weeks or months, so that the preceding statement ("the interior of our buildings will be what remains of our city life") was a prescient projection of a state of great fear indeed. A very different response assumes that by 2020 "China will have surpassed the West in environmental innovations, transportation efficiency, and urban planning schemes . . . . There will be more freedom of speech and more education for all, and the countryside as a peaceful alternative to city living will be preferred and protected." More akin to the intergenerational equity theme is the following:

> I hope China will develop into a country in which more people can have a share of the resources it has, where less energy is wasted and ways are found to curb the growing pollution. I hope the economic development of China will not cut into the rich physical culture and heritage,[18] so as to leave something for our children they can be proud of. I really hope I can still be a part of that, and that I can enjoy the beautiful country it will be.[19]

These deliberately anonymous responses display the pulse of the individual urban dweller in China when asked in 2015 to just look five years ahead. In contrast, large organizations, governments, corporations and other entities are often tasked and faced with the problem of having to look much further out. Elements of uncertainty abound when doing so, which is where the Monte Carlo Simulation[20] would come in, but that is not my concern with this intermission.

* * * End of Intermission * * *

Probably the oldest and most well-established nation-level agency tasked with forecasting, modeling, auditing, and making recommendations for the well-being of future generations can be found in Finland. Perhaps not surprisingly, on the OECD Better Life Index (the accepted matrix to evaluate quality-of-life indicators), Finland always ranks in the top five of all nations. On the Committee for the Future's website we find the following opening statement:

---

[18] The Chinese phrase is 大自然和文化遗产.
[19] From comments by interviewees, in *Urban China*, op. cit.
[20] On the Monte Carlo Simulation, which addresses and attempts to average out factors of risk and uncertainty, see "What is the Monte Carlo Simulation?" at https://www.ibm.com/topics/monte-carlo-simulation.

"The Committee for the Future is an established, standing committee in the Parliament of Finland. The Committee consists of seventeen Members of the Finnish Parliament. The Committee serves as a Think Tank for futures, science and technology policy in Finland. The counterpart cabinet member is the Prime Minister. The Committee was established in 1993."[21]

As the elder brother among siblings, Finland's Committee for the Future was host to The World Summit of the Committees of the Future in October 2022. Besides the Finnish hosts, this summit was attended by the following representatives:

    Committee of Research, Innovation and Digitalization, Parliament of Austria
    The House of Commons Standing Committee on Industry and Technology, Parliament of Canada
    Committee of the Future, Science, Technology and Innovation, National Congress of Chile
    Economic Affairs Committee, Parliament of Estonia—Riigikogu
    The Future Committee, Parliament of Iceland—The Althing
    Committee for the Future, Parliament of Lithuania—Seimas
    ICT Committee and Future's Committee, Congress of Paraguay—Congreso
    Committee of Sustainable Development Goals, Innovation and Futures Thinking, Congress of the Philippines
    Committee for Digitalisation, Innovation and Modern Technology, Parliament of Poland—Sejm
    Committee of Science, Technology, Research and Innovation, National Assembly of Thailand
    The Special Futures Committee, General Assembly of Uruguay
    Committee for Science, Technology and Environment, National Assembly of the Socialist Republic of Vietnam

---

[21] Eduskunta Rijksdagen/Committees https://www.eduskunta.fi/EN/valiokunnat/tulevaisuusvaliokunta/Pages/default.aspx. Accessed Sept. 6, 2023.

Note the absence of the world's largest economies, including China's. Although, the summit's mandate was not content with crumbs from the Finnish prime minister's table:

> The questions raised by the Committee for the Future of the Finnish Parliament are related to the relationship between the Earth's limited natural resources and technological development, the future of algorithm-based communication, humanity in 2222, and the importance of citizens' future skills, hope and trust for social development.

These are not exactly minor details when it comes to addressing mankind's state of future existence, not to mention well-being. Humanity in 2222 might sound a tad remote, especially from the angle of intergenerational equity (which seldom looks beyond the next three generations, i.e., the next sixty to ninety years), but Path 2222, as it is called, encompasses the next 200 years and, based on background material researched by the various committees, mankind will experience highly disruptive technological interventions of a radical magnitude in very short order.

According to the Finnish Summit Report of 2022, subsequent generations will experience (and in the Summit's view, no doubt benefit from) "neural networks and deep learning, robotisation of traffic and logistics, new imaging and positioning solutions, proliferation of artificial intelligence-powered platform services, improvement of genome transcription and editing, development of solar power, speech recognition and synthetic speech technologies, as well as dozens of other radical solutions that will all produce changes, already over the coming decades, both in the ways in which many sectors of industry work and in how people's day-to-day life is organized."[22] As a mere sidebar, the Summit report questions

---

[22] Summit Report, 64.

assumptions about the development of the human body (and brain), with future generations spending extended periods of time in digital and even virtual environments, which "is an unprecedented situation for our species."[23]

Further challenges arrive in the form of anonymously launched, path-dependent algorithms, resource scarcity, climate anxiety and burnout, targeted disinformation, loss of trust in representative decision-making bodies, etc. The Summit suggests, therefore, a new type of approach to resiliently and adequately deal with disruptive technologies or, more simply, with just really messy weather: training in *eco-social intelligence*: "An eco-socially intelligent person is capable of critical and systemic analysis, has mastery of collaborative learning and nonviolent communication skills; s/he values, in particular, ecological and interpersonal factors and a meaningful life."[24]

In a recent (January 2023) policy brief that bears the seal of Oxford University entitled *Towards a Declaration for Future Generations*, the authors comply with a proposal made in the UN's Our Common Agenda (September, 2021): namely, that every state should (eventually, urgently) compile its own Declaration for Future Generations. The text on hand appears to constitute a working paper (therefore, the nomenclature "policy brief") directed towards wordsmithing the official British version. In the Executive Summary page, a vital link is established outright between the UN's Sustainable Development Goals and a "broader governance transformation," highlighting the hope, if not the urgent necessity, that

---

[23] Summit Report, 65.
[24] In other words: everyone turn to Buddhism or Taoism in their search for inter-personal competence and mindful nimbleness. Just kidding. To bring the sequence of Future Summits up to date: there was a follow-up Summit in May 2023, in Vilnius (Lithuania). Preparation for the NATO Summit followed in the same city one month later. Other Commissioners for the Future include those authorized by the Knesset, from 1999 to 2006, then abolished/defunded; Gibraltar; and Lithuania.

A Declaration on Future Generations requires accompanying institutionalisation. Specifically, countries should create a "voice" for future generations in the UN system, such as a Special Envoy or High Commissioner, as well as a forum in which nations can share experiences regarding how to better safeguard future generations in their domestic systems.[25]

Since we do not (yet) have the "required institutionalization" in evidence with any government on planet Earth, in order to "game out" such a scenario, we will have to resort to fictitious accounts of a Ministry for the Future. Luckily, Kim Stanley Robinson published a book under exactly this title not so long ago.[26] Hailed as "One of Barack Obama's favorite books of the year" and filed under the Science Fiction section by the Library of Congress, the book should probably be read as anything *but* science fiction. While not explicitly addressing intergenerational equity or justice, Robinson's Ministry for the Future is the primary agency of institutional change on a global scale, and, since natural, climate-change driven agents of change do not recognize state lines, it amounts to the most consequential global actor in human history. In an interesting bifurcation of responsibilities, the Ministry (located by Robinson in Geneva, Switzerland) actually has two branches, one that operates "above board," engaging in diplomacy with world leaders from all sectors (finance, policymaking, environment, etc.) and eventually extracting all sorts of concessions and regulatory changes (buy-ins) that add up to meaningful measures to address climate change, environmental decline, resource scarcity, overpopulation, food insecurity, and social instability. There is, however, another shadow branch within the ministry, a seemingly more sinister, covert black-ops branch, carrying out assassinations of, say, un-compliant captains of industry, such as

---

[25] *Towards a Declaration* 2021.
[26] Robinson 2020, now in its 5th printing.

weapons manufacturers, and bringing down a few airliners, on the logic that the aviation industry is one of the largest polluters of the earth's atmosphere. In a 2022 interview with the German left-leaning journal TAZ, Robinson was asked if he had lost trust in government by pairing a decidedly nongovernmental and mostly lethal approach to problem-solving with in a ministry that is part of the weighty (but mostly toothless) sprawl that is the United Nations. In his response, Robinson declares himself a pacifist who believes in the rule of law. On the other hand, he goes on to state that the next decades will most likely bring much misery, anger, and despair, due to the glacial slowness of the democratic process when key powerful figures can be easily bought. And while Robinson admires Chenoweth's *Why Civil Resistance Works*,[27] he also sees a useful place in the conversation about mankind's future for a publication like "How to Blow Up a Pipeline" by the Swedish philosopher Andreas Malm.[28] Maybe we need both approaches, he says.[29] Forging the connection between a blown-up pipeline, climate activists, and Kim Stanley Robinson's fiction, the journalist Eva Horn, on October 15, 2022, asked in the center-right *Frankfurter Allgemeine Zeitung* (FAZ) if activist members of Germany's so-called Extinction Rebellion had not, in all likelihood, blown up Russia's North Stream 2 pipeline in the Baltic Sea.[30]

Shifting gears, a note on demographics: Article 28 of the Constitution ("Great Law of Peace") of the Iroquois Nation of North America advises leaders to "look and listen for the welfare of the whole people and have always in view not only the present but also the coming generations, even those whose faces are yet beneath the surface of the ground—the unborn of the future." Demographically speaking, the elders, in an orderly fashion, hand the reins over to

---

[27] Chenoweth and Stephan 2011.
[28] Malm 2021.
[29] TAZ 2021.
[30] Horn 2022.

the next generations, having trained them properly to handle affairs of the tribe or nation, as required. What, then, happens if the older generation, for example, clings to power and continues to make decisions which, advertently or not, unfailingly serve their own self-interests—when they refuse to act in the interests of other parts of the demographic spectrum (never mind the unborn)?

As the 2023 Oxford Policy Brief correctly notes,

> The majority of people yet to be born this century will be born and live in the Global South.[31] In particular, Africa is projected to see the largest increases in fertility. A call to consider future generations in international governance is, then, in large part a call to consider the Global South—bolstering existing efforts to adequately represent Global South interests on the international stage.

Just this fact alone is a strong indicator of a new world order. The Brief continues, "These projections also suggest that most people who will live in the twenty-first century belong to future generations. Indeed, projecting even further forward, it appears entirely plausible that *future generations far outnumber all those who have ever lived*: that the great majority of people have yet to be born."[32] Michel Foucault would no doubt recoil at this outlook.[33]

On a more granular scale, we wish to introduce the fact that China is aging fast and that the country's birth rate at present is the lowest of any country with a population of over 100 million. Several highly industrialized nations have an almost equally low birthrate. Never mind Japan, where the population over eighty has already breached the 10 percent threshold. In fact, if Russia continues down the negative fertility trajectory it has been on for over a decade now, it will, mathematically speaking, come to an end much sooner than

---

[31] *Toward a Declaration*, 8.
[32] *Toward a Declaration*, 8.
[33] See chapter One.

any other nation. On an even more granular scale, let us take a look at Philippe Van Parijs' discussion on "The Disfranchisement of the Elderly, and Other Attempts to Secure Intergenerational Justice."[34] Van Parijs leads with an argument introduced vigorously by Douglas J. Stewart, who in 1970 published a very controversial editorial in the *New Republic*:

> There are simply too many senile voters and their number is growing. The vote should not be a privilege in perpetuity, guaranteed by minimal physical survival, but a share in the continuing fate of the political community, both in its benefits and its risks. The old, having no future, are dangerously free from the consequences of their own political acts, and it makes no sense to allow the vote to someone who is actuarially unlikely to survive, and pay the bills for, the politician or party he may help elect . . . I would advocate that all persons lose the vote at retirement or age 70, whichever is earlier.[35]

Having thus directed the reader to solid quicksand, Parijs dryly continues by stating the obvious: "One generation later [counting from Stewart's opinion piece from 1970], the concern that the elderly are becoming politically too powerful has taken, in a number of countries, unprecedented proportions." This perception is especially true in China, although Guo Guangwu tries to argue otherwise, when writing in May 2023 on behalf of the Asia Society on the rise of Xi Jinping's Young Guards. (We will get back to Guo soon.) The fact of the matter is that China's leaders on average live to the ripe old age of eighty-eight (based on the last available data from 2008). There is no number more auspicious, and over the final third of their lives and careers these leaders enjoy extraordinary healthcare coverage,

---

[34] Parijs 1998.
[35] Stewart 1970. [Nylan: replace age with race, and Stewart nearly repeats the argument made by William F. Buckley in his 1965 Cambridge Union debate with James Baldwin.]

for example, in the hands of doctors at Beijing's Military Hospital 301, which in 2019 unwisely launched an ad campaign (quickly deleted after a firestorm erupted) boasting that in 2005 it had started a project called "981 Health Project for Leaders" aiming to prolong the lives of senior leaders to no less than 150 years.[36] Other hospitals and specialty clinics in China have in the past advertised their life-prolonging services on a more modest scale of a mere 120 years.

For his part, Parijs embarks on a very interesting historical study regarding *Generational Shares* "in the continuing fate of the political community." Of course, he asks the prime question first: "Suppose we know what social justice is, what political institutions should we attempt to put into place in order to achieve it as closely and safely as possible?" As we have seen, the Summit for Future Generations is grappling with the same issue. Let us now assume that Parijs' view regarding social justice has a smidgen of merit: "social justice demands that, subject to the protection of certain individual rights, the worst off should be as generously endowed with socioeconomic advantages, resources, opportunities, real freedom (or whatever other magnitude is chosen to express a person's 'situation') as is sustainably feasible across successive generations." There are more generous approaches to social justice—Léon Bourgeois' *Solidarité* from 1896 comes to mind—and there are meaner and leaner, cost-benefit, bean-counting versions, but Parijs will suffice for now. Parijs argues convincingly that the elder proportion of the electorate, for example, has better representation and more powerful posts and connections, while at the same time moving along path-dependent, long-established, and, of course, age-differentiated self-interests. A quick look at AARP tells the story: with 33 million members above the age of fifty, it is the "biggest organization in the United States apart from the Catholic

---

[36] Quickly deleted, but archived on Twitter/X.

Church."[37] One out of four voters is a member, and it can count on an active volunteer corps of 350,000 senior citizens when it is time to go to the polls. Meanwhile, the disconnect between generations only keeps growing, enhanced by the fact that "geographical and social mobility loosens the ties between generations, in part because both the proportion of households currently without dependent children and the proportion of people who are and will remain childless keeps increasing."[38] This is already the case in China, where tens of millions of able-bodied migrant workers leave their children behind in the villages with their aging parents, a scale of generational disconnect which is unprecedented in the history of humanity. What naturally follows such intergenerational dislocations, according to Parijs (who ignores China), is "that some urgent action needs to be taken in industrialized societies in order to prevent major intergenerational injustice." Furthermore,

> We cannot reasonably expect such action from their democratic systems, because of the growing weight of increasingly selfish elderly voters. If we care about intergenerational justice, what should we do? Reshape our democratic institutions in . . . such a way that older members of the electorate either possess less power or exercise it less selfishly.[39]

What about the "generational share" in other countries? A lengthy and passionate discussion revolves around voting rights for minors. It was somewhat fixed at age twenty-five in most countries after WWII, but in countries such as Brazil and Nicaragua, sixteen-year-old teenagers can go to the polls. After his release from prison, Nelson Mandela went one step further and proposed voting rights for those who were fourteen (which was not approved). In post-revolutionary

---

[37] Parijs 1998, 288. Contrast AARP 1992.
[38] Parijs 1998, 298.
[39] See Parijs 1998, 299.

Iran, surprisingly, the voting age stood at fifteen until 2007, when it was raised to eighteen. According to Article 3 of China's elections laws (adopted December 2, 1986), eighteen is also the age when "All citizens of the People's Republic of China . . . shall have the right to vote and stand for election, regardless of ethnic status, race, sex, occupation, family background, religious belief, education, property status or length of residence."[40] Common sense (i.e., the "underlying principle," as Parijs calls it) dictates that "people should be empowered to influence decisions in proportion to the extent to which they are likely to have to bear the consequences of these decisions."[41] Legal scholars and social scientists have long questioned the legitimacy of state authority which is based solely on what is deemed *adulthood*.[42]

Alternative scenarios have over time been put forward by a great number of interested and very diverse parties, such as the so-called proxy vote: should parents be legally allowed to vote on behalf of their underage children? Or should voters with degrees get more votes? Never mind age, how about gender coupled to life expectancy? Or ethnicity? Which segment of society, in other words, has a constitutionally encoded, proportionally fair, and legitimate share when it comes to, say, mid-term decision-making? I am afraid at this particular stage we encounter contradictions and disconnects everywhere we look. Since it is short-termism that drives modern democracies, any constitutional amendment—be it a change in voting rights, establishing a new ministry with cabinet level powers, or putting in place the legal framework that allows minors to press charges and make claims on their own future—will require a serious transformation of the established institutions, as chapter One suggests. Parijs, writing in the late 1990s, emphasizes that such

---

[40] http://www.asianlii.org/cn/legis/cen/laws/telotnpcalpcotproc944/. Accessed Sept 12, 2023.
[41] Parijs 1998, 305.
[42] Parijs 1998, 311n48.

a transformation is precondition for greater equity towards the end of his study on intergenerational justice and generational shares: "Indeed, taking such steps before it is too late may prove of crucial importance to prevent social justice from turning ever more into a sheer dream, as the rules of the political game inexorably drive our societies away from anything resembling it."[43]

Scaling down from the global to the China local, let us return to the above-mentioned analysis by Guo Guangwu entitled "Generational China in the CCP Leadership." Surveying the political playing field and looking for generalities as well as outliers, Guo comes up with some sobering insights: "CCP's new top leaders anointed at the 20th Party Congress were older than those inaugurated 5, 10, or 20 years ago. The average age of the 175 members of the Politburo Standing Committee (PSC) selected in October 2022 was 65.1, compared with 62.9 in 2017, 63.1 in 2012, and 62.0 in 2002." Although these age increments may appear to be small, we may have ossification instead of rejuvenation. Xi Jinping deliberately delays the promotion of younger cadres, Guo argues, in order to consolidate his own power. On the other hand, a closer look at the almost three thousand delegates strong of the National People's Congress reveals a small number of representatives under the age of thirty. The Yunnan delegate Tie Feiyan 铁飞燕 was only twenty-two when she was elected.[44]

In a section devoted to Future Governance, Guo looks at future leaders in the financial and technology sectors, two highly important considerations where ideological loyalty must be matched by innovative acumen and a flexible, globally conscious mindset. To no one's surprise, the leaders in the first of the two fields are of very "average" age, for China at least. Most if not all on Guo's list were

---

[43] Parijs 1998, 327.
[44] On Tie Feiyan, see http://global.chinadaily.com.cn/a/201403/25/WS5a2fb3bca3108bc8c6728b4f.html.

born in the late 1960s or early-to mid 70s, while those assuming state authority in the tech arena exhibit a different (i.e., slightly younger) age profile. Guo's conclusion is short and concise, if not perhaps the whole story:

> Age is a significant factor in CCP politics, and a younger generation has emerged at the national and provincial levels in the latest round of power redistributions following the 20th Party Congress. Whereas Xi spent the past decade sidelining younger cadres, his calculus appears to have changed after his decisive victories over rival factions, although he has retained some elder leaders at the top of the party hierarchy. This trend has changed the dynamics of the CCP's personnel politics, and it will likely continue to have a significant impact on CCP elite politics and China's governance in the years and decades to come.[45]

Guo's story is "not the whole story," however, if only because there is the small matter of the Communist Youth League of China (CYL), an organization that not long ago boasted a membership of about 90 million in the fourteen to twenty-eight year-old bracket, but is now reduced to just over 70 million, still a formidable number by any measure. Add to that the 130 million members of the Young Pioneers, which covers the ages from five to fourteen, and we arrive at an enormous base layer of young people that are shaped by the state, or, in a narrower sense, by the Communist Party and its understanding of itself. Introducing Karl Mannheim and his seminal essay on "The Sociological Problem of Generations" at this point seems relevant. Mannheim held the view that a younger generation, especially in a rapidly accelerating world, does not fight the same fight as the older generation: "While the older people may still be combating something in themselves or in the external world in such fashion that

---

[45] Guo 2023.

all their feelings and efforts and even their concepts and categories of thought are determined by that adversary, for the younger people this adversary may be simply nonexistent: Their primary orientation is an entirely different one."[46] If the youth is blocked by a much more powerful ideological (and to a degree ossified) narrative, its "freshness" loses focus and intensity while being subverted and coopted. The Communist Young League, which boasts a history of almost a century,[47] for its part serves as a "proving ground" for future leaders, and has indeed produced a great number of them, such as Hu Jintao, Li Keqiang, and many others.

Xi Jinping, who himself is not a product of the Youth League, has in fact sidelined the youngsters' influence on thoughts and proceedings of the Party in recent moves, in part by radically defunding the Youth League by almost two-thirds since he came to power. In a book of various speeches and edicts published in 2017, "Xi lambasted the youth league for 'chanting empty slogans' and chided its officials for their 'bureaucratic and arrogant air' as far back as June 2013."[48] In his eyes, "the youth league's grass-roots organisations 'may appear to have covered [a great part of the population] but in fact they are not of any use and exist only in name.'"[49] Nine years later, on May 11, 2022, Xi Jinping "hailed the contributions made by young communists over the past century, and called on them to offer energy and creativity to push forward national rejuvenation." He further stated that the Youth League had achieved success, precisely because it had upheld the leadership of the Party, reinforced faith in communism and socialism, committed itself to national rejuvenation, and remained rooted in

---

[46] Mannheim 1928, 178.
[47] It was founded back in 1925 as the Chinese Socialist Youth League.
[48] See Gan 2017.
[49] See Gan 2017.

Chinese youth.⁵⁰ Under the guise of praise we find a straightjacket, however. Forging the minds of China's youth is one of Xi's greatest matters of concern (Stalin's "engineering the soul" comes to mind). In the same May speech, Xi therefore delineated the roles of the Youth League as follows:

> Inculcating ideology and educating the young for/in support of the party, "a school for young people to learn socialism and communism with Chinese characteristics"
> "Uniting and leading young members of the Youth League to consciously obey the call of the party"
> Being a bridge between party and youth, between the Young Pioneers and the party (described respectively as vanguard, shock brigade, and reserve force), a "trilogy of life" for young people to pursue political progress
> "Being courageous in self-revolution, and always becoming an advanced organization that closely follows the party"⁵¹

Just six weeks earlier, the State Council Information Office of China had published its first-ever White Paper dedicated to the next generation entitled "Youth of China in the New Era."⁵² For the uninitiated, the title's temporal marker "in the new Era" points to the time when Xi Jinping came to power, at the eighteenth CPC National Congress in October 2012. There can be no newer "new era" than the Xi-era. A thorough investigation into the contents and intentions of this White Paper would fill more pages than are available to me, but suffice it to say that, colloquially speaking, it is a self-serving, rigidly utilitarian set of formulas and therefore only to be regarded

---

[50] State Council: Xi tells Chinese youth to contribute energy, creativity to rejuvenation; Updated: May 11, 2022 08:59. For the Chinese text, see the *People's Daily* from May 11, 2022. The English version, published by The State Council Information Office of the People's Republic of China of *Youth of China in the New Era* is accessible at https://english.news.cn/20220421/ad0c7490f6db42f2bd6539794f3ca1af/c.html.
[51] State Council.
[52] First-ever, to our knowledge. See note 44 above for the English version.

as a useful document in the sense that it inverts the mechanism of generational obligations: here the youth are firmly required to oblige the elders, envisioned not as their parents but as the Party elders and the line they chart. Shot through with the usual inflated optimism—youth are the "beacon of hope" and "vanguard in the rejuvenation process," "youth have never wavered in their determination to love the Party," youth have "iron will and boundless courage," etc.)—the timing of its compilation and its public release in April, 2022 could not have been worse. The very first paragraph leads with "The New Era: Great Times with Ample Opportunities," all the while tens of millions were under Covid lockdown. On May 4, 2023, a year (and many excess deaths) later, China's August Leader addressed the youth unemployment situation (i.e., the exact *lack* of ample opportunities) by recommending that they "eat bitterness," a generationally paternalistic piece of advice, if ever there was one.[53] Meanwhile, by the time of this writing, China's youth unemployment rates are at such historic levels (over 20 percent) that the government—usually so eager to gather data and broadcast statistics, some exaggerated—no longer publicizes any youth employment data.

The White Paper reads like a time capsule, albeit an interesting one, for sure, as it reflects on the progress being made since the founding of the PRC, and rightly so. The tables and graphs certainly are impressive. To learn that 88 percent of Chinese youth are capable of managing their emotions as of 2021, or that "More than 20,000 young people have been honored as Positive and Kind Youth for exuding positive youthful energy" or that, "As of the end of 2021, more than 90 million people aged between 14 and 35 had registered at the volunteering platform"[54]—these are important and comforting pieces of information. It comes as no surprise, then, that Xi Jinping's

---

[53] *People's Daily*, May 4, 2023.
[54] Chinavolunteer.mac.gov.cn.

government has great plans for China's youth: "a basic mechanism for youth work from the central level to the local level has been generally put in place, and a preliminary policy system for youth development with Chinese characteristics has taken shape." That mechanism and system looks like this:

To be sure, this type of growth into a (next/future) generation "with high aspirations, moral integrity, professional competence, a good sense and a broad mind" will be brought about under the watchful eye of the Party, percolating down and into all aspects of an individual's private life and professional career: It is hoped that

Table 2

Middle- and Long-term Youth Development Plan (2016-2025)	
	Overall Objectives
中长期青年发展规划 （2016—2025 年）	By 2020, a preliminary policy system and work mechanism for youth development with Chinese characteristics will be in place. The theoretical and political literacy of the vast number of youth, and their all-round development will be further improved. They will have the opportunity to play a full role as a new driving force and pioneer in securing a decisive victory in building a moderately prosperous society in all respects. By 2025, the policy system and work mechanism for youth development with Chinese characteristics will be more developed. The young people will have greater theoretical and political literacy, significantly upgrade their all-round development, and they will grow into a generation with high aspirations, moral integrity, professional competence, a good sense and a broad mind, and an enterprising spirit who can shoulder the important responsibility of realizing the Chinese Dream of national rejuvenation.

Table 3

Areas of Youth Development	Key Projects
Theoretical Literacy and Moral Standards	Young Marxists Training Project
Education	Youth Core Socialist Values Study Project
Health	Youth Physical Health Improvement Project
Dating and Marriage	Youth Internship Plan
Employment and Entrepreneurship	Youth Choicest Cultural Works Project
Culture	Youth Internet Civilization Development Project
Social Integration and Engagement	Young Chinese Volunteer Campaign
Safeguarding Legitimate Rights and Interests	Youth Ethnic Unity and Progress Promotion Project
Preventing Juvenile Delinquency	
Social Security	

Tables 2 and 3, from the White Paper, "Youth of China in the New Era," issued by the State Council Information Office of the People's Republic of China, in April 2022.

the "more than 150,000 youth organizations [that] have been set up, covering all counties" will guarantee the desired outcome.

As in the West, but for different reasons, "universal values" do not have much currency in contemporary China. In fact, there are long-standing campaigns against such "packaged" values, insofar as they are identified with "the West." Every aspect of life is (indeed, must be) infused "with Chinese characteristics." It is therefore a bit curious that we see the White Paper discussing "common values" within the context of a globalized environment:

> They [the youth] actively draw inspiration from the experience and achievements of other countries and civilizations. They work along with their peers from around the world to build a global community of [a] shared future, and advocate peace, development, equity, justice, democracy and freedom, which are the common

values of humanity, for the purpose of creating a better future for all.⁵⁵

To complete the recent Communist Youth League timeline, a few months later, in October 2022, it became clear that Xi Jinping had no intention at all of rewarding the so-called success of the Communist Youth League with any significant leadership posts at the 20th Peoples' Congress. During the reshuffling of top posts within the party, not one candidate who had participated in the Youth League was considered to fit the bill. Observing what had transpired in Beijing, Martin Quinn Pollard (Reuters) decided on a rather flashy but probably accurate headline on the matter: "China's Xi deals knockout blow to once-powerful Youth League faction."⁵⁶ For his article, Pollard invited a couple of informed opinions, among them Dali Yang, a political scientist at the University of Chicago, who weighed in saying, "As a party-led organization, the League has lost its clout as the place for grooming leaders." The most damning judgment on the Communist Youth League's status change, however, came from senior China watcher Cheng Li, who simply noted that "they are completely defeated." A statement may pack rhetorical punch through its sheer grammatical simplicity, but certainly one cannot with a single sentence (or speech) undo 100 years of organizational structuring and layering and grooming of talent, nor call millions of young people "defeated."⁵⁷ The actual plan Xi Jinping has for China's youth (whether organized in a "league" or in the Pioneer system) harkens back to the Mao-era, when any such bodies, under the guidance of the Communist Party, were transformed into mass organizations that could be mobilized

---

⁵⁵ One has to wonder if the Chinese version of the White Paper includes this particular clause. It is "for internal circulation only" so we cannot say.
⁵⁶ Pollard 2023.
⁵⁷ Although, there is a term for exactly that demographic status: the lost generation. China's leaders certainly would never admit that the nation had suffered such a generational cave-in.

for whatever campaign the leadership might deem necessary. Mao, who often made use of the country's youth to outsource and stage ideological struggles during the Cultural Revolution when he was not using them as cheap mass labor, understood that "Socialist youth" would be an experience that shaped people in specific ways. In 1953, four years after the founding of the PRC, Mao said, "New China must care for her youth and show concern for the growth of the younger generation. Young people have to study and work, but they are at the age of physical growth. Therefore, full attention must be paid both to their work and study and to their recreation, sport and rest."[58] Two years later, we have Mao issuing this statement:

> The young people are the most active and vital force in society. They are the most eager to learn and the least conservative in their thinking. This is especially so in the era of socialism. We hope that the local Party organizations in various places will help and work with the Youth League organizations and go into the question of bringing into full play the energy of our youth in particular. The Party organizations should not treat them in the same way as everybody else and ignore their special characteristics. Of course, the young people should learn from the old and other adults, and should strive as much as possible to engage in all sorts of useful activities with their agreement.[59]

The operative word in that last sentence? *Useful*. We are very close to entering through the gates of utilitarianism, where the libertarian philosopher Jan Narveson waits to tell us that "having children is normally a matter of moral indifference," but that in a utilitarian regime "we must be obliged to produce as many children as possible, as long as their [projected] happiness exceeds their misery."[60] What

---

[58] Talk at the reception for the Presidium of the Second National Congress of the Youth League (June 30, 1953).
[59] "Youth Shock Brigade," Introductory note.
[60] Narveson 1967, 62, 67.

would a younger Pan Yue 潘岳[61] or a slightly older Greta Thunberg have to say about the meaning of that particular adjective when applied to the young generation of today? China's youth is certainly not defeated, although many have decided to "lie flat" (*tang ping* 躺平) and to be a tad less useful to the Party, and, ironically, its rejuvenation efforts, for a while at least.

Some numbers and dates: 2035, 2045, 2050, 2060

We have already seen that environmental experts do not shy away from big numbers. The Year 2222 is a prime example. Two hundred years into the future, where will things stand, they ask? We cannot say, but with large nuclear arsenals, an ozone layer that has thinned, the potential impact of GHG on the Jet Stream, with AI and CRISPR (clustered regularly interspaced short palindromic repeats, which allow gene editing), our decision-making platform has changed dramatically in recent years. As Stephen Bickham succinctly put it, "We did not have the responsibility for the future that we do now before we had the capacity to destroy it."[62]

Good decision-making at this juncture of human history appears to be of the essence. Or does it? Let's take another near-2222 scenario, this one concerned with depletion, which was articulated by the British philosopher Derek Parfit in 1982 about the world a century later:

---

[61] Pan Yue was deputy director of China's State Environmental Protection Administration (SEPA) and an outspoken critic of China's destructive environmental practices. As a senior official with SEPA, he advocated for a better balance between economic development and natural resource management. Over time it was felt that he made too much "troublesome commotion" (*nao* 闹) in that post and so he was eventually moved to another position within the party apparatus.

[62] Bickham 1981.

Suppose that, as a community, we must choose whether to deplete or conserve certain kinds of resources. If we choose Depletion, the quality of life over the next two centuries would be slightly higher than it would have been if we had chosen Conservation, but it may later be much lower. At this much lower level people's lives would, however, still be well worth living.[63]

So argues Derek Parfit in perfectly sensible fashion, juxtaposing two quality-of-life scenarios against two different temporalities. Parfit proposes a similar equation by weighing risky energy policies (with nuclear, the riskiest of all) with less risky but more polluting ones (coal comes to mind). Which of these does more harm, and over what stretches of time? With nuclear, it is entirely feasible that a single catastrophic event occurs that kills thousands of people. With coal, we can be certain that it shortens the lives of millions of people (not just those of miners).[64] Which road are we to choose, then, keeping in mind the well-being of future generations vs. the self-interest of the present generation?[65] That is a question of both morality and of economics. In a capitalist system, these two aspects of the single problem behave like oil and water—they don't mix. Unless, of course, a third, powerful agent enters the fray: necessity. Necessity may be driven by external factors (e.g., the realities of climate change triggering staggering financial and social costs), or by internal factors (e.g., a moral consciousness that translates into a self-censoring set of codes, regulations, and laws). Most philosophers and political realists would argue that the weight of the internal factor is weak, while the weight of reality is as strong as it gets. At this juncture, we

---

[63] Parfit, Derek. "Future Generations: Further Problems", *Philosophy & Public Affairs*, Spring, 1982, Vol. 11, No. 2 (Spring, 1982), 113–172.
[64] Such nuclear disasters did happen, even if Parfit was writing before Tchernobyl and Fukushima.
[65] The Chinese for the first term is *daiji guanhuan* 代际关怀; and, for the second, is *bendai liji zhuyi* 本代利己主义.

may recall what Eugene Linden has to say about reality in relation to the environment, especially on a temporal scale.[66] Linden posits four separate clocks (reality, science, finance/corporate world, and public awareness), an intriguing construct, especially when considering policymaking. Reality is *now* and instantaneous. Science, on the other hand, is always grappling to understand reality, and thus it tends to lag far behind, by some measure of time (two years on average in the atmospheric sciences, according to Linden, an unrealistic time-frame for data-driven work).[67] Finance and the corporate world deny, stall, and deflect; they are the masters of time, as they make it seem to stop. However, as happens more often these days, this tier of "players" gets caught by reality, a global copper or oil crisis, for example. As a saying attributed to Ayn Rand goes, "You can ignore reality. However, you cannot ignore the consequences of ignoring reality." Reality, as one of the four clocks, ticks in the realm of public opinion or awareness, which draws from the scientific community and corporate spin in almost equal measure. Regrettably, public awareness, not to mention official action (writing law, implementing policies, instituting new gov agencies, etc.), almost always lags far behind the science, both in its first responses and in its demands for consequential actions.

Necessity usually belongs more into the very first category of "now." One does not (or should not) delay a response to an emergency, not if the consequences may cause, for example, insurers to threaten to pull out of much of a state (as is the case in California and in Florida, and soon will be elsewhere) because they are no longer willing or able to underwrite the risks (fire, floods, earthquakes) which, looking forward, are likely to be larger than the capitalization of any single company

---

[66] Linden 2022.
[67] Many of today's environmental insights took forty years or more to develop, including that of "keystone species." See https://ny.pbslearningmedia.org/resource/nat38-discovery-of-keystone-species-vid/the-serengeti-rules-media-gallery/

itself.[68] If, therefore, necessity requires restrictions on the depletion of certain, perhaps finite resources (something any neoliberal or pro-libertarian thinker vehemently denies on principle),[69] then we find ourselves obliged to act, lest our lives and, potentially, in an extreme case scenario, the lives of future generations, may no longer be worth living. (In a more generous scenario, future lives would simply be harmed or restricted, but they would still be worth living.)

Many of those writing about obligations towards future generations draw a line in the sand, temporally speaking. Parfit, who was not adverse to moving two hundred years through time in his equations, reeled in his time horizon and accepted no responsibility whatsoever to generations that far removed from our own. So did the philosopher of law Martin Golding (1930–2020). The latter "asserts that because distant future generations lie outside of our moral community, we have only very limited obligations to those generations. Instead, our primary obligations are to our contemporaries and to our immediate descendants." And further along in the argument, Golding questions "what one generation owes to those generations with whom it will not share a 'common life.'"[70] The "eco-economist" Robert Heilbroner agrees: "It is the absence of just such a bond with the future that casts

---

[68] Without insurance, nobody will build anymore, and nobody will want to manufacture anything anymore.

[69] Narveson 1967, which, according to Parfit, "pioneered" the discussion on future generations. Narveson in a later paper (1995), opines, "Current 'Environmentalists' evidently think of resources as natural. Identifying them with quantities of stuff—oil, say, or land. And they suppose that such resources must be finite in amount and therefore scarce, so that when we use any of these we leave less—less for others. This way of thinking is, I argue, entirely wrong. Resources for people are not finite; they expand with human thought and effort, *without upper limit*. There are no global shortages of anything that we have to worry about, nothing requiring the imposition of extra-market controls on our use of the stuff of the world. All environmental policies based on such premises are consequently ill-conceived, and bound to work only harm" (italics not in the original).

[70] Quoted from Auerbach 1991, 73.

doubt on the ability of nation states or socioeconomic orders to take now the measures needed to mitigate the problems of the future."[71]

Xi Jinping, for his part, maintained his own view on the subject of depletion and conservation. Moving from the urban to the otherworldly, Xi in a speech from 2017, issues a clear and coherent message, if not a path forward. "Man and nature form a community of life; we, as human beings, must respect nature, follow its ways, and protect it. Only by observing the laws of nature can humankind avoid costly blunders in its exploitation. Any harm we inflict on nature will eventually return to haunt us. This is a reality we have to face."[72] The reader should at this point perhaps be reminded that China, not unlike the West, has had a long history of trying to bend the laws of nature through large-scale geoengineering interventions.

In an article from March 2006 entitled "Two Mountains, Three Phases—China's ecological dialectics,"[73] Xi speaks of a goal for all mankind (sic!): to possess a gold mountain (Jinshan 金山) and a green mountain (Lüshan 绿山). The mountains are metaphors for economic development and ecological environment. They are contradictory to each other but can be dialectically united. The three phases attached to these mountains consist of Phase 1, when the earth's carrying capacity is sorely tested and even disregarded; Phase 2, when contradictions between economic pursuits and resource scarcity break wide open, and conflict ensues; and Phase 3, when the sciences addressing the challenges of the ecological frontier function as the economic driver; they are the new economy's "power source." This type of circular economy (it's actually a stretch to call it that)

---

[71] Heilbroner 1980, 135.
[72] Xi Jinping 2017 (Oct. 18), "Secure a Decisive Victory." One wonders if the Chairman is aware of the costs and logistics involved in the remediation of a legacy superfund site, aka an environmental "blunder" committed by private actors or SOEs (state owned enterprises).
[73] Generally referred to as "Liang shan lun" 两山论 ("Two Mountains Doctrine"), first articulated in 2020.

requires three preconditions: a) the science is advanced enough to repair the harm that was done; b) the wealth accrued during the first phase is enough to carry out improvements; and c) that the chain of values in the interim has been enhanced, which is to say that the next generation's relationship with planet Earth is in fact different (protectionist in the widest sense) from the preceding generation's, the one that went on a rampage of extraction and destruction, in the name of nation building, GDP growth, and industrialization.

None of these three categories—logical, ethical, or financial integrity—can be guaranteed or should be taken for granted, however, which makes Xi's Two-Mountains theory a bit of a house of cards. (Strictly speaking, the theory is not his; he simply appropriated the analogy and made it his.[74]) Furthermore, there is no scenario built into this "theory" whereby the generation which has to shoulder the cleanup would actually be the possessor of presumptive rights and claims against the "pioneer" generations. The succession of law suits against such presumptive rights generated in Switzerland (alluded to in the Introduction) or Montana (Held vs. Montana, described in chapter One), just to pick two prominent cases, is only accelerating, as indicated earlier, and it will perhaps at some not too distant point in time fulfill two premises: firstly, a series of precedents will be set on the local or regional level which will find its way all the way up to the highest national court (the US Supreme Court, say, in the United States), where a case about precedents will set the tone for everything that follows from it. Second, never mind national (mostly Anglo-American) law; we will undoubtedly see many similar cases winding their ways through supra national and international courts.

---

[74] A good introduction to the history and legacy of this concept—preceding Xi Jinping by quite a few years—can be found in the article *Green Waters and Green Mountains* by the China Media Project dated April 16, 2021. See https://chinamediaproject.org/topic/two-mountains-theory/

The headline to this section promised numbers and dates, and let us start with an easy one: 2035. In a somewhat perplexing move, China got a head start towards 2035, for in Beijing and elsewhere, 2035 has already happened, not only on paper, but also "in the field." To explain: the usual planning-for-the-future strategy lies with the Five-Year Plans (FYP). With the help of Russian experts, the first such plan was implemented in 1953 and lasted until 1957. At present we are in the middle of FYP14 (2021–2025). The FYP include initiatives and directives that address all aspects of the country's economic, political, social, cultural, agriculture, and now also ecology-oriented goals, for instance, carbon neutrality, low emissions manufacturing, a pilot for an emissions trading system, product life cycles, and better environmental monitoring. These Plans, in other words, represent a comprehensive collection of sweeping agendas, meant to reach all the way from the capital to the smallest village. In each FYP, one of the most important target agendas always relates to land use, which includes agriculture and food security. The latter is a difficult subject, one that Xi Jinping has declared to be "the foundation of national security" in a speech at the annual Central Rural Work conference in December 2022. As Xi pointed out, "Once something's wrong with agriculture, our bowls will be held in someone else's hands and we'll have to depend on others for food. How can we achieve modernization in that case?"[75]

In 2019, in addition to the short-term Five-Year Plan, the State Council launched a new set of plans, the so-called Comprehensive Territorial Masterplans, to cover the timespan of three FYP, from 2020 to 2035, with a particular focus on land use and land coverage.[76] Not all aspects of this spatial masterplan comply with the time frame

---

[75] Zuo 2023.
[76] The Party Congress ratifying these new spatial plans took place in Beijing from Oct. 26–29, 2020.

stipulated in the title. There is one particular item of business that does not fall into that bracket, the aforementioned category of agriculture, i.e., food security. The temporal label attached to agriculture in this set of new plans is *forever* (*yongjiu* 永久). State authorities seem finally to have understood that the future of the nation is at an inflection point, especially with regard to its ecological well-being, having looked at the looming triple threats of urban sprawl, "mounting external containment and [geopolitical] uncertainty," plus climate change that causes not only catastrophic floods but also accelerates desertification in China, with these trends reducing the amount of arable land in the PRC.[77]

All 2035 Plans issued on the national, provincial, county, and municipality level (several thousands in total), are custom-tailored, localized strategic plans, yet they exhibit an identical structure and similarly politicized wording. Matching targets and agendas with national development guidelines ensure that disparate communities, although competing against each other in every field of human endeavor, are nevertheless "on the same page" where national (or Party) priorities are concerned. One tactical approach to achieving a goal is to streamline procedures. The 2035 plans therefore contain the maxim *duo gui he yi* 多规合一, which can mean ideally "different regulations to fuse into one," but more often, within a large bureaucratic apparatus such as the PRC's, points to the avoidance of policy sprawl, for which China is Exhibit A, even if these days this form of governmental malpractice is widely shared among many nations.[78] Ergo, the language of section 7 of the

---

[77] Zuo2 2023. Never mind the atrocious amount of soil and water pollution, which has a detrimental impact on produce quality and public health.
[78] China actually has a commendable regulatory framework when it comes to environmental protection. As of 2014, by Wang Zhihe, et al, "China enacted nine laws on environmental protection (such as the Water Pollution Prevention Law, the Solid Waste Pollution Prevention and Control Law, and the Radioactive Pollution Prevention and Control Law) and seventeen laws on resource efficiency (including the Renewable Energy Law, the Cleaner Production Promotion Law, and the Water Law). To this can be added fifty relevant administrative laws and regulations on environmental protection."

Jiangxi Province territorial masterplan for 2035 is summarized in English as "Organizing Attractive Territorial Area and Building a Picturesque Jiangxi with Characteristics of Revolution, Green and History."

A closer look at the China of the year 2035 gives a clearer picture of "the world we want." From an environmental perspective, the holistic view of mountains, streams, forests, fields, lakes, grasslands and seas as an interdependent system is commendable.[79] Parts of this system will surely always remain open to negotiation (or transgressive practices by illegally operating actors), but now every province, county and municipality in the nation has been given a set of definitive red lines for aspects such as "forever" securing land for agricultural use (given in minimum acreage), environmental protection zero-tolerance thresholds, urban sprawl (literally, "piercing urban limits"), heightened water resource controls, "red" wastewater management.[80] To be given a set of guidelines and to be able to act on them are of course two different things entirely. China suffers from a traditionally feeble bureaucratic enforcement system, although unannounced inspections of construction sites, industrial plants and public projects increased, ironically perhaps, during the pandemic years.

The overall aim of the 2035 plans is to build a "beautiful China," which is not only a slogan, but a necessary ingredient of a new civilization in the making. This new civilization, in which the next generation plays a critical role, at least according to the aforementioned White Paper,[81] will be firmly planted in the ecological sphere, in

---

In addition, 660 local government regulations and 800 national standards related to environmental protection." What is critical is how these laws and regulations are enforced and adjudicated in the courts, which is where China still falls short. The above is cited from Wang Zhihe et al. 2014.

[79] The Chinese reads, 落实山水林田草湖海生命共同体的整体系统观.
[80] These five phrases in Chinese are (1) 永久基本农田; (2) 生态保护红线; (3) 城镇开发边界三条控制线作为不可逾越的红线; (4) 水资源开发利用控制红; and (5) 水功能区限制纳污红线.
[81] Youth of China in the New Era Section III. "Shouldering Heavy Tasks and Responsibilities.

balance with nature, with the result a completely harmonious society with a shared vision for all of humanity, by Xi Jinping's account. This is all part and parcel of the China Dream (*Zhongguo meng* 中国梦), Xi's platform slogan in November, 2012, shortly after his inauguration as president. On the occasion of the national Youth Day in May 2013, "President Xi Jinping encouraged young Chinese people to dare to dream, work assiduously to fulfill the dreams and contribute to the revitalization of the nation. He said the young generation with firm will, strong sense of responsibility and great professional competence is the hope of realizing the Chinese dream." Didactically, Xi added one conditional clause: "A nation will be prosperous if its young generation is ambitious and reliable."[82]

Fast forward to 2035, and not much will seem predictable, let alone reliable. Stephen Bickham, however, writing long before Beautiful China, the China Dream, and Ecological Civilization were put on the banners of Xi's new era, makes an interesting point that concerns Marxism and its dreams:

> Marxism provides another example of a system in which obligation to future generations is a central doctrine. . . . The commitment of the Marxist is to bring about on earth a perfect society, but a contemporary Marxist realizes it is very doubtful that he will live to see the new promised land. One of the factors which has given the Marxist movement its powerful tone of idealism is its requirement to sacrifice for the future.[83]

I suppose it can be said with a fair degree of confidence that the number of young people buying into "the dream" or any of the other party slogans has fallen precipitously since the Covid pandemic. The number of young people "required" by Xi and the Politburo

---

[82] Xinhua News Agency. May 5, 2013.
[83] Bickham 1981.

for the doubtless necessary sacrifice of nation-building, national rejuvenation, and so on, might still be high, however.

It is no secret that China's society in record time has become one of the most inequitable in modern history.[84] The 2035 plans attempt to reverse this, in theory. Laudably, the large gulf between urban and rural is being recognized. Four pronouncements address this problem, in one way or another:

> "For 2035, reduce the differences between urban and rural, and equalize efforts at public services."
> "For 2035, match people's incomes with economic growth; raise the level of access to services in equal measure" (for all ages and all income groups).
> "For 2035, realize equity (or equality) in the people's ability to participate in governance, and fairly (or justly) guarantee the development of [evenly distributed?] authority.
> "For 2035, make further steps towards a fair (or just) society (*shehui gongping* 社会公平)."[85]

Both the gender pay gap and unequal access to education are items of further concern. To call this a Territorial Masterplan is to some degree a misnomer, as the agenda includes a host of social (not only spatial) issues that bear resolving. And, meanwhile, there are a number of obvious problems with the 2035 plans, most notably on a conceptual level, the absence of Karl Marx himself, although that no longer surprises. Remember that Marx' approach to, say, agriculture, was anything but sanguine:

> All progress in capitalistic agriculture is the progress in the art, not only of robbing the laborer, but of robbing the soil; all progress

---

[84] See the Gini-coefficient report for 2023, on the PRC.
[85] These extracts are based on a lecture given by Thomas Hahn at UC Berkeley on October 13, 2022.

in increasing the fertility of the soil for a given time, is a progress towards ruining the more lasting sources of that fertility.[86]

For Marx, the same applies for forestry and other land uses, so that for environmental industries, the rate and intensity of extraction must always outpace that of restoration. In Marx's view, for instance, "The development of civilization and industry in general has always shown itself so active in the destruction of forests that everything that has been done for their preservation and production is completely insignificant in comparison." For Marx, the accrual of surplus resources (e.g., surplus capital in capitalist societies, such as the PRC is now) deeply depend on the above-mentioned imbalances between resources, labor, and added or accrued value (i.e., surplus value). Since capitalist modes of production disturb "the metabolic interaction between man and the earth," the only long-term remedy is to replace capitalism with a different economic model.

A "natural" response to extractive and destructive models would be, of course, an environmental counter-movement. As Paul Robbins in his *Political Ecology* notes,

> Finally then, green materialism insists that such ongoing pillage of the environment must ultimately result in a political response. Just as the exploitation of labor leads to a labor movement, the exploitation of nature must result in an environmental movement. In capitalism's excess, therefore, lie the seeds of more sustainable and equitable practices.[87]

Just to be clear: China professes to a system of state capitalism (Mao said so himself)[88], so Robbins' words do apply here. After roughly two decades of national and international E-NGO's involvement in

---

[86] Marx 1976 rpt., 637–38. Shades of Elvin (?).
[87] Robbins 2012, 58.
[88] Mao Zedong. "On State Capitalism," *Selected Works*, Written comment on a document of the National Conference on Financial and Economic Work held on July 9, 1953.

Chinese development projects (with varying levels of success), these same organisations (mostly run by young people) have less and less operational influence in the PRC.[89] The 2035 plans exclude these non-state actors altogether.

At the same time, climate change is a serious problem, especially for coastal cities such as Wenzhou, Ningbo, Fuzhou, Tianjin, and Shanghai (cf. Florida and Hawai'i) that require costly adaptation and mitigation measures. A good number of cities have incurred heavy debts and are on the brink of or already beyond insolvency, which means the coming two or three decades will be very challenging, and it probably won't get much better thereafter, even if China is carbon neutral by 2060 (which seems highly doubtful).[90] Land use and land coverage, the main subject of all the 2035 plans, will witness the largest adjustments since probably the establishment of the Peoples Communes in the late 1950s/early 1960s. Changes to the land, especially unfavorable ones (think of desertification, water contamination, land grabs by developers, commodity flow inefficiencies, temporary emergency requisitioning, zoning), have been the number one cause of social unrest.

On the other hand, it is also entirely possible that perhaps one of the eight targets China envisions to reach by 2035 might be realizable in real time and space. According to my aggregate of various 2035 Spatial Masterplans issued by the Government, those eight are:

1. a country full of vitality and innovation;
2. a country famous throughout the world for its opening-up;
3. a convenient and interconnected country;
4. a sharing country that is inclusive and livable;
5. a green and low-carbon country;

---

[89] E-NGO = Environmental non-governmental organization.
[90] The introduction of a property tax (first proposed back in 2003) has not yet generated reliable municipal income streams aside from a number of pilot programs.

6. a smart country that is safe and efficient;
7. a charming and happy country of humanity; and
8. a country with developed intelligent manufacturing.

This all sounds very much like Wales' Well-Being Act from 2015, except for the importance placed on China's "face" and international reputation, in prominent second place; otherwise, the reason for the similarity is easy to trace, as the Chinese version is also derived from the United Nations Development Agenda (2015–2030). Insofar as this picture partakes of utopianism, perhaps the Russian philosopher Ivan T. Frolov (1926–1999) can help us out. An early proponent of the "ecological civilization" concept now so popular in China,[91] Frolov advanced the dialectically stringent argument "that although struggles to create a more ecologically rational world ran the risk of utopianism, since they necessarily got ahead of the development of material-social forces, the severity of the global ecological threat nevertheless demanded a 'rational realism' that was utopian-like in character."[92] Elements of utopianism are required for vision, scenario building, analysis, and imagination;[93] all age groups possess at least one or two of these faculties, which means the conceptual development of a utopian society could be placed on (almost) anyone's shoulders. The implementation of such a society, however, is another subject altogether.

Since the last few pages have oscillated between 2035 and "Forever", let us lower our sights for the moment somewhere in the middle, in the year 2060, say. In several contexts the term "scenario" has come up, and in 2021, Shell Oil, in the business of extracting, refining, and selling fossil fuels, released a document intended to provide a *scenario* for China in 2060. Entitled "Report on Carbon Neutrality for China's

---

[91] The "ecological culture" slogan originated in the Soviet Union.
[92] "Global Problems and the Future of Mankind" (1982), cited in Foster 2015.
[93] See Forstater 2004.

Energy System in 2060,"[94] the well-designed cover collage at its center sports a picture of a young mother with her child, somewhat bizarrely but delicately examining the stalk of a plant; the abbreviation "AI" also makes an appearance in its own box on the cover, as does a Chinese stone lion and a wind turbine.[95] Shell, a company that clearly intends to be still in the fossil fuel energy supply business in 2060, lays out a complex path of interdependencies to align itself with China's energy security goals, as well as Xi Jinping's pledge for carbon neutrality by that year. Some of the interdependencies are beyond Shell's control (e.g., reforestation in China, a national priority) and others are beyond China's control. And yet the Report goes into great detail about how many trees have been planted during the current fourteenth FYP, and how that translates into the potential for carbon sequestration by natural means going forward.[96] The more trees the country plants, the better for Shell, as the higher carbon capture capacity by arboreal means allows Shell, with any other emissions-spewing company, to stagger its output accordingly, especially in what of late has become the largest and fastest growing energy market on the planet. Out of Shell's control and mostly out of China's control are the climate targets set by politicians in Paris, Copenhagen or Rio.[97] The company is quite candid about such matters, and tries to play both sides, the market and the latest climate science.[98] However, the report downplays the clear fact that the 1.5 degree Celsius global warming ceiling that

---

[94] The Chinese is: 中国能源体系2060 碳中和报告.
[95] See Shell.
[96] Shell, 35, says, "Forests provide biomass energy and act as natural carbon sinks" 森林可提供生物质能源并充当天然碳汇.
[97] See CarbonBrief: "The fossil fuel giant stresses that its scenarios are not intended as forecasts, projections or indeed business plans. Despite being a major oil-and-gas producer, it also states that meeting global climate targets is 'not within Shell's control'."
[98] Shell's CEO in a recent interview made the following bizarre claim: "I am of a firm view that the world will need oil and gas for a long time to come. As such, cutting oil and gas production is not healthy." See Mathis 2023.

world leaders had agreed upon at the Paris meeting is incompatible with oil and gas production and consumption on the current scale.

Shell is, of course, only one major player in the global sphere of energy supply. China, on the other hand, once positioned itself as a leader in renewable energy (which is also clearly stated in the Scenario Report), and has instituted the 2060 Program, which includes two pledges:[99] the first, made by Xi Jinping at the Paris Climate Conference in 2015, was to flatten the curve of greenhouse gas by 2030 and the second, to become carbon neutral by 2060, announced in 2020. (Those pledges preceded Xi's announcement in 2023, that he would open hundreds of *new* coal-burning plants, which demolished his credibility with the environmentalists.)[100] Environmentally speaking, three words must accompany any pledges: necessary, feasible, and plausible, but neither of the two pledges adequately addresses all these three terms with any degree of specificity. One therefore has to assume that the pledges are as aspirational as their implementation is actually vital. Whether they are technically feasible or financially plausible, only time will tell. It will be for the next generation to find out, a generation which may very well find itself in a more equitable and just environment, as long as everyone lives in Wales or Finland.

This short exposé will finish by picking up on an unassuming phrase used above in the context of the 2015 Wales act, namely, a "shared vision" "for a future worth living, and designing a set of *pathways* to get there." The language of pathways is part and parcel of a broader theoretical framework now employed by economists, statisticians, and planners to chart plausible outcomes under what/if conditions. These so-called SSPs (Shared socioeconomic pathways),[101] first formulated around 2016, usually come in a set of five. On a global

---

[99] That is, of course, before Xi announced in 2023 that he would open 200+ *new* coal-burning plants. See immediately below.
[100] This promise seems to have been made to help Russia in the Ukraine war.
[101] *Gongheng shehui jingji lujing* 共享社会经济路径 in Chinese.

scale, we need to differentiate between different visions of different pathways (SSP1 to SSP5, as laid out below). All pathways have a certain degree of plausibility, but that degree changes considerably once scaled down from the global to the national and especially the local. Besides a spatial axis, the SSPs also operate on a temporal axis, namely, they extend until at least 2050, and on occasion, the pathway modeling stretches out towards 2100. Let us dive deeper...

In a 2022 research article, a research group out of Lanzhou (Gansu province, in China) mapped out dependencies of economic development within the triangular box of climate change, economic activity, and deployed technologies.[102] NB: the deployed (i.e., currently in use) technologies under consideration by this research group do not include AI, let alone a potential AGI[103], which is not only a unique accelerant, but might very well turn out to be the defining techno-social dimension of the twenty-first century. Be that as it may, let's take a bird's eye view at the SSPs. Again, keep in mind that the "underlying SSP narratives depict... five typical global situations differentiated by climate change mitigation and adaptation challenges."

SSP1 (sustainability): The world has made progress in sustainability, and the rapid development of low-income regions means that the emphasis on economic growth shifts toward a broader emphasis on human well-being and better environmental conditions, even at the expense of somewhat slower economic growth over the long-term. The world faces low mitigation and adaptation challenges.

SSP2 (middle-of-the-road): The world follows a path in which social, economic, and technological trends do not shift

---

[102] Jiang, et al. 2022.
[103] An AGI (aka Artificial General Intelligence) empowered entity, would have cognitive, reasonings, and problem solving powers.

markedly from historical patterns. Moderate challenges arise in terms of both mitigation and adaptation.

SSP3 (fragmentation): This path involves a fragmented world with regional conflicts and competitiveness. The world is characterised by a high degree of poverty and faces significant mitigation and adaptation challenges.

SSP4 (inequality): This path describes a highly unequal world in which large numbers of poor people in various regions face significant adaptation challenges, whereas advanced wealthier regions have developed alternative technologies to reduce their mitigation challenges.

SSP5 (conventional development): Under this path, the world is growth-oriented and uses conventional technologies (especially energy conversion technologies based on fossil fuels). Therefore, it faces significant mitigation challenges.[104]

As is evident from the above, a higher degree of equality and socio-spatial justice leads to slower growth overall, but does not pose "significant" mitigation and adaptation challenges (SSP1 vs. SSP5). In other words, under the shared socioeconomic pathway #1, the world would count (relatively) fewer heat-related deaths, a reduced pace of desertification in places like the Hexi Corridor in NW China, fewer and less severe wildfires in California, and a slowing of the melting of glaciers everywhere. As well-read historians, we place SSP1 on the over-optimistic side. Some would argue that we live squarely in a SSP3 or even SSP4 world. Somewhat counter-intuitively, if we were to take the separation of the 5 SSPs as equidistant from each other (in a socioeconomic sense at least), to get from SSP3/4 to SSP1 does *not* lead through SSP2 since we cannot and should not rely on historical patterns of growth and development. Those patterns got us into the present pickle in the first place.

---

[104] Jiang et al. 2022, 2577.

Basing its modeling for 2050 on statistical yearbooks, the Gansu study takes China's recent population census data and other growth indicators to chart startingly different pathways for a China in 2050. Those differences exhibit themselves in GDP per capita growth, which all decline under any SSP, but SSP5 would mean only 1 percent growth by 2050, in contrast to a "healthier" 5 percent under SSP1. Yet the historical growth patterns that have favored the coastal provinces and the capital region over the past three decades no longer hold true under any of the SSPs. With the somewhat surprising exception of Fujian province, which consistently ranks highly within any scenario modeled against the 2050 time horizon, the central and western provinces catch up to the coastal provinces when it comes to GDP per capita growth. Equally surprisingly, Beijing and Guangdong no longer rank in the top ten national growth engines under any of the SSPs once we've reached the year 2050.

While the Gansu study is only one sophisticated method of charting a "shared vision" for the future, there is still the little understood matter of attribution. What is "attribution"? Let us say that, historically speaking, the province of Gansu had x amount of precipitation and that an averaged graph of the monthly distribution of rainfall over the past forty years does not display any significant non-linear deviations. Let us further assume that just in the past decade, those historical patterns of precipitation no longer apply, and that our hypothetical graphs and charts show either slight or significant deviation. Questions then arise. In which measurable way does climate change contribute to the change in historical patterns of rainfall, of growing seasons, of bird migration schedules, etc.? Will Gansu's Dunhuang and the Mogao Caves become flooded?[105] How can we attribute global warming as a factor to precipitation anomalies

---

[105] Dunhuang archeologist Fan Jinshi 樊锦诗 expressed such concerns about increased precipitation in her conversation with Xi Jinping and his entourage in August 2019.

in Gansu, or anywhere else for that matter, in probabilistic terms and with a fair degree of accuracy? This is the question of attribution, i.e., the now rather well developed analytical tool set to determine to which degree climate change contributed to, say, sextreme weather events.

It goes further than that, though. Attribution methods also model the predictability of future occurrences of climate events in theory and in practice. How probable (i.e., statistically predictable) was the so-called hundred-year flood which wiped out the Ahr Valley in Germany in 2022, taking over 100 lives with it? And how probable will be such an event in, say, 2050 or 2099? The numbers don't look promising. Using a more traditional statistical formula, in a +2 degree C world, the likelihood of such an event reoccurring is X, while in a +4 degree C world the likelihood is Y, where Y is exponentially—not linearly—higher. Especially high-density urban clusters or corridors (something that China has been very fond of developing over the past three decades) are especially vulnerable to exponential, non-linear weather event curves, but the urban climate profile in high-density cities is not well understood scientifically, beyond the heat island phenomena, in large part because urban climate adaptation in cities around the world has just recently started to be assessed (ergo the "knowledge gap"),[106] and up to now the data collected has not been entered into any form of systematic record keeping down to the neighborhood level, or gated community level, so that it can be analyzed mathematically.[107] Hence, adaptation measures or post-facto

---

[106] It would help if the municipal public works, transportation, and water and sewage departments would, on general principle, employ so-called climate adaptation managers to coordinate efforts, but again, that has only happened on a provisional basis in merely a handful of cities to date.

[107] This knowledge gap (the lack of big data describing many different places) is one of the key topics discussed in Stechemesser 2024. Out of over 1,500 climate initiatives implemented between 1998 and 2022 across 41 countries in six continents, the authors identified only 63 policies (or 69, as emended in the study's *Results* section) that successfully reduced total emissions of CO_2. At the same time, as noted earlier in the

mitigation cannot be accurately assessed in terms of costs, which are always higher by a large multiplier in urban areas. Yet, despite the uncertainties, we are in no doubt that in a +4 degrees C world, cities like Wuhan, Phoenix AZ, Cairo, New Delhi or even Madrid would become well nigh unlivable.[108]

Recall that in the year 1950 (May 3–5), in the aftermath of the Donora sulfur dioxide emissions disaster in Pennsylvania, the reality of "blunders" and ecological plunder was addressed in the form of the first United States National Technical Conference on Air Pollution. And while China was busy with the Great Leap Forward, the Russian geophysicist Mikhael Ivanovitch Budyko published his pathbreaking book, *Heat Balance of the Earth* (1958), a classic that earned him the Lenin Prize.[109] Three years later, in 1961, while nobody in the western world was looking, Budyko and the climatologist Yevgraf Yevgrafovich Fedorov called the "All-Union Conference on the Problem of Climate Modification by Man" in Leningrad, to address the emerging problem of climate change—the first such conference in the world. That same year, Budyko presented his paper "The Heat and Water Balance Theory of the Earth's Surface" to the Third Congress of the Geographical Society of the USSR, in which he arrived at his famous conclusion that anthropogenic climate change was now inevitable under business as usual, a prediction that foretold and corresponds to the above SSP5. His conclusion: that human energy consumption needed to be curtailed. Fedorov, meanwhile, in 1962, as a member of the Presidium of the Supreme Soviet of the USSR and head of the Institute of Applied Geophysics of the State Committee of the USSR

Introduction, the lack of perfect knowledge is no excuse for the decision not to engage in climate activism.

[108] +4 degrees C globally translates to an increase of about 8 or 9 degrees C on the local urban scale.

[109] Budyko would be awarded the Blue Planet Prize in 1998 for his contributions to the understanding of climate and energy-related science.

on Hydrometeorology and Control of the Natural Environment, already raised the critical issue of sea level rise with the melting of the Greenland ice sheet.[110] Since advanced Soviet science happened mostly behind the so-called Iron Curtain, in a fragmented world such as imagined above in SSP3, and was highly guarded as state secrets, there was a lamentable delay in the transmission of the accumulated knowledge of some of the world's leading climate scientists to a wider, global audience.

The seemingly random preceding paragraph on Soviet-era science serves a specific purpose: it supplies good reasons not to defragment our knowledge, our decision-making, our policies. In the co-authors' view, it shouldn't matter where this knowledge and policies were first conceived (national security should be subordinate to planetary security), as long as its discrete elements, pertinent as they continue to be, are shared in a timely manner and without political gaming among a global community of "pathfinders." By "pathfinders," we mean, "we the people," equal in rights and equal in our quest to live in peace and with the "right to dignity."[111] In this context, it would be commendable indeed if we can be thanked by the next generation for leaving the world intact. Which begs the question, "Is it possible to make the world a better place by creating additional happy people?"

A question such as this lies at the very heart of the new field of population ethics,[112] as it considers how to **value** different populations and/or future generations. Adding the uncertainty of climate change into the equation, population ethics becomes a highly relevant line of inquiry because choices about climate change policies affect both the size of future populations and the quality of life for future people. Pursuing this line of inquiry, we may end up in the territory of Parfit's

---

[110] See Foster 2015, for a very interesting discussion on the contributions of Soviet science to the ecological crisis.
[111] Xi Jinping 2017, 44.
[112] The Chinese term is *renkou lunli* 人口伦理.

famous Repugnant Conclusion (this conclusion, in very choppy moral waters, allows "that any loss in the quality of lives in a population can be outweighed by a sufficient gain in the quantity of lives"),[113] but we may also eventually stumble upon a new theory of beneficence (a Theory X, in Parfit's lingo, yet to be formulated) as a perfectly viable and acceptable solution.

---

[113] Fumagalli 2024, 85. Parfit says, "For any possible population of at least ten billion people, all with a very high quality of life, there must be some much larger imaginable population whose existence, if other things are equal, would be better even though its members have lives that are barely worth living." For more on Parfit's Repugnant Conclusion, see the *Stanford Encyclopedia of Philosophy* (https://plato.stanford.edu/entries/repugnant-conclusion/). Equating to something like a theory of beneficence—"theory X," in Parfit's lingo—is able to solve the Non-Identity problem and thereby bypass the Repugnant Conclusion.

Conclusions

Michael Nylan

There are only a few points that need to be emphasized in my conclusion to our joint venture. First, as Rebecca Solnit and Thelma Young Lutunatabua stress, it is "Not Too Late" to stabilize the environment if we all work together, each contributing to the effort as the person's talents and situation permits. As Solnit writes, "Difficult is not the same as impossible," and thoughtful action on climate change, if belated, is also accelerating on many disparate fronts. Many individuals and groups excuse their inaction on climate change by claiming that they as individuals can't possibly change the story, so why make an effort to do so? Historians, by contrast, know that people's hearts and national policies can and do change on a dime, also that history seldom changes without collective efforts for a common purpose. Moreover, once we begin to really see, as the Ancients did, that there are no self-made success stories in the world and every shining achievement reflects patient hard work over long periods by many (often invisible or dead) people, we are free to discern, nay revel in our glorious intergenerational dependencies. So let each of us vow, arm and arm with Zhuangzi and Wendell Berry, to try our best to "Let It Be Spring with Everything."[1] We can make it happen, and besides we have no other alternatives but to try, unless

---

[1] The phrase *wu wei chun* 物為春 comes from chapter 4 of the *Zhuangzi* ("De chong fu" 德充符); the translation is by Burton Watson. All of Wendell Berry's work is relevant here, but particularly, perhaps, *A Continuous Harmony* (1972).

we are determined right now to disavow all that we love. As T.S. Eliot wrote, for us mere mortals, "There is only the trying—the rest is not our business." At the end of the day, I like to channel a god in my pantheon, John Oliver, the comedian, who said this:

> Nihilism is completely useless. The coward's way out. So you work through that. And I have found, generally, that the light at the end of the tunnel—albeit that light might be smaller than you like it to be ideally—is that there are activists making small, incremental progress on the ground.[2]

As Vaclav Havel wrote, "It's not the conviction that something will turn out well, but the certainty that something makes sense [that should prompt action], regardless of how it turns out." And, as a favorite gloom-and-doom expert Leonard Cohen puts it, "Ring out the bells that still can ring/ forget your perfect offering. There's a crack, a crack in everything. That's how the light gets in."[3] The point is, cold and broken we may be, but we will never see where those cracks lie, unless we push against them as hard and as fast as we can.

Thomas Hahn here

And I'm afraid we can't. Or we can, but we won't. Because we are running out of time, simply speaking. And we are running up against a rather large number, too. 2.4 trillion dollars, to be exact. That is the amount the developing world will need by 2030 to address climate change—not as a one-off, but every single year. So said Sultan al Jaber, the host of the 2023 COP meeting, in an op-ed in *Fortune*.[4] So far,

---

[2] *The New York Times*, Sunday Magazine (Oct. 6, 2024), Interview by Lulu Garcia-Navarro with John Oliver, 13.
[3] Cohen's "A Broken Hallelujah" (renamed and revised as "Anthem").
[4] Sultan al Jaber. "COP 28 president: 'It's time to transform climate finance—and bridge its $2.4 trillion gap." *Fortune Magazine*, (Sept. 28, 2023). Michael Nylan counters: Can

committed funds range around 100 billion per year. How do we arrive at such numbers is not the issue in this conclusion, but the good Sultan is, interestingly, quite optimistic that within the next seven years the gap of 2.3 trillion USD can be bridged. It will take "concerted effort from governments, international financial institutions, and the private sector to reform the current financial architecture and better align global and domestic financial flows with the world's climate goals." Sultan al Jaber and those that move in high finance will have to start writing very large checks, very soon. The science no longer can be doubted, yet green finance platforms still have a long way to go.

As someone prone to throwing a wrench into proceedings, I recommend Arthur Schopenhauer's essays on pessimism. After all, Schopenhauer opined that

> If children were brought into the world by an act of pure reason alone, would the human race continue to exist? Would not a man rather have so much sympathy with the coming generation as to spare it the burden of existence, or at any rate not take it upon himself to impose that burden upon it in cold blood? (see his essay "On the Sufferings of the World," first published in German in his *Parerga und Paralipomena* in 1851).

Michael and Thomas

Naturally, under Trump, things just got a lot harder for everyone.[5] But perhaps we (Americans in particular) needed to be smack up against that high wall, before we could be persuaded to see that the

---

the head of a major fossil fuel producing country be trusted with the final analysis of our existential crisis? I doubt it, particularly as his calculation is based on a steady-state world such as has *never existed*, except in balance sheets and projections.

[5] For a good overview of climate deregulation under Trump, see the PBS "Newshour" segment for April 21, 2025, entitled "How the Trump Administration is Dismantling Climate Protections." The segment interviewed Bill McKibben, a leading climate activist,

wall is there for us, too. With that realization, that we are part and parcel of this negative spiral, maybe enough of us will learn to turn away from our endless array of amusements to direct sufficient will to resolving the disastrous trends all around us. We may be white, but we, too, are targets of the latest form of white supremacy that styles itself as a moralizing populism. And though we, as political people, will doubtless continue to spend way too much time tracking short-term political wins and losses, we also realize that deep commitments to climate solutions require a whole different level and quality of commitment going forward, if we are to leave the next generations a world fit for living in.

who made one serious error of fact: McKibben said that it was Americans who had first measured climate change, when it was actually Soviet scientists under Stalin.

Further Readings

(compiled by Michael Nylan and Thomas Hahn)

Over time, thousands of publications, big and small, have weighed in on Chinese notions of the environment. No single human being, no matter how motivated, can possibly read them all. Michael Nylan and Thomas Hahn have read a fair number of these publications, however, with some of them insightful and some quite dreadful. The following baker's dozen therefore represents a quirky selection of books, essays, and other types of media that Michael Nylan and Thomas Hahn have found edifying or entertaining, while conducting our research for this volume.

As so many of our notes cite Chinese sources, we have focused "Further Reading" on English-language sources. And as one of our themes is intergenerational equity, we think it only right to begin by acknowledging two pioneering works organized by four impressive scholars that tie the environment to philosophical concerns: *Nature in Asian Traditions of Thought: essays in environmental philosophy* (1989), eds. J. Baird Callicott and Roger T. Ames; and *Confucianism and Ecology: the interrelation of Heaven, Earth, Human* (1998), eds. Mary Evelyn Tucker and John Berthrong. The former is a wide-ranging first stab at the philosophical dimensions of the problem throughout East and South Asia; the latter is more focused on China, Japan, and Korea, with Neville's essay "Orientation, Self, and Ecological Posture" (26,5–73) a particular delight to those intent upon figuring out what ritual actually has meant in the Sinosphere.

Readers need not be daunted by the booklist, because often reading the Introduction, Conclusion, and a chapter or two will furnish sufficient insights on any given topic. Alongside the books reviewed below (in no particular order) are a handful of essays, documentaries, and podcasts that we heartily recommend. NB: with East Asian names, sometimes the family name comes first and sometimes last, according to local conventions of the publishing houses. For the benefit of English-only speakers, the family name ("surname") has been rendered in **bold**, to obviate confusion.

1. For international law as it relates to the environment, there can be no single better reference guide than Edith **Brown Weiss**' *Establishing Norms in a Kaleidoscopic World* (2011), based on a series of lectures that Brown Weiss delivered at The Hague Academy of International Law. The term "kaleidoscopic" points to the fragmented state of the world since the year 2000, where bottom-up attempts by assorted entities (individuals, *ad hoc* coalitions, informal groups, transient networks, among others) are confronted with unprecedented efforts at top-down control—unprecedented because the level of state control that is now possible far surpasses that of *any* earlier era, thanks to technological advancements; also, that so many attempts and efforts, for good and for ill, cross national borders with abandon.

    Because her analysis of simultaneous movements toward greater integration and greater fragmentation is realistic, her proposed "solutions" will likely strike readers as achievable. Her overall recommendation is to reconceptualize public international law so that it is "more inclusive of other actors and additional forms of law, in addition to binding agreements and obligations to report," in light of the emerging norms of human dignity, transparency, anti-corruption, equity (especially intergenerational equity), and accountability to which lip-service is paid, at least, by

EuroAmerican institutions (39) ostensibly dedicated to the avoidance of harm. Within philosophy, Brown Weiss puts herself firmly in the camp of the constructivists, who believe "that through interaction and communication, actors generate shared knowledge and shared understandings that become the background for subsequent interactions and new social norms that help shape how actors see themselves, their world, and their interests." We are teachable, in other words, and "what we do in one place, either individually or cumulatively, can significantly affect both the local and the global resilience and integrity of our planet" (38), so we should cling to the slogan, "think globally, act locally." Meanwhile, we must not ignore the staggering price tag of inaction and climate densialism that Brown Weiss, like David Wallace-Wells (see below), provides.

2. *Not Too Late: changing the climate story from despair to possibility,* co-edited by Rebecca Solnit and Thelma Young Lutunatabua (2023), fits easily into the pocket or purse, and it rocks. Mostly impressively to me, it reminds us that we are all, in effect, indigenous people now, prey to the worst abuses of crony capitalism (or should we call it imperialism), while distinguishing hope from the blind optimism blithely believing that "technology will fix the problem" (see 5). Keeping to the Middle Path, we are "to recognize that what is unlikely is not impossible, just as what is likely is not inevitable" (6). In twenty-eight short essays by twenty-three authors, there is no whitewashing in sight, only callouts of companies that routinely "greenwash." Uncertainty is what we've got, and with uncertainties we will deal, if we decide to try to participate in shaping a better future world. But "An Extremely Incomplete List of Climate Victories" (92–102) helps to offset the near-daily funk we all experience when scanning the news. So do the facts and figures generously supplied in this volume and the

bracing conversation suggesting that, lest we lose our humanity, "Imagination is a Muscle" we need to deploy along with grief, to fend off atrophy (151–57).

3. For a crash course on the intergenerational equity issues analyzed by rival groups of philosophers, nothing surpasses the co-edited *Intergenerational Justice* (2009), and the follow-up *Intergenerational Justice* (2017), edited by Meyer alone. My personal favorites are chapters 2 and 8 ("Libertarian Notions of Intergenerational Justice" and "What Do We Owe to Future People as a Matter of Social Justice?"), in part because I see future-oriented and libertarian views are so hip right now with smart millennials who are unthinking. As for the Libertarian claims, "full self-ownership," the fundamental Lockean claim for each person, ignores two obvious facts about today's world: first, we are all reliant on many other people from the womb into old age, which reliance creates a panoply of obligations, like it or not; and second, there is by now no "unowned" part of the planet to which any fully "choice-capable person" can claim an exclusive or appreciably better right. (No wonder Thiel and Musk would have all of us aim for Mars.) Historically, libertarianism has always been rooted in a strong "choice-protecting" conception, a conception almost always understood to imply that, at any given time, only those who are capable of *then* making choices *then* have rights, in a clear denial of even minimal equity within a given social unit. Once we fully consider the practical limitations placed by Locke and Kant on who is "choice capable" and hence fully "moral," we begin to see how shockingly easy it has been to formulate rationales for so many land-grabs seized from indigenous groups dubbed "not yet moral," including Native Americans, Jews, and Palestinians. Life as a contract, in essence, becomes life adjusted to suit the interests of the current powers-that-be. Not only

do the intertwined concepts of "choice" and "contract" deny the signal importance to human dignity of life-transcending calls; they also deny the possibility of incremental harm over generations. Americans, for their parts, cannot help but recall that the Founding Fathers did not deem their slaves to be equals to themselves, nor their women. By valid contracts, they were instead property whose lives would be determined by their "owners."

4. For sheer readability, nothing beats David Wallace-Wells' *The Unhabitable Earth* (2019), whose author confesses that he had no interest whatsoever in climate questions until he got a commission to look into the issue. Perhaps his newness to the debates was an advantage, for the book is chockfull of startling information, even for those claiming climate awareness. For example, as a historian, Nylan did not know that "the majority of the burning has come since the premier of *Seinfeld*" or that "since the end of the Second World War, the figure is about 85 percent" (4), or that "Fifteen percent of all human experience throughout history. . . belongs to people *alive right now, each walking the earth with carbon footprints*" (8). Sadly, teachers of climate do come to know that current overpopulation exceeds the "carrying capacity" of the planet, resulting in direct heat, desertification, flooding, "unnatural" natural events, plastic panics, polluted oceans, and dried-up aquifers *all at once*, with climate migrants projected to be one billion people soon (7). In sum, "everything we know of as civilization is so fragile that it has been brought to the brink of total instability by just one generation of human activity" (220). The book manages to make it abundantly clear that, contrary to Jerry Brown's "new normal" pronouncement, the climate change we are witnessing is (a) not normal and (b) no longer new.

Cascading events caused by climate change effectively mean that the real estimates of the death toll for climate change is 150 million (25 Holocausts) (28). (Europe alone estimates that 50,000 died in 2023 from climate change.) Given the direness of the situation and the imminence of the onset of mutually-assured destruction, one would think this book would be a real downer, but Wallace-Wells, like other smart writers, keeps emphasizing that it is **we** who are staging climate catastrophes by our inaction, and just as surely, by a multitude of actions **we** can stop climate events (31) from happening at this pace and this scale. This is a question of will, in other words. Quoting two climate writers, Wallace-Wells concludes, "The problem, it turns out, is not [even] an overabundance of humans but a *dearth of humanity. . . . If humanity is the capacity to act meaningfully within our surroundings, then we are not really, or not yet, human.*" Xunzi couldn't have said it more succinctly on the eve of unification in China in 221 BC. We need to think "like a people, one people, whose fate is shared by all," since we can't choose the planet, the only place "any of us will ever call home" (228).

5. James Miller's *China's Green Religion: Daoism and the Quest for a Sustainable Future* (2017) is a tour de force, even if its central premise is dubious, insofar as the worldview and values he ascribes in his writings exclusively to Daoism appear in a broad range of classics and masterworks in early imperial and medieval China. If these and other "facts" and characterizations presented by Miller seem woefully outdated, that does little to diminish his basic insights. Miller also has a way with words, particularly in chapter 8, where he lays out a vision that goes well beyond mere "sustainability" to describe the conditions that both human and non-humans need to flourish. By this vision, humans are not to "save" the world or Nature. Rather

people are to learn how to practice a distinctive role in the cosmos that helps them help all other things to flourish, given that Daoist (or to Nylan, classical) beliefs posit "the capacity of nature to produce growth and change from within itself" (163). That begins a transformation that is profoundly aesthetic and spiritual (even religious?), affecting how people "sense, feel, and cognize their location in space and time"—a "transfiguration" in Miller's terms—that can happen not only within individuals but across communities that come to appreciate their bonds with the living earth and the lively celestial order. Justifiable complaints about Miller's lack of citing the basic secondary sources (e.g., Kuriyama's *Expressiveness of the Body* and Deborah Sommer's work on the *ti* body) do not preclude Miller from mostly arriving at his destination.

6. Many people recommended that I take a good look at Chia-ju Chang's edited volume entitled *Chinese Environmental Humanities: practices of environing at the margins* (2019). I was initially put off by what I saw as a number of outright factual errors, with the most egregious casting Tao Yuanming as a peasant poet. Equally annoying were the editor's contortions positing a suitable "traditional" (i.e., premodern) derivation from the modern neologism for "environment." After giving book a second look, I find most of the fourteen chapters in the book to be engaging, even if surprisingly few of the chapters bridge the divide between "modernity and tradition," despite the editor's ambitious claims to do this. In this collection of presentist essays, one stellar exception is Stephen Roddy's chapter devoted to three cultural conservative scholars whose impulse was to distrust the "smash all" May Fourth modernizers. Other chapters that challenge "tradition" as unitary include Christopher K. Tong's bracing analysis of the two terms "Chinese" and "sustainability," and the first half of

Winnie Yee's account of Hong Kong's self-image as financial center. (The second half of Yee's essay reads like a case study in George Monbiot's *Regenesis: feeding the world without devouring the planet* [2022], as a fine exploration into the real-life promises and perils of multigenerational organic farming communities.)

7. Iza Ding's *Performative States* (2022) challenges many presuppositions that Euro-Americans entertain, most importantly, that there can be no accountability for official acts outside of their familiar democratic "checks and balances." Based on field work done in 2015 in a big town south of the Yangzi River (named "Lakeville"), Ding ably demonstrates that mid-ranking officials in China feel acute pressure to perform from on high and from below, but they may lack the means to implement the policies and, in some cases, the requisite authority to decide which of several competing directives is Party policy. (Meanwhile, thanks to a volley of Supreme Court decisions, American citizens begin to wonder how much accountability they enjoy in our supposedly democratic system.)

Ding's distinction between "substantive governance" ("delivering the fruits of effective rule") vs. "performative governance" ("the state's deployment of visual, verbal, and gestural symbols of good governance for the audience of citizens") proves crucial, in that citizens must discern the difference if they are to begin to hold an administration accountable for its actions and inactions (7). Mainly, Ding ascribes national problems to "lack of capacity" (cf. Michael Mann's "infrastructural power"); however, one wonders if that analysis can be correct. Meanwhile, she gives relatively short shrift to local resistance among Party members and non-Party actors to platitudinous Party directives.

Under Xi Jinping, the government has ostensibly become "service-oriented" (*fuwuxing zhengfu* 服務型政府), but Xi's twin preoccupations—encouraging economic growth and preventing political unrest via "structural optimization" and a sharply controlled state media—have left many disgruntled parties, inside and outside the Party, even as the Chinese Communist Party under Xi seeks to reverse the trend toward greater fragmentation of authority that has characterized the post-Mao era.[1] With the green economy, as with every other sector, corruption is tolerated, and the political incentives dangled before the moneyed classes undermine efforts to put a true price tag on environmental malfeasance. Add to that Xi's recent warm embrace of Putin's war effort in Ukraine, which has led to Xi's building hundreds of new coal plants to burn Putin's output, and the future now looks grim for environmental improvements within the People's Republic of China, although China is investing meanwhile in green energy. (China accounted for 95 percent of the world's new coal power construction in 2023, with such construction up fourfold since 2019, according to the Global Energy Monitor. The remaining 5 percent is distributed among twenty-one countries, of which eleven have one project and are on the brink of achieving the "no new coal" milestone.)

8. Anyone interested in the environment should read Kim Stanley Robinson's *The Ministry for the Future* (Orbit/ Hachette, 2020), for the roadmaps (plural) it deftly marshals and the questions about tactics that it insistently raises. A UN-funded ministry (underfunded, quite predictably) wrestles with forms of eco-terrorism (salutary and not), a host of material and psychological uncertainties, and the intransigence of the world's Central Banks, after twenty million people die during a sustained period of 38 degrees Celsius in Lucknow, India.

---

[1] In 2022, around 19.23 million people were working for state and local governments in the United States. In the PRC, in July of 2024, 99 million Party members (some 7 percent of the population) work for the government.

How long will it take until we know that "No one is safe until we all are secure"? Nylan found the opening nearly unbearable to read, but long before page fifty she was hooked, for the novel considers a slurry of strategies to which various actors beginning with nation-states, the rich, and the righteous may resort in the very near future, with the specter of one hundred million people (or is it a billion?) as climate migrants looming.

Unsurprisingly, perhaps, none of the technological fixes work because they take too long to test and scale up, although clusters of geoengineering attempts manage to ameliorate the worst of the mess. By contrast, the application of the financial carrots and sticks transform populations quickly, even if the old adage says, "Easier to imagine the end of the world than the end of capitalism." What, in the end, will produce a new structure of feeling adequate to meet the challenges of a new material situation, given the co-dependency of nation-states and the chief market players, emboldened by the laws crafted at the behest of the wealthiest? How to crank the Great Turn? Is euthanasia not necessary for the rentier class, as John Maynard Keynes suggested already in the 1930s?

Robinson's analysis of the United States, China, France, and Germany is astute, if he imagines (wrongly) that the Hindu nationalists will be ejected from India speedily, and he buys the Chinese arguments that they are trying, trying, trying to clean up the world. Throughout, the theme is "too little, too late," with one clear message ("The invisible hand never picks up the check," 411), and several lyrical scenes bathed in Alpenglow. As a historian, Nylan was trained to "follow the money"; here readers have to follow the feelings, too. Besides, it's hard not to love a novel that invokes the gentle *Local Hero* film (1983) to illustrate our unholy mess, or one whose survey of the dysfunctional and craven international "order" is this precise, even if its portraits of India and Hong Kong are ridiculously rosy.

9. *All We Can Save: truth, courage, and solutions for the climate crisis* is an anthology of poems, essays, reminiscences, and letters "midwived" by feminist writers and edited by Ayana Elizabeth Johnson and Katherine K. Wilkinson; the book has a website offering further resources for teaching, thinking, and organizing (www.allwecansave.earth/circles). The editors and authors believe that "the climate movement is only as strong as the relational web between us, which needs to be nurtured." Part of that nurturing means bringing to light aspects of history that have been ignored, for example, the pathbreaking work of Eunice Newton Foote who, in 1856—three years before John Tyndall (widely credited as the "founder of climate science")—theorized that changes in carbon dioxide in the atmosphere could affect the earth's temperature. And part means showcasing what the editors call the "feminist climate renaissance," through a chorus of sixty female voices rooted in compassion, creativity, and collaboration who welcome all to the fight and the companionate feast. The emphasis on reframing conversations and reshaping minds until we manage to lift each other up will inspire many, regardless of gender or sexual identities, to summon the courage to deny fashion and money their supreme hold on our psyches. At that point, together, we can finally roll up our sleeves and start to chart an unmapped future with the potential for greater equality around the globe. This book pairs well with David Brooks (2025) on the need for a civic uprising.
10. For those with a practical bent, the *Guide to Chinese Climate Policy* (2022) published by the Oxford Institute for Energy Studies will doubtless come in handy, especially, as the preface reasonably argues, "There is no solution to climate change without China." Chock full of charts, tables, graphs, maps, and statistics, the guide is divided into three main parts: 1. Background, a part that includes such chapters as "Chinese

Emissions of Heat-Trapping Gases" (it doesn't look pretty) and "Impacts of Climate Change in China" (not pretty either); 2. Domestic Policies, which addresses a huge range of subjects, including hydropower, wind, and solar technologies; nuclear power; emissions trading (nominally launched in 2017, but officially implemented four years later, in 2021); rapid urbanization; green finance; food systems; forestry, clean energy research and development, and so on; and 3. Foreign Policies, that is, CCP policies with a global impact (or "step shift," as the authors call it), such as the Belt and Road initiatives.

Together these three parts make a densely woven tapestry of policies aimed at the domestic energy resource markets, with some of greater consequence and some of lesser. Their cumulative effect surely has made a difference, in China and beyond, since 1993, when China became a signatory to the United Nations Framework Convention on Climate Change (UNFCCC). For thirty years now, the PRC has sought allies around the globe in promoting green technologies, although, paradoxically, it claimed for over a decade after signing the UNFCCC agreements to be exempt from emissions control mandates. The fact that China is engaged in (and indeed prioritizes) developing "industries for the future" is already highly consequential, given the hazards which lie ahead. This volume is serious in its methodology and in its stock-taking dimensions.

11. Rivoli's *The Travels of a T-shirt in the Global Economy* (second edition, 2008) is enjoyable to read and highly informative, even if, as an economist, she was oddly blind to quite a few economic trends, intent as she is upon telling a "happy story": that worker and consumer, as well as China and the United States, each depend on the other for their well-being. Some of the destruction wrought is occluded by the language of choice:

female factory workers find life in the city, no matter how restrictive, less onerous than life in the countryside, so they walk with their feet. Scant mention is made of their 80- to 100-hour work-weeks, of the vulnerability of the female workers (many underage) not only to their bosses but also to market forces. But astute readers will not miss the big picture, which includes a "race to the bottom," with aging populations in both China and the United States complicating the narrative. What clearly didn't happen, to Rivoli's surprise: rising prosperity has not brought greater personal freedom or a larger civil space to the factories in south China. But why would we think it would? That's Voodoo economics by another name.

12. *Remains of the Everyday: a century of recycling in Beijing*, by Joshua Goldstein (2021), reminds us that nothing is "waste" unless the society deems it so, and in the early twentieth-century, nearly everything (including night soil) in China was repurposed and so of value. As a historian, Nylan loved the descriptions of old Beijing's methods of waste disposal. Many moderns will want to skip to chapters 6–8 and the addendum entitled "Wither Beijing's Recyclers" (159–263). Since January 2018, Beijing has shut its ports to the garbage of the rest of the world for recycling, with the goal to refuse all foreign waste (recyclable or not) by the end of 2020. Meanwhile, the state-licensed recycling infrastructure has moved at a snail's pace, even in the capital, for good reasons, as well as bad.

As Goldstein explains (and Iza Ding disputes, see above), the CCP deftly manufactures public opinion and then claims to bow to it, finding the right labels (e.g., "foreign garbage") to elicit widespread support for what it wants to do. As a case study, the state promotion of Wang Jiuliang's *Plastic China* (*Suliao wangguo* 塑料王国) perfectly exemplifies those practices, as the state made the film appear to be a "spontaneous" public sensation before it censored it, in a typical example of warring propaganda departments. After all, "Ecological Civilization" must find a way to align environmental protection with corporate interests and economic development, which is no small feat. The result: many of the informal recyclers are now officially "out of a job," but nonetheless come out of the woodwork frequently enough to save the day when the normal metropolitan waste-removal routines falter. Only time will supply us with the end of this intriguing tale.

13. Julia Thomas's edited volume, *Altered Earth: getting the Anthropocene right* (2022), is a remarkable achievement in a number of ways, expressing a certain optimism that humanity has the sway and wherewithal to extract itself from the "singular situation" we now find ourselves in, namely, a man-made new geosphere that may become ungovernable and create massive harm to our species within a generation or two. To reverse what otherwise might become a hopeless state of affairs ("the bleak enormity of our collective destructiveness") and to get things back on track (or "right" in moving toward what is accurate, balanced, and just) (1, 5), distinguished historians of science, researchers of climatology, writers, and ecologists have joined together to "open vistas on our common personal dilemma" (4), consciously illuminating the "scratchy textured way in which this new knowledge is being cobbled together" from multiple academic disciplines (5) too often working in academic silos. As the essay contributors are united in their intention to help people develop better habits of decision-making, which they see culminating in an exploration of "mutualistic cities, greater equity, and new political forms" (15, 232), their disparate voices are bound to appeal to a broad spectrum of readers.

Two works by Annie Proulx are marvelous to read anytime, even in bed: *Fen, Bog, and Swamp* and Proulx's novel, *That Old Age in the*

Hole (New York: Scribner, 2002), which follows a hog farm worker (Bob Dollar) in his life in the hard-scrabble Texas panhandle.

Five short pieces highlight issues within and beyond the Chinese tradition, serving as excellent teaching tools:

1. Paul D'Ambrosio, "Rethinking Environmental Issues in a Daoist Context," explains that, strictly speaking, Dao (not to mention Daoism) is at odds with modern environmentalism, for Dao includes not only what EuroAmericans call "Nature," but human beings as well. D'Ambrosio goes on to suggest, counter-intuitively, "it is precisely because the Daoists have no conception of "nature" that they have so much to offer (contemporary) environmentalism." Daoism, D'Ambrosio says, offers a new perspective in its focus on "things" of all types and on efficacious action, and its distrust of "mechanical thinking" and impractical and unnecessary technological fixes.
2. **Ni** Peimin, "Seek and You Will Find It; Let Go and You Will Lose It" (2014), like Nuyen (below), begins with a conundrum: why is it that the Universal Declaration of Human Rights has brought about so few real reforms in institutional arrangements? Ni first considers the question of how a Confucian regards outrageous treatment inflicted on him: he first questions whether his own conduct has been at fault, worries that he, perhaps, has not done his very best, and only when there has been no improvement does the Confucian begin to understand his tormentor as "less-than-human," but still worthy of just treatment by the tormented, who chooses not to treat others in unjust ways. Ni reminds us that the Kongzi of the *Analects* wishes his disciples to learn their limits, and he cautions them against the notion that they should be engaged is disparaging others, rather than seeking to protect others from others' depredations.

3. Ahn Tuan **Nuyen**, "Confucian Role-Based Ethics and Strong Environmental Ethics" (2011) divides philosophical approaches to Confucian teachings into three types: (1) virtue-based; (2) role-based; and (3) obligations-based, with which he lumps (a) deontology and (b) consequentialism/ utilitarianism, neglecting to consider political realism of the sort promoted by Raymond Geuss in his works. Arguing that resort to universal human rights talk has not gotten us very far, it being subsumed into the neoliberals' "To Get Rich is Glorious," Nuyen argues that "For a Confucian, to be in a social relation is to incur obligations within a network of social relations, but also to expect benefit from the obligations incurred by others in the social relation with you." Moreover, "The only 'universal' and 'fundamental' obligation in Ru thinking is 'commit oneself to fulfilling the [multiple] roles that constitute' the person to the best of one's ability" (558), in a constructive and particularized fashion, so that Confucius prefigures Charles Taylor. Why, then, do so many self-identified "Confucians" (not to mention others) refuse to see that inflicting harm on the environment is inflicting harm on themselves?
4. Lynn White, Jr., "The Historical Roots of Our Ecological Crisis," is still worth reading, insofar as he, as a historian of science, makes a strong argument that our environmental crisis cannot be reduced to our own technological ability to degrade the environment, but rather is essentially the product of our Western worldview. Both the Christian religion and the Scientific Revolution offered justifications for human hegemony over plants and animals. Religion says that this arrangement is God's design. Natural selection explains that human triumph is "the survival of the fittest"—a term coined by Herbert Spencer and later adopted by Charles Darwin as an alternative to "natural selection" (49).
5. Ilaria Maria Sala's "Soil is Home to a Vibrant World" ably reframes our thoughts about soil, so that we see in it a part of

the interconnected, self-regulating system that is Earth. "We owe many of Earth's defining features—its breathable atmosphere, blue sky, mineral diversity, ocean chemistry and wildfires—to life. Over time, Earth and life, much like soil and the organisms that maintain it, formed a single evolving system that has endured for billions of years. The living earth beneath our feet mirrors our larger living planet." The challenge before us, then, is not simply to amend Earth's soils, but to revitalize them before they're lost forever. Two core principles can guide this shift: minimizing soil disturbance and emphasizing biodiversity. Once again, we see science just catching up with ancient insights.

Of course, Nylan likes D'Ambrosio's conclusions, because they concur with hers in her "Humans as Animals" essay; and Nuyen's comments on networks fit with her own analysis in a chapter in a forthcoming (early 2026?) *Cambridge History of China*, devoted to "Confucianism" (a misnomer that she prefers to call "classical learning"). Both Nylan and Hahn are of the school that believes ideology shifts, sometimes with surprising rapidity, when other factors (economic, social, scientific, diplomatic) change, but ideology unquestionably matters in the short-term, as we see in voting blocs in recent elections. Put another way, moral arguments are not to be dismissed; it's just that our morality so often reflects our non-moral situations. (Of course, we encounter the moral argument again in Parfit's famous Non-Identity argument, i.e., the unknown quantity and quality of future, distant generations.) And to show just how quirky our choices are, we co-authors are both ardent filmgoers, but neither of us particularly likes reading *about* film. But for those who want a book about Chinese films devoted to environmental issues, see *Chinese Eco-cinema*, edited by Sheldon H. Lu and Jiayan Mi (2009), where some individual essays are admittedly quite wonderful.[2]

---

[2] We co-authors prefer the essays on Hong Kong, but that may just reflect our greater familiarity with Hong Kong.

Podcasts and TV shows:

1. "The Serengeti Rules" (PBS documentary, https://ny.pbslearningmedia.org/resource/nat38-discovery-of-keystone-species-vid/the-serengeti-rules-media-gallery/keystone animals), on the vital role that keystone species, animal and vegetable, play in land restoration projects, which necessitates the reintroduction of human predators into the environment in many populated areas. Last accessed Oct. 8, 2024.

2. "Under the Dome": the self-financed documentary about pollution in China made in 2015 by the former CCTV (China Central Television) journalist Chai Jing 柴静 (b. 197b), which purportedly garnered over 150 million viewings before its removal by the Party on the third day. The documentary is still banned in China.

3. Jia Zhangke, "Still Life" (in Chinese, Sanxia haoren 三峡好人) asks us to consider the internal displacement caused by the building of the massive Three Gorges Dam (Li Peng's signature project): whole towns and villages were demolished or submerged under water to make way for the new river patterns created by the geoengineers, producing monumental displacement of individual people. Unlike most of Jia's oeuvre, *Still Life* was approved by the Chinese Film Bureau and the State Administration of Radio, Film, and Television, and co-produced by the state-operated Shanghai Film Studio. Jia suggested that this film received state support because "the impact of the Three Gorges project is phenomenal. It's not something the government can cover up."[3] Hope he's right.

---

[3] *The New York Times*, "Blurring Reality's Edge in Fluid China," *The New York Times*, Jan. 20, 2008 (byline Dennis Lim).

4. "Burning" (2021): a documentary by Oscar-winning producer Eva Orner shows the political, economic, social, and cultural background to the man-made fires that rampaged through Australia in 2019–2020, with a clarity that "The Guardian" rightly says, "boils your blood and rattles your bones," laying to rest the polite fiction that these fires were nothing special, since "fires in Australia are a constant" and "every year there are bushfires." The key villains are identified—with Rupert Murdoch's News Corp spewing forth massive disinformation campaigns, and the "ideologically flexible" [i.e., unprincipled] politician Scott Morrison in the lead—but the movie contains gentler narratives as well, with trees as "arcs of time," and climate activists as vital contributors to changing climate change.
5. Highly recommended is a radio interview on Radio Canada/Canadian Broadcasting Company: https://www.cbc.ca/radio/quirks/indigenous-scientist-earth-medicine-1.7178030, where an indigenous ecologist, Jennifer Grentz, talks about why we need to save the planet. Amanda Buckiewicz interviewed for CBC News. The transcript of the interview was posted: Apr 19, 2024 12.08 pm PDT.
6. The best analysis of the disastrous case reviewing Chevron (the US Supreme Court's decision in Loper-Bright) is https://www.youtube.com/watch?v=j3w8-d_fnqE, John Oliver's analysis of the monumental Chevron decision, which is strongly anti-expert/technocrat, when it comes to environmental equity.
7. For those with German language skills or translations tools at hand, there is probably nothing better to learn from than the annual Extreme Weather Congress, organized for the past fourteen years by the German Weather Service and other state agencies. This series, supplemented in 2024 for the first time by a climate management conference, is the broadest and most informative forum on climate change we know

of. Local, national and international experts from all walks of life—finance, community governance, climate modeling, oceanography, atmospheric sciences, soil and forestry experts, inland water transportation managers, satellite system operators, and the arts—come together for three days to present the latest findings, trends, tools, and policies in their respective fields. Bridging scientific knowledge, state planning, and public curiosity, this congress is a highly successful vehicle for communication. Among the many specialists who have participated in this forum over the years, we urge readers to look out for these names, whose speeches are models in every way: Mojib Latif, Hermann Held, and Tobias Fuchs. All sessions for the past four years can be found on Youtube.

And finally, here's a word for you readers, if you don't know it already: Etuaptmumk. It's a Mi'kmaq word, and its etymology and English translation were featured in a Canadian Broadcast program. The translation was given as, "The gift of multiple perspectives." May we all come to enjoy such immense blessings.[4] And for an uplift, check out the Green Ship sent by Fortescue to New York harbor in mid-October of 2025.

---

[4] See https://www.kuow.org/stories/two-eyed-seeing-as-a-way-to-decolonize-western-science.

A Chronology Replete with Acronyms

UNITED NATIONS,[1] A Multilateral Forum

1919–20 Founding of the **Permanent Court of International Justice** (PCIJ), in the wake of World War I, under the League of Nations, Article 14. The onset of World War II effectively ended this body, which met last in December, 1939.

1945–1947 England and the United States convened a committee of well-respected jurists to oversee the establishment of a comparable body in 1943, near the end of World War II. At Dumbarton Oaks, an alliance of China, the Soviet Union, the United Kingdom, and the United States, agreed upon the necessity to have a court of international law. April-June 1945, at the San Francisco Conference, fifty nations agreed to the establishment of a new court under UN Charter. The **International Court of Justice** took on its first case in 1947, involving Corfu, two years after the PCIJ archives were turned over. The composition of the court is to follow Article 3, which states that no two judges may be nationals of the same country. According to Article 9, the membership of the court is supposed to represent the "main forms of civilization and of the principal legal systems of the world." This has been interpreted to include common law, civil law, socialist law, and Islamic law, while the precise meaning of "main forms of civilization" continues to be hotly contested.

1948 **Universal Declaration on Human Rights** envisions individuals having such fundamental rights as the rights to nationality.

1949 First court case decided by the **International Court of Justice,** Corfu Channel (U.K. v. Albania).

1950 First **United States National Technical Conference on Air Pollution** convened by President Truman (May 3–5). Resulted in first drafts of the Clean Air Act.

1961 Russian geophysicist Mikhael I. Budyko and the climatologist Yevgraf Fedorov organized the "**All-Union Conference on the Problem of Climate Modification by Man**" in Leningrad, to address the emerging problem of climate change—the first such conference in the world.

---

[1] Four stages of work at the United Nations on climate change are listed in chapter 1.

1966 **International Human Rights Covenants**. These rights explicitly allow for the right to self-determination (including determination of political status); the right to social and economic development; and the right for nation-states to utilize their own natural resources as they choose.

1972/1973 **Stockholm Declaration** formally, Principle 21 of the United Nations "Stockholm Declaration"; UN Doc. A/CONF.48/14 (1972); revised UN Doc.A/CONF.48/14/Corr. 1 (1973). Cf. the 1972 Declaration on the Human Environment listing twenty-six Principles; Action Plan with 109 recommendations. (As the Conference produced the Declaration and Action Plan, these are often conflated.) Notably, the Stockholm Declaration did not seek to formulate legally binding provisions, only voluntary guidelines. Principle 21 reaffirms the rights of sovereign states "to exploit their own resources pursuant to their own environmental policies," but also "the responsibility to ensure that activities within their jurisdiction . . . do not cause damage to the environment of other states . . . beyond their national jurisdiction." Because the Stockholm Declarations links a state's rights to its obligations, it is widely considered an "environment-supporting" declaration.

1974 Resolution 1803 (VII), which proclaims "the right of peoples and nations to permanent sovereignty over their natural wealth and resources," whose violation is "contrary to the spirit and principles of the Charter of the United Nations and hinders the development of international cooperation and the maintenance of peace." This seems, at this point, "to reflect the state of customary law existing in this field,"[2] as opposed to Resolution 3281.

December 1974 **Resolution 3281** (XXIX), Chart of Economic Rights and Duties of States, proclaimed by the UN General Assembly, declares that "every sovereign state has permanent sovereignty over its wealth, natural resources, and economic activities," undercutting Resolution 1803, even as it called on all states, in the case of shared natural resources, to use and exploit those resources in a manner that avoids harming the legitimate interests of others. A proposal to amend Resolution 3281, by inserting a "good faith" clause into Article II, failed to pass the General Assembly.[3] (This resolution was adopted without the assent of the most prominent Western countries, and without general consensus among the

---

[2] Perrez 1996, 1196-97. Resolution 1803 is seen as a "carefully worked out compromise" (ibid.,), supported by all the major powers, as well as by the formerly colonized sovereign states.

[3] Much of the debate in this period centered over "nationalization" of the states' assets, but that is not the case now.

states with respect to its most important provisions, especially provisions that bore upon questions of nationalization of a state's assets.)

1982/1994 United Nations **Convention on the Law of the Sea** (UNCLOS) provides a legal framework for the adjudication of disputes on all maritime matters. The agreement supposedly came into force in 1994, when Guyana became the 60th nation-state to ratify the convention.

1987 United Nations "Report of the World Commission on Environment and Development: Our Common Future" (aka the **Brundtland Report**): defines "sustainability" in the broader sense, as involving the management of human impact on the environment, to meet humans' present and future needs, via a negotiated balance of environmental preservation and capitalist development agendas: "Sustainable development is not a fixed state of harmony, but rather a process of change in which the exploitation of resources, the direction of investments, the orientation of technological development, and institutional change are made consistent with future as well as present needs."

1992 **Rio de Janeiro Conference on Environmental and Development** (UNCED), which sought to ways to coordinate responses to international environmental problems. The Rio Declaration basically reaffirmed the Stockholm Declaration, but weakened it, declaring that states have "the sovereign right to exploit their own resources pursuant to their environmental *and developmental* policies," an added caveat that has been subject to dispute. The so-called Rio Paradox is this: the challenge to "fully and indissolubly integrate environment and development" is identified, but no guidelines are given. Many argue that the "right to a wholesome environment" embodied in the Stockholm Declaration was jettisoned in favor of "a right to development,"[4] with the support of developing countries, to resolve the question of compensation for nationalization of resources, and to undermine (a) freedom of treaty assumptions; and (b) the principle of *pacta sunt servanda* ("contracts/treatises/acts are to be kept"). Nonetheless, the Rio "Convention on Biodiversity" recognized it as a "common concern" of humankind, and the Convention was signed eventually by 196 states.

1992–1994 **United Nations Framework Convention on Climate Change** (UNFCCC), signed May 9, 1992; went into force March 21, 1994.

1998 Establishment of the **International Criminal Court**, adopted July 17, under the Rome Statutes. Leading up to that, the United States was one

---

[4] Guruswamy 1995.

of the driving forces behind the use of an International Criminal Tribunal to prosecute leaders of the former Yugoslavia and later of Rwanda. Yet, in Rome, the United States joined six other states in voting against the ICC treaty, lest American soldiers or their leaders be prosecuted by the ICC. Key objections included the ability of the ICC to bypass the Security Council, which would lessen the role of the United States in that system, wherein the United States is one of five permanent members whose veto power can stop Security Council motions. Meanwhile, the American Bar Association told the US Congress that "the Treaty of Rome contains the most comprehensive list of due process protections which has so far been promulgated."

1997–2005 **Kyoto Protocol** to the United Nations Framework Convention on Climate Change, issued December 10, 1997; went into force February 16, 2005; first commitment period 2008–2012.[5]

2001 International Law Commission, Draft Articles on the Responsibility of States for Internationally Wrongful Acts (DASR). China enters the World Trade Organization WTO.

July, 2002 The **International Criminal Court** (ICC) is established with the intention to serve as the "court of last resort." The ICC complements existing national judicial systems and may exercise its jurisdiction only when national courts are unwilling or unable to prosecute criminals. It lacks universal territorial jurisdiction and may only investigate and prosecute crimes committed within member states, crimes committed by nationals of member states, or crimes in situations referred to the Court by the United Nations Security Council. Practically speaking, those provisions prevent US citizens from being charged by the court.

2007 **Intergovernmental Panel on Climate Change** (IPCC) established.

2008 **UN Human Rights Council (UNHRC) adopts the first resolution explicitly tying human rights to climate change.** Resolution 7/23, UN Doc. A/HRC/7/78 (March 28).

2011/2012 United Nations **"Guiding Principles on Business and Human Rights"** (UNGP), Nov. 4, 2011; "Corporate Responsibility to Respect Human Rights" (Dec. 2, 2012 For information see the White Paper

---

[5] The United States of America failed to ratify the Protocol; multiple powers (e.g., Canada, Japan, Russia) withdrew from it; other polluting powers (e.g., China and India) refused to commit themselves to any emission reduction obligations.

CS351315_-_Human_Rights_Whiteaper_Final (available for download in pdf form).

2012, June UN **Conference on Sustainable Development** (often called **Rio + 20**) issues a report called "The Future We Want" that appreciably weakened the 1992 Rio Declaration, saying that states have a right to develop their own resources:"to exploit their own resources pursuant to their environmental and development policies, and the responsibility to ensure that activities within their jurisdiction or control do not cause damage to the environment of... areas beyond the limits of national jurisdiction." See UN Framework Convention on Climate Change (UNFCCC).

2021 United Nations paper, "Our Common Agenda," in September.

2023 A **High Seas Treaty** was added to the 1982 Convention as a legally binding instrument to protect ocean life in international waters. Greenpeace called this "the biggest conservation victory ever."

2015–2030 United Nations Development Agenda.

2020–2030 United Nations Decade of Action. Mobilizing government and non-government actors to engage in realizing seventeen sustainable development goals. Goal No. 10 refers to reducing inequalities across a variety of socioeconomic sectors.

2022, July 5: President Biden's Executive Order 14008 created a government-wide "Justice40" Initiative with the goal of delivering to underserved and disadvantaged communities 40 percent of the overall benefits of federal investments in climate and clean energy, including relevant investment in the Bipartisan Infrastructure Law (passed, with bipartisan support, and signed on Nov. 15, 2021), with an emphasis on making investments in clean energy, transportation, and infrastructure upgrades to make them more resilient to extreme weather events.

2024 The World Meteorological Organization (WMO) confirms that 2024 is the warmest year on record.

2024, May, The International Tribunal for the Law of the Sea affirmed that greenhouse gas emissions pollute the marine environment, and ruled that both public actors and private companies can now be sued.

2025, January 20 Trump is elected and on Day 1 formally withdraws from the Paris Accords (for the second time). Firings at the EPA, the General Accounting Office overseeing the budget, and a host of other government agencies swiftly follow after USAID, as Elon Musk cheerfully takes a chainsaw, by his own account, to the federal government. Sales of electric cars plunge.

2025, July 4 The Inter-American Court of Human Rights declared that the climate crisis is a human rights emergency that triggers human rights obligations for nations and businesses, most especially in the fossil fuel industry.

2025, July 23 The International Court of Justice ruled that states and corporations may be held liable for policies that undermine climate science.

Bibliography

Primary Sources in Classical Chinese

Analects/Lun yu 論語. References follow the standard paragraphing found in Ruan Yuan's *Shisan jing zhushu* (Preface 1815), accessed through https://hanchi.ihp.sinica.edu.tw/ihp/hanji.htm.

Art of War: References follow *The Norton Critical Edition of the Art of War*, ascribed to Sun Tzu. Translated by the Berkeley Translation Team, led by Michael Nylan. New York: W.W. Norton & Company, 2022.

Bohu tong 白虎通 (White Tiger Discussions). Tradit. ascribed to Ban Gu 班固. References follow *Bohu tong zhuzi suoyin* 白虎通逐字索引, ICS Concordance Series/ CHANT. Hong Kong: Shangwu yinshuguan, 1995 (Classical works no. 21).

Changes classic 易經. Anonymous. References follow *Zhouyi zhuzi suoyin* 周易逐字索引, ICS Concordance Series/ CHANT. Hong Kong: Shangwu yinshuguan, 1995 (Classical works no. 8).

Cui Shi 崔寔. *Zhenglun* 政論. In *Hou Hanshu* 52.1725-33; cf. *Tongdian* 通典, "Shihuo, shang 食貨, 上: Tianzhi, shang" 田制 section, accessible online in https://ctext.org/tongdian/zhs

Dunhuang Xuanquan: *Dunhuang Xuanquan Han jian shicui*, edited by Zhang Defang 張德芳 and Hu Pingsheng 胡平生. Shanghai: Shanghai guji chubanshe, 2001.

Fan Shengzhi shu 氾勝之書. In *Liang Han nongshu xuandu: Fan Shengzhi shu he Simin yueling* 兩漢農書選讀: 氾勝之書和四民. Beijing: Nongye chubanshe, 1979.

Gongyang 公羊. Anonymous. References follow *Gongyang zhuan zhuzi suoyin* 公羊傳逐字索引, ICS Concordance Series/ CHANT. Hong Kong: Shangwu yinshuguan, 1995, Vol. 31.

Guo Xiang 郭象 (d. ca. 312). *Zhuangzi zhu* 莊子注. [See Richard John Lynn's translation.]

Guoyu 國語. References follow the *Guoyu zhuzi suoyin* 國語逐字索引, ICS Concordance Series/ CHANT. Hong Kong: Shangwu yinshuguan, 1999. See also Wei Zhao.

Hanshu 漢書. Compiled by Ban Gu 班固 (32–92), Ban Zhao 班 (45 – ca. 116), et al. References follow the punctuated edition, annot. by Yan Shigu 顏師古. Beijing: Zhonghua shuju, 1962.

Liji 禮記 (*Rites Record*) *Liji* 禮記. References follow *Liji zhuzi suoyin* 禮記逐字索引, ICS Concordance Series/ CHANT. Hong Kong: Shangwu yinshuguan, 1992.

Lunheng 論衡. Compiled by Wang Chong 王充 (27-97?). References follow Huang Hui 黃暉, compiler, *Lunheng jiaoshi* 論衡校釋, 4 vols. Beijing Zhonghua shuju, 1990 rpt. of 1938 edition.

Lüshi chunqiu 呂氏春秋. Attributed to Lü Buwei 呂不韋. In *Lüshi chunqiu jiaoshi* 呂氏春秋校釋. Edited by Chen Qiyou 陳奇猷. Shanghai: Xuelin chubanshe, 1984. The standard paragraphing follows *Lüshi chunqiu* 呂氏春秋逐字索引, ICS Concordance Series/ CHANT. Hong Kong: Shangwu yinshuguan, 1994.

Mencius/Mengzi 孟子. References are to the standard paragraphing found in Ruan Yuan.

Qianfu lun 潛夫論. sBy Wang Fu 王符. References follow *Qianfu lun zhuzi suoyin* 潛夫論逐字索引, ICS Concordance Series/ CHANT. Hong Kong: Shangwu yinshuguan, 1995. Hu

Qin jiandu heji (ni) 秦簡牘合集(貳), edited by Chen Wei 陳偉. Wuhan: Wuhan daxue jianbo yanjiu zhongxin, 2014.

Quan Hou Hanwen 全後漢文. In *Quan Shanggu Sandai Qin Han Sanguo Liuchao wen*. 全上古三代秦漢三國六朝文, compiled by Yan Kejun 嚴可均. Taipei: World Books, 1961.

Ruan Yuan 阮元. *Shisan jing zhushu, fu jiaokanji* 十三經注疏附校勘記 (preface 1815). Beijing: Zhonghua shuju, 1980; accessible online through Scripta Sinica (https://hanchi.ihp.sinica.edu.tw/ ihp/hanji.html).

Rites Record; see *Liji*.

Shangshu/Documents classic: References follow the translation of the Han-era *Documents*, generated and translated by Michael Nylan and He Ruyue. Seattle: University of Washington Press, 2026.

Shangshu dazhuan 尚書大傳 (*Great Commentary to the Documents*). Tradit. Fu Sheng (fl. 221-180 BC) and Zheng Xuan (127-200). References follow

Shangshu dazhuan zhuzi suoyin 尚書大傳逐字索引, ICS Concordance Series/ CHANT. Hong Kong: Shangwu yinshuguan, 1995 (*Jing* 經 9).

Shiji 史記. Compiled by Sima Qian 司馬遷, et al. References follow the punctuated edition. Beijing: Zhonghua shuju, 1972.

Shuoyuan 說苑: Compiled by Liu Xiang 劉向 (d. 7 BC). References follow Eric Henry, *Garden of Eloquence/Shuoyuan*. Seattle: University of Washington Press, 2021.

Wei Zhao 韋昭: In *Guoyu Wei Zhao zhu* 國語韋昭註. Taipei: Wenyi yinshuguan, 1944.

Xunzi 荀子. References follow the standard paragraphing found in *Xunzi yinde* 荀子引得. Sinological Index Series Supplement no. 22. Beijing: Harvard-Yenching Institute, 1950. For a translation, see also Hutton.

Yinqueshan Han mu jujian 銀雀山汉墓竹简. Edited by the Yinqueshan Han Tomb Bamboo Slips Compilation Team 銀雀山汉墓竹简整理小组. Beijing: Wenwu chubanshe, 1975.

Yinwan: *Yinwan Hanmu jiandu* 尹灣漢墓簡牘. Compiled by the Liangyungang City Museum. Beijing: Zhongshu shuju, 1997.

Yuelu 嶽麓: *Yuelu shuyuan cang Qin jian*, 1–3 vols. 嶽麓書院藏秦簡. 壹一叁. Compiled by Chen Songchang 陳松長. Shanghai: Shanghai cishu chubanshe, 2018.

Zhuangzi 莊子: References follow *Zhuang jishi* 莊子集釋, annot. Guo Qingfan 郭慶藩. Taipei: He-Luo tushu chuban shushe 1974 rpt. of Qing compilation.

Modern Secondary Sources

A More Equal Wales. 2015. https://www.futuregenerations.wales/a-more-equal-wales/.

AARP. 1992. *Justice Across Generations. What Does it Mean?* Edited by Lee Cohen. Washington: American Association of Retired Persons.

Aklin, Michaël and Matto Mildenberger. 2020. "Prisoners of the Wrong Dilemma: Why Distributive Conflict, Not Collective Action, Characterizes the Politics of Climate Change." *Global Environmental Politics* 20 (4): 4–27.

Alberti, Caroline. 2024. "The Cost of Inaction." *Climate Policy Initiative*, January 4. https://www.climatepolicy initiative.org/the-cost-of-inaction/ (Accessed for the second time, April 19, 2025).

Amann, Diane Marie. 2002. "The United States of America and the International Criminal Court." *American Journal of Comparative Law* 50: 381–404.

Anderson, Greg. 2018. *The Realness of Things Past: Ancient Greece and Ontological History.* Oxford: Oxford University Press.

Anderson, Jon Lee. 2025. "Letter from Brazil." *The New Yorker*, April 7. https://www.newyorker.com/magazine/2025/04/14/the-brazilian-judge-taking-on-the-digital-far-right.

Anti-SLAPP: Reporters Committee for Freedom of the Press. https://www.rcfp.org/anti-slapp-legal--guide/#:~:text=As%20of%20July%202024%2C%2034,%2C%20New%20Jersey%2C%20New%20Mexico%2C.

Applebaum, Anne. 2024. *Autocracy, Inc.: The Dictators Who Want to Run the World.* New York: Doubleday.

Arzate-Mejía, R. G., and I. M. Mansuy. 2022. "Epigenetic Inheritance: Impact for Biology and Society, Recent Progress, Current Questions and Future Challenges." *Environmental Epigenetics* 8, no. 1. November 5. https://doi.org/10.1093/eep/dvac021.

Auerbach, Bruce Edward. 1991. *Intergenerational Justice: A Conceptual History and Analysis.* University of Minnesota, Ph.D. dissertation.

Baba Rieko 馬場理惠子. 2007. "Toki no hôrei: ZenKan tsukirei kô" 時の法令: 前漢月令考, *Shisô* 史窓 064: 1–12.

Badmington, Neil. 2022. "Review of Graham Robb and Peter Watson." *TLS (Times Literary Supplement)*, 6217, May 27.

Bajpai, Kanti, and Evan A. Laksmana. 2023. "Asian Conceptions of International Order: What Asia Wants." *International Affairs* 99, no. 4: 1372–81.

Bandursky, David. 2023. "What does Xi Jinping Mean by 'Forever'?" *China Media Project*, University of California, Berkeley, August 30.

Beck, Hans, and Griet Vankeerberghen, eds. 2021. *Rulers and Ruled in Ancient Greece, Rome, and China.* Cambridge: Cambridge University Press.

Begley, Sharon. 2007. "The Truth About Denial." *Newsweek*, August 2007, 23.

Beijing Review. 2021. Accessed online at https://www.bjreview.com/Documents/202112/t20211228_800271137.html (Accessed September 11, 2023).

Benatar, David. 2006. *Better Never To Have Been: The Harm of Coming into Existence.* Oxford: Clarendon Press.

Benite, Z. Ben-dor, S. Geroulanos, and N. Jerr, eds. 2021. *The Scaffolding of Sovereignty: Global and Aesthetic Perspectives on the History of a Concept.* New York: Columbia University Press.

Berry, Wendell. 1972. *A Continuous Harmony: Essays Cultural and Agricultural.* New York: Harcourt, Brace, Janovich, Inc.

Bickham, Stephan. 1981. "Future Generations and Contemporary Ethical Theory." *Journal of Value Inquiry* 15: 169–77.

Bielenstein, Hans. 1980. *The Bureaucracy of Han Times.* Cambridge: Cambridge University Press.

Biermann, Frank, and Ingrid Boas. 2007. "Preparing for a Warmer World: Towards a Global Governance System to Protect Climate Refugees." *Global Environmental Politics* 10, no. 1: 60–88 ("Plan 25").

Bittle, Jake. 2023. *The Great Displacement: Climate Change and the Next American Migration.* New York: Simon & Schuster.

Bodde, Derk. 1975. *Festivals in Classical China: New Year's and Other Annual Observances, during the Han Dynasty, 206 B.C.-A.D. 220.* Princeton: Princeton University Press.

Bourgeois, Léon. 1896/1902. *Solidarité.* Paris: Armand Colin.

Bridle, James. 2022. *Ways of Being: Animals, Plants, Machines: The Search for a Planetary Intelligence.* New York: Macmillan.

Brindley, Erica. 2021. "The Concept of 'Educational Transformation' and its Relationship to Civilizing Missions in Early China." *Journal of Chinese History* 中國歷史學刊 5, no. 1 (January): 1–21.

Brooks, David. 2023. "What is Happening is Not Normal: America Needs an Uprising that is Not Normal." *The New York Times*," April 18, A23.

Brown Weiss, Edith. 1988. *In Fairness to Future Generations: International Law, Common Patrimony, and Intergenerational Equity.* Tokyo: United Nations University.

Brown Weiss, Edith. 1990. "Our Rights and Obligations to Future Generations for the Environment." *The American Journal of International Law* 84, no. 1 (January): 198–207.

Brown Weiss, Edith. 2002. "Common but Differentiated Responsibilities in Perspective." *Proceedings of the Annual Meeting (American Society of International Law)*, 96 (March 13–16): 366–68.

Brown Weiss, Edith. 2020. *Establishing Norms in a Kaleidoscopic World.* Leiden: Brill.

Burkett, Maxine A. 2013. "The Nation Ex-Situ." In *Threatened Island Nations: Legal Implications of Rising Seas and a Changing Climate,* edited by Michael B. Gerrard and Gregory E. Wannier, 89–122. Cambridge: Cambridge University Press.

Carbon Brief. 2023. "Analysis: Shell Admits 1.5C Climate Goal Means Immediate End to Fossil Fuel Growth." April 20. https://www.carbonbrief.org/analysis-shell-admits-1-5c-climate-goal-means-immediate-end-to-fossil-fuel-growth/ (Last accessed September 17, 2023).

Carbon Brief. "China Responsible for 95 % of New Coal Power Production." https://www.carbonbrief.org/china-responsible-for-95-of-new-coal-power-construction-in-2023-report-says/ (Last accessed September 5, 2024).

Carson, Rachel. 1962. *Silent Spring.* Boston: Houghton Mifflin.

CBC: Canadian Broadcasting Company, interview with Jennifer Grentz, an indigenous ethnologist.

Chang, Chia-ju. 2019. *Chinese Environmental Humanities: Practices of Environing at the Margins.* London: Palgrave/MacMillan.

Chapman, Jesse. Forthcoming (late 2025/early 2026?). ""The Body and the Body-Politic in Guo Xiang's *Zhuangzi zhu.*" In *Global Reception of the Classic ZhuangziI: Early Commentaries,* Tobias Zern and Mark Csikszentmihalyi, eds.

Chen Guyuan 陳顧遠 (1896–1981). 1934. *Zhongguo guojifa suyuan* 中國國際法溯源. Shanghai: Shanghai Commercial Press.

Chen Guyuan 陳顧遠 (1896–1981). 1964. *Zhongguo fazhi shi gaiyao* 中國法制史概要. Taipei: Sanmin shuju, 1964.

Chen Guyuan 陳顧遠 (1896–1981). 2021. *Anthology of Chen Guyuan (Volume 3): Anthology of Chen Guyuan's [Writings on] Law.* Beijing: Commercial Press.

Chen Sudong 2018. "*Hongfan wuxing zhuan* zaiyi sixiang xilun: yi Zhanguo Qin Han *wuxing* jishi Yueling wenxian wei beijing." 洪范五行傳災異思想析論: 以戰國秦漢五行及時月令文獻為背景, *Suzhou daxue xuebao* 蘇州大學學報 6: 184–94.

Chenoweth, Erica, and Maria J. Stephan. 2011. *Why Civil Resistance Works: The Strategic Logic of Nonviolent Conflict.* New York: Columbia University Press.

Cloud, Morgan. 2018. "Property is Privacy: Locke and Brandeis in the Twenty-first Century." *American Criminal Law Review* 55, no. 37: 37–75.

Clunas, Craig. 1996. *Fruitful Sites: Garden Culture in Ming China.* Durham, NC: Duke University Press.

Cohen, Leonard. 1984. "A Broken Hallelujah." Revised 1994, under the title "Anthem."

Constantino, Nicholas. 2021. "Pretending to be Good: Explaining *wei* in the Xunzi." *Philosophy East and West.* Project MUSE. https://doi.org/10.1353/pew.0.021.

Cornell Law. Cf. Anti-SLAPP: Reporters Committee for Freedom of the Press. https://www.rcfp.org/anti-slapp-legal--guide/#:~:text=As%20of%20July%202024%2C%2034,%2C%20New%20Jersey%2C%20New%20Mexico%2C.

Corradini, Piero. 1995. "Ancient China's 'Ming tang' 明堂: Between Reality and Legend." *Rivista degli studi orientali* 69, Fasc. 1/2: 173–206.

Crone, Patricia. 1989. *Pre-Industrial Societies.* Oxford: Blackwell.

Csikszentmihalyi, Mark. 2004. *Material Virtue: Ethics and the Body in Early China.* Leiden: Brill.

D'Ambrosio, Paul. 2013. "Rethinking Environmental Issues in a Daoist Context: Why Daoism is and is Not Environmentalism." *Environmental Ethics* 35, no. 4: 407–17 [found at Philpapers].

Despeux, Catherine. 2003. "Bien débuter en la vie, L'education pré-natale en Chine." In *Éducation et instruction en Chine: I,* edited by Christine Nguyen Tri and Catherine Despeux, 61–98. Paris: Éditions Peeters.

Ding, Iza. 2022. *Performative States: Public Scrutiny and Environmental Governance in China.* Ithaca: Cornell University Press.

Du Zhengsheng 杜正勝. 2013. "Bianhu qimin zhi bu qi: yifen liangqian duo nian qian sifa wenshu jieshi de shehui" 齊民之不齊: 一份兩千多年前司法文書揭示的社會, *Gudai shumin shehui* (op. cit).

Duit, Andreas, Peter H. Feindt, and James Meadowcroft. 2016. "Greening Leviathan: The Rise of the Environmental State?" In *Environmental Politics* 25, no. 1: 1–23.

Durkee, Allison. 2024. Ohio v. Environmental Protection Agency." *Forbes*, June 28. https://www.forbes.com/sites/alisondurkee/2024/06/28/supreme-court-corrects-epa-opinion-after-gorsuch-confuses-laughing-gas-with-air-pollutant/

Dynamic City Foundation 动态城市基金会: see *Urban China*.

Earth Org. https://earth.org/greenwashing-companies-corporations/ Last accessed September 4, 2004).

Ehrenreich, Barbara. 2009. *Bright-Sided: How Positive Thinking is Undermining America*. New York: Picador.

Elvin, Mark. 2006. *The Retreat of the Elephants: An Environmental History of China*. New Haven: Yale University Press.

European Court of Human Rights. https://www.echr.coe.int/ (last accessed September 15, 2023).

Federal Constitutional Court of Germany. 2021. Judgment on Neubauer et al. versus Germany.

Federal Sustainable Development Act (S.C. 2008, c. 33), Canada.

Feinberg, Joel. 1980. "The Rights of Animals and Unborn Generations." *Rights, Justice, and the Bounds of Liberty: Essays in Social Philosophy*. Princeton: Princeton University Press.

Feindt, P. H. 2013. "Encircling the Commons. Property Rights, Political Authority and the Liberal Environmental State." Paper Presented at *Green Leviathan, Ecological Insurance Agency, or Capitalism's Agent? Revisiting the Ecological State in the Anthropocene*, ECPR Joint Sessions, Mainz, Germany, March 11–16, 2013.

Feng Wenwen 馮聞文. 2016. *Qin Han teshu shehui fuli yanjiu* 秦汉特殊社会福利研究 [Notes on Social Welfare in Han]. Wuhan daxue, Ph.D. dissertation.

Fingarette, Herbert. 1969/2000. *Self-Deception, with a New Chapter*. Berkeley: University of California Press.

Fingarette, Herbert. 1983. "The Music of Humanity in the Conversations of Confucius." *Journal of Chinese Philosophy* 10, no. 4 (December): 331–56.

Fingarette, Herbert. 2023. *Confucius: The Secular as Sacred*, with a new preface by Michael Nylan. Hannacroix, NY: Apocrophyle Press.

Fisher, Mark. 2009. *Capitalist Realism: Is There No Alternative?* Winchester: Zero Books.

Forstater, Mathew. 2004. "Visions and Scenarios: Heilbroner's Worldly Philosophy, Lowe's Political Economics, and the Methodology of Ecological Economics." *Levy Economics Institute Working Paper* 413 (October).

Forster, E. M. 1910. *Howard's End*. Reissued in 2000 by Penguin/Random House.

Foster, John Bellamy. 2015. "Late Soviet Ecology and the Planetary Crisis." *Monthly Review*, June 1. https://monthlyreview.org/2015/06/01/late-soviet-ecology-and-the-planetary-crisis/#en37 (Last accessed Sept. 12, 2022).

Foucault, Michel. 1966. *Les mots et les choses*. Paris: Gallimard. English version *The Order of Things: An Archaeology of the Human Sciences*. New York: Random House, 1970.

Foucault, Michel. 1994 (trans.). *Order of Things, an Archaeology of the Human Sciences*. New York: Vintage Books.

Fowler, Michael Ross, and Julie Marie Bunk. 1996. *Law, Power, and the Sovereign State: The Evolution and the Application of the Concept of Sovereignty*. University Park, PA: Pennsylvania State University Press.

Friedman, Daniel Butler. 2024. "Silent Revolution: The Rockefeller Foundation's Invisible Influence on the Model Penal Code" *Harvard Law Review* 59.2/ C.R.-C.L. L. REV. (Feb. 1), 45 pages.

Fumagalli, Robert. 2024. "A Dissolution of the Repugnant Conclusion." *Journal of Applied Philosophy* 41, no, 1 (February): 85–105.

Gan, Nester. 2017. "Latest Xi Jinping Book Gives Clues on Decline of Communist Party's Youth Wing." *South China Morning Post*, September 23. Accessed online at https://www.scmp.com/news/china/policies-politics/article/2112461/latest-xi-jinping-book-gives-clues-decline-communist (Last accessed Sept. 16, 2023; since removed).

Garland, Merrick B. 2023. "Remarks at the American Bar Association Annual Meeting Before the House of Delegates, Aug. 7, in Denver, Colorado." Accessed online at https://www.justice.gov/opa/speech/ attorney-general-merrick-b-garland-delivers-remarks-american-bar-assocation-annual#.

Geaney, Jane. 2002. *On the Epistemology of the Senses in Early Chinese Thought*. Albany: State University of New York Press.

Gerrard, Michael: see NY TIMES (May 20, 2023).

Geuss, Raymond. 2008. *Philosophy and Real Politics.* Princeton: Princeton University Press.

Gini co-efficient for 2023. Accessed online at https://data.worldbank.org/indicator/SI.POV.GINI?locations=CN.

Global Times (a state-sponsored Chinese outlet). 2023. "China Always Part of Developing World and a Member of the Global South, says Senior Chinese Official at G77+China Summit" (September 15).

Goldstein, Joshua. 2021. *Remains of the Everyday: A Century of Recycling in Beijing.* Berkeley: University of California Press.

Gonsalves, Ralph E. 2015. "Transforming Our World: The 2030 Agenda for Sustainable Development." Prepared Remarks at the United Nations 7th Plenary Session, on September 25. Included in UN document A/70/L.1, the Agreement on a Set of 17 Goals and 169 Targets to Come into Effect on January 1, 2016, Replacing the Millennium Development Goals Set in 2000.

Goody, Jack L. 2006. *The Theft of History.* Cambridge: Cambridge University Press.

Gosseries, Axel, and Lukas H. Meyer. 2009. *Intergenerational Justice.* Oxford: Oxford University Pres.

Greene, Jamal K. 2021. *How Rights Went Wrong: Why Our Obsession with Rights Is Tearing America Apart.* New York: Mariner Books (a division of HarperCollins).

Grote Stoutenburg, Jenny. 2013. "When Do States Disappear? Thresholds of Effective Statehood and the Continued Recognition of 'Deterritorialized' Island States." In Threatened Island Nations: Legal Implications of Rising Seas and a Changing Climate, edited by Michael B. Gerrard and Gregory E. Wannier, 57–88. Cambridge: Cambridge University Press.

Gudai shumin shehui 古代庶民社會. 2013. Edited by Hsing I-t'ien 邢義田 and Liu Tseng-kuei 劉增貴. Taipei: Zhongyuan yanjiuyuan.

Guo Guangwu. 2023. *The Rise of Xi Jinping's Young Guards: Generational Change in the CCP Leadership.* New York: Asia Society.

Guruswamy, Laksham. 1995. "International Environmental Law: Boundaries, Landmarks, and Realities." *National Resources & Environment* 10: 42, 46.

Hampshire, Stuart. 2018. *Justice is Conflict.* Princeton: Princeton University Press.

Hansen, James, et al. 1981. "Climate Impacts of Increasing Carbon Dioxide." *Science* 213, no. 4511 (August 28): 957–66.

Harari, Yuval Noah. 2016. *Homo Deus: A Brief History of Tomorrow.* London: Harville Secker, 2016; New York: Harper, 2017 rpt.

Hawkins, Amy. 2023. "China Spent 240 Billion on Belt and Road Bailouts from 2008 to 2021, Study Finds." *The Guardian,* March 28. See https://www.theguardian.com/world/2023/mar/28/china-spent-240bn-belt-and-road-debts-between-2008-and-2021 (Last accessed September 19, 2024).

Heather, Peter and John Rapley. 2023. *Why Empires Fall: Rome, America, and the Future of the West.* London: Allen Lane/Penguin Books.

Heilbroner, Robert. 1980. *An Inquiry into the Human Prospect.* New York: W.W. Norton & Co.

Heilbroner, Robert. 1996. *Visions of the Future.* Oxford: Oxford University Press.

Henry, Eric. 2022. *Garden of Eloquence/Shuoyuan, by Liu Xiang.* Seattle: University of Washington Press.

Hirase Takeo. 2005. *Toshi kokka kara Chūka e: in shū shunjū Sengoko* 都市国家から中華へ: 殷周春秋戰国. Tokyo: Kodansha. [A Chinese translation by Li Yanhua 李彥樺 was published in 2018 under the emended title of *Cong chengshi guojia dao Zhonghua* 從城市國家到中華.].

Hitchens, Christopher. 2001. *The Trial of Henry Kissinger.* London, New York: Verso.

Holmes, Brooke. 2010. *The Symptom and the Subject: The Emergence of the Physical Body in Ancient Greece.* Princeton: Princeton University Press.

Horn, Eva. 2022. *Was, wenn es Klimaaktivisten waren?* Accessed online at https://www.faz.net/aktuell/feuilleton/debatten/eva-horn-ueber-sabotage-an-nord-stream-18386063.html.

Hölscher, Katharina, and Niki Frantzeskaki, eds. 2019. *Transformative Climate Governance: A Capacities Perspective to Systematize, Evaluate, and Guide Climate Action.* Cham, Switzerland: Palgrave/ Macmillan.

Hou v. Bd. of Land & Natural Res. 2015. Supreme Court of Hawai'i. 363 P.3d 224, 136 Haw. 376 (Haw. 2015) (Last accessed online at https://casetext.com/case/hou-v-bd-of-land-natural-res).

Hsiao, Harry Hsin-i. 1973. *A Study of the Hsiao-ching: With an Emphasis on its Intellectual Background and its Problem.* Harvard University, Ph. D. dissertation.

Hull, Isabel V. 2006. *Absolute Destruction: Military Culture and the Practices of War in Imperial Germany.* Ithaca: Cornell University Press.

Hulsewê, A. F. P. [Anton]. 1987. "Han China: A 'Proto-welfare' State: Fragments of Han Law Discovered in North-west China." *T'oung pao* 73, no. 4/5: 265–85.

Hutton, Eric. 2014. *Xunzi: The Complete Text, Translated and with an Introduction.* Princeton: Princeton University Press.

ILC: International Law Commission. Accessed online at https://www.un.org/law/ilc, reprinted in Crawford, James. 2002. *The International Commission's Articles on State Responsibility: Introduction, Text, and Commentaries.* New York: United Nations.

Ivanhoe, P. J. 1991. "A Happy Symmetry: Xunzi's Ethical Thought." *Journal of the American Academy of Religion* 59, no. 2 (July): 309–22.

Jackson, Robert H. 1945. "Opening Statement, the Nürnberg Trials.": see Garland 2023.

Jameson, Fredric. 1994. *Seeds of Time.* New York: Columbia University Press.

Jiang, Daiwei, Yixing Chang, Fanglie Zhong, Wenge Yao, Yongnian Zhang, Xiaojiang Ding, and Chunlin Huang. 2022. "Future Growth Pattern Projections under Shared Socioeconomic Pathways: A Municipal City Bottom-up Aggregated Study Based on a Localized Scenario and Population Projections for China." *Economic Research Ekonomska Istraživanja* 35, no. 1: 2574–95.

Kahneman, Daniel. 2011. *Thinking, Fast and Slow.* New York: Farrar, Strauss, and Giroux.

Kaniewski, Daniel. "Disaster Resilience Is a Trillion-Dollar Challenge, Here's what FEMA Can Do to Help." https://www.nibs.org/blog/disaster-resilience-trillion-dollar-challenge-heres-what-fema-can-do-help.

Kenkel, Carly D. 2024. "Want to See Coral Reefs Grow? Freeze Them." *The New York Times*, Opinion, Sat. August 17, A19.

Khayutina, Maria. 2010. "Royal Hospitality and Geopolitical Constitution of the Western Zhou Polity (1046/5-771 BC)." *T'oung Pao* 96, no. 1–3: 1–73.

Kirsch, Adam. 2023. "Why More People want Human Extinction: Climate Change, an AI 'Singularity', and Merging with the Cosmic Flow of Data." *South China Morning Post Magazine*, 29 (Jan.); rpt. in https://michel-foucault.com/2023/02/07/adam-kirsch-why-more-people-want-human-extinction-climate-change-an-ai-singularity-and-merging-with-a-cosmic-flow-of-data-2023/ (Last accessed Sept. 15, 2023).

Kissinger, Henry. 2001. "The Pitfalls of Universal Jurisdiction." *Foreign Affairs* 80, no. 4 (July/August), 86–96.

Kreps, David M. 1990/2003. "The Problems of Game Theory." *Game Theory and Economic Modelling,* online edn, Oxford Academic, November 1. https://doi.org/10.1093/0198283814.003.0005 (Last accessed September 16, 2024).

Kriss, Sam, and Ellie Mae O'Hagan. 2017. "Tropical Depressions: On Climate Change and Human Futilitarianism." *The Baffler* (September).

Kuriyama, Shigehisa. 1999. *The Expressiveness of the Body, and the Divergence between Greek and Chinese Medicine.* Cambridge, MA.: Zone.

Lacal, Irene, and Ventura Rossella 2018. "Epigenetic Inheritance: Concepts, Mechanisms and Perspectives." *Frontiers in Molecular Neuroscience* 11. https://www.frontiersin.org/journals/molecular-neuroscience/articles/10.3389/ fnmol.2018.00292.

Lewis, Martin W., and Kären Wigen. 1997. *The Myth of Continents: A Critique of Metageography.* Berkeley: University of California Press.

Li Zehou. 1999. "'Subjectivity and Subjectality': A Response." *Philosophy East and West* 49, no. 2: 113–19.

"Liang Shan lun." 2020. Xi Jinping doctrine. Accessed online at https://en.wikipedia.org/wiki/Clear_waters_and_green_mountain.

Linden, Eugene. 2022. *Fire and Flood: A People's History of Climate Change from 1979 to the Present.* New York: Penguin/ Random House.

Lipscomb, Benjamin J. B. 2021. *The Women Are Up to Something: How Elizabeth Anscombe, Philippa Foot, Mary Midgley, and Iris Murdoch Revolutionized Ethics.* Oxford: Oxford University Press.

Liu Ming 劉鳴 (aka Raymond Liu). 2022. *Yueling yu Qin Han Shijian zhixu* 月令與秦漢時間秩序. Xi'an: Xibei daxue chubanshe.

Liu Tseng-kuei 劉增貴. 2013. "Handai zangsu Zhong de shiri Xinyang" 漢代葬俗中的時日信仰. In *Gudai shumin shehui*, 325–60. op. cit.

Lloyd, Geoffrey. 1990. *Demystifying Mentalities.* Cambridge: Cambridge University Press.

Locke, John. 1679. *The Second Treatise of Government.* The edition consulted was edited by C.B. MacPherson, for Hackett, 1980.

Loewe, Michael. 2011. *Dong Zhongshu, a "Confucian" Heritage and the Chunqiu fanlu.* Leiden: Brill.

Loewe, Michael. 2021. "Land Tenure and the Decline of Eastern Han Government." In *Technical Arts*, 49–100. op. cit.

Lu, Sheldon, and Jiayan Mi, eds. 2009. *Chinese Eco-cinema.* Hong Kong: Hong Kong University Press.

Lu Xiqi 魯西奇. 2021. *Zhongguo gudai xiangli zhidu yanjiu* 中國古代鄉里制度文化. Beijing daxue chubanshe.

Lujan v. Defenders of Wildlife, 504 U.S. 555 (June 12). 1992. See https:// www.law.cornell.edu/wex /standing#:~:text=Standing%2C%20or%20l ocus%20standi%2C%20is,law%20or%20action%20being%20challenged (Last accessed November 9, 2024); also https://supreme.justia.com/cases /federal/us/504/555/.

Lü Simian 呂思勉. 2005. *Lü Simian dushu zhaji* 呂思勉讀書札記, 3 vols. Shanghai: Shanghai guji chubanshe rpt. of collected earlier works.

Lynn, Richard John. 2022. *Zhuangzi: A New Translation of the Sayings of Master Zhuang as Interpreted by Guo Xiang.* New York: Columbia University Press.

Mac Cumhaill, Clare, and Rachael Wiseman. 2022. *Metaphysical Animals: How Four Women Brought Philosophy Back to Life.* New York: Doubleday.

MacIntyre, Alasdair. 1981. *After Virtue: A Study in Moral Theory.* Notre Dame, Ind.: University of Notre Dame, (with multiple reprints).

Maffesoli, Michel. 2005. Quoted in the UNESCO's "Final Report" of the International Workshop "Paths to Dignity," held at UNESCO House, Paris, Nov 14–15.

Malm, Andreas. 2021. *How to Blow Up a Pipeline.* London: Verso.

Malouf, Amin. 1998. *In the Name of Identity: Violence and the Need to Belong.* Translated by Barbara Bray. New York: Arcade.

Mannheim, Karl. 1928. "The Sociological Problem of Generations" (English translation of the 1928 original entitled "Das Problem der

Generationen"). In *Younger than Jesus: The Generation Book*, edited by Lauren Cornell, et. al., 163–95. New York: New Museum; Göttingen: Steidl, 2009.

Marlon, Jennifer et al. 2022. "Yale Climate Opinion Maps. 2021." Yale Program on Climate Change Communication, February 23. Accessed online at https://climatecommunication.yale.edu/visualizations-data/ycom-us/.

Marx, Karl. 1976 rpt. *Capital, vol.1*. London: Penguin.

Marx, Willem. 2025. "Suddenly Miners Are Tearing Up the Seafloor for Critical Metals." *Scientific American,* April 15. https://www.scientificamerican.com/article/miners-are-pulling-valuable-metals-from-the-seafloor-and-almost-no-one-knows/ (Last accessed April 18, 2023).

Mars, Neville, and Adrian Hornsby. 2008. *The Chinese Dream*. Rotterdam: 010 Publishers.

Mathis, Will. 2023. *Bloomberg,* on March 2, 2023. Accessed online at https://www.bloomberg.com/news/articles/2023-03-03/shell-ceo-says-cutting-oil-and-gas-production-is-not-healthy#xj4y7vzkg (Last accessed September 3, 2023).

McAdam, Jane. 2011. "Swimming Against the Tide: Why a Climate Change Displacement Treaty is Not the Answer." *International Journal of Refugee Law* 23: 2–27.

McInerney-Lankford, Siobhan. 2013. "Human Rights and Climate Change: Reflections on International Legal Issues and Potential Policy Relevance.". In *Threatened Island Nations*, 195–242. op. cit.

McKibben, Bill. 1989. *The End of Nature*. New York; Random House.

McKibben, Bill. 2016. "A Pipeline Fight and America's Dark Past." *The New Yorker*, September 6.

Meyer, Lukas. 2017. *Intergenerational Justice*. London: Routledge.

Meyer, Lukas, and Dominic Roser. 2007. *Intergenerationelle Gerechtigkeit - Die Bedeutung von zukünftigen Klimaschäden für die heutige Klimapolitik*. Zürich: Bundesamt für Umwelt.

Midgley, Mary. 2011. *The Myths We Live By*. London: Routledge.

Miller, James. 2017. *China's Green Religion: Daoism and the Quest for a Sustainable Future*. New York: Columbia University Press [available through JSTOR].

Miller, Ryan W. 2016. "How the Dakota Access Pipeline Battle Unfolded." *USA Today*, December 2.

Ministry for the Future: see Robinson, Kim Stanley.

Molina, J. Michelle, and Donald K. Swearer, eds. 2010. *Rethinking the Human.* Cambridge, MA: Center for the Study of World Religions.

Monbiot, George. 2022. *Regenesis: Feeding the World without Devouring the Planet.* London: Penguin.

Morgan, T. J. H., and K. N. LaLand. 2012. "The Biological Bases of Conformity." *Frontiers in Neuro-Science,* June 14: 1–7. PMCID: PMC3375089.

Monte Carlo Simulation: *What is Monte Carlo Simulation?* Accessed online at https://www.ibm.com/ topics/monte-carlo-simulation.

Mullick v. Mullick: The Bombay High Court, April 28, 1925. Accessed online, on September 16, 2024, at https://indiankanoon.org/doc/290902/.

Narveson, Jan. 1967. "Utilitarianism and New Generations." *Mind* 76 (January): 62–72.

Narveson, Jan. 1995. "Resources and Environmental Policy." *Two Papers on Environmentalism II. Center for the Study of Ethics in Society Papers* 29. Accessed online at https://scholarworks.wmich.edu/ethics_papers/.

Neville, Robert Cummings. 1998. "Orientation, Self, and Ecological Posture." In *Confucianism and Ecology: The interrelation of Heaven, Earth, Human,* edited by Mary Evelyn Tucker and John Berthrong, 265–73.

Nieboer, Jeremy. 2003. *Climate Eco-Socialism.* Bruges: The Bruges Group.

Noreña, Carlos. 2011. *Imperial Ideals in the Roman West: Representation, Circulation, Power.* Berkeley: University of California Press.

NPR/ (see also PBS). https://www.npr.org/2023/08/23/1194710955/montana-youth-climate-ruling-could-set-precedent-for-future-climate-litigation (on Held v. Montana).

NPR/ (see also PBS). https://www.thirteen.org/programs/nature/kalahari-wilderness-without-water-ld4tas/ (on keystone species and their role in environmental restoration).

NPR/ (see also PBS). https://ny.pbslearningmedia.org/resource/nat38-discovery-of-keystone-species-vid/the-serengeti-rules-media-gallery/ (on keystone species and their role in environmental restoration).

NPR/ (see also PBS). https://www.pbs.org/video/trump-agenda-climate-1745271281/ (on keystone species and their role in environmental restoration).

NRDC news. 2021. https://www.nrdc.org/news-and-commentary

NY TIMES. 2023. *The New York Times.* March 20. Accessed online at www.nytimes.com/2023/03/24/climate/montana-youth-climate-lawsuit.html, citing Michael Gerrard, Director of the Sabin Center for Climate Change Law at Columbia University.

NY TIMES. 2023. "Swiss Women Sue the Government over Dangers of Climate Change." *The New York Times,* August 7, A13. Print edition.

NY TIMES. 2023. "Extreme Heat Harms Mental Health, With Link to a Rise in Suicides, Scientists Say." *The New York Times,* August 10, A1 (by-line Apoorva Mandavilli).

NY TIMES. 2023. Claire Cameron, "Opinion: We Thought We Were Saving the Planet but We Were Planting a Time Bomb." *The New York Times,* September 15/17, Print edition (SR 5) by the shorter title: "We Were Planting a Time Bomb."

NY TIMES. 2024. "Extreme Weather Threatens Global Gains in Education." *The New York Times,* August 15, A10 (by-line Somini Sengupta).

NY TIMES. 2024. "A Struggling Iowa Farmer Trades its Hogs for Mushrooms." *The New York Times,* August 15, A11 (by-line Cara Buckley).

NY TIMES. 2024. "New Study Re-evaluates Worst Case Scenario for Antarctica's Thwaites Glacier." *The New York Times,* August 21, A10 (by-line Raymond Zhong).

NY TIMES. 2024. "Judge Blocks E.P.A. From Using Civil Rights Law in Pollution Case." *The New York Times,* August 23 (by-line Lisa Friedman).

NY TIMES. 2024. "South Korean Court Orders Country to Step Up Action on Climate Change." *The New York Times,* August 29, (by-line Choe Sang-Hun).

NY TIMES. 2024. "Has the Tide Turned for Tiktok, Telegram, and X?." *The New York Times,* September 11.

Neimanis, Astrid, and Rachel Loewen Walker. 2014. "'Weathering': Climate Change and the 'Thick Time' of Transcorporeality." *Hypatia* 29, no. 3 (Summer): 558–75.

Ni Peimin. 2014. "Seek and You Will Find It; Let Go and You Will Lose It: Exploring a Confucian Approach to Human Dignity." *Dao: A Journal of Comparative Philosophy* 13 (May 7): 173–98 [also found at PhilPeople; Academia.edu].

Nussbaum, Martha C. 2017. *Not for Profit: Why Democracy Needs the Humanities.* Princeton: Princeton University Press.

Nussbaum, Martha C. 2024. *The Monarchy of Fear: A Philosopher Looks at Our Political Crisis.* New York: Simon & Schuster.

Nuyen, Ahn Tuan. 2011. "Confucian Role-Based Ethics and Strong Environmental Ethics." *Environmental Values* 20, no. 4: 549–66 [found at PhilPapers].

Nylan, Michael 1992. *The Shifting Center: The Original "Great Plan" and Later Readings.* Monumenta Serica Monograph Series, 24.

Nylan, Michael 1993. *"The Canon of Supreme Mystery" by Yang Hsiung.* Albany: State University of New York Press.

Nylan, Michael 1996. "Confucian Piety and Individualism." *Journal of the American Oriental Society* 116, (January–March): 1–27.

Nylan, Michael 2001. "Boundaries of the Body and Body Politic in Early Confucian Thought." In *Boundaries and Justice*, edited by David Miller and Sohail Hashmi, 112–35. Princeton: Princeton University Press.

Nylan, Michael 2005. "Toward an Archaeology of Writing, Ritual, and Public Display in the Classical Era." In *Text and Ritual in Early China*, edited by Martin Kern and Benjamin Elman, 3–49. Seattle: University of Washington.

Nylan, Michael 2008. "Beliefs about Seeing: Optics and Moral Technologies in Early China." *Asia Major* 21, no. 1: 89–132.

Nylan, Michael 2010a. "Yin/yang, Five Phases, and *qi*." In *China's Early Empires*, 398–414. Cambridge: Cambridge University Press.

Nylan, Michael 2015. "Lots of Pleasure, Little Happiness To Be Seen: The Case of Early China." *Philosophy East and West* 65, no. 1 (January): 196–226.

Nylan, Michael 2018. *The Chinese Pleasure Book.* New York: Zone Books.

Nylan, Michael 2019. "Humans as Animals and Things in pre-Buddhist China." *Religions,* online journal. Accessed online at religions-495627.

Nylan, Michael 2021. "On *Hanshu* 'Wuxing zhi' 五行志 and Ban Gu's Project." In *Technical Arts in the Han Histories*, 213–80. Albany: State University of New York Press.

Nylan, Michael 2022. "Sihai wei xue" 四海為學. Zoom lecture organized by Paul d'Ambrosio (October 7). Series available on Youtube.

Nylan, Michael 2025. "Xunzi and the Greek Xunzi, Aristotle." *Oriens Extremus* 59: 61–118, in special issue entitled 'Beyond Orientalism'.

Nylan, Michael 2025b. "The Common Good in Early China in Context." *Journal of Asian History*, 59, 1–24.

Nylan, Michael 2026a. "Entangled Pasts." Chapter in *A Global History of Confucianism: The Cambridge History of Confucianism*, Vol. I, edited by Kiri Paramore (forthcoming).

Nylan, Michael. 2026b. "Xunzi on *de* 德, *dao* 道, and *daode* 道德," *Xunzi: A Reception History*, edited by Winnie Sung (forthcoming in 2026). Berlin: De Gruyter.

Nylan, Michael, and Nicholas Constantino. 2022. "On the Rites and Rites Controversies in Mid-Eastern Han." In *Autour du Traité des rites: de la canonisation du rituel à la ritualisation de la société* [English title: *All about the Rites: From canonised ritual to ritualised society*], edited by Anne Cheng and Stéphane Feuillas, 241–84. Paris: Maisonneuve et Larose. The text also appears onthe College de France Website, Accessed online at https://books.openedition.org/cdf/12918.

Nylan, Michael, and Trenton Wilson. 2022. "A Brief History of Daring." In *Emotions across Cultures: Classical Greece and China*, chap. 4, edited by David Konstan and Yang Huang, 75–142. Berlin: de Gruyter.

Nylan, Michael with Trenton Wilson (forthcoming). "Deng Sui, a Complex Figure." accepted by *Early China* in the spring of 2025.

Nylan, Michael, and Shoufu Yin. 2026. "Consequential Voting and Public Expression before 1350 in China," accepted for a new *Cambridge History* devoted to democracy before 1350.

Nylan, Michael, and Michael Loewe, eds. 2010. *China's Early Empires, a Reappraisal*. Cambridge: Cambridge University Press.

NZZ (Neue Zürcher Zeitung): https://www.nzz.ch/english/beijing-targets-women-in-efforts-to-boost-birth-rate-ld.1843460 (Last accessed April 23, 2025).

Olberding, Garret P. 2023. *The Exercise of the Spatial Imagination in Premodern China, Shaping the Expanse.* Berlin: de Gruyter.

Oreskes, Naomi, and Erik M. Conway. 2012. *Merchants of Doubt - How a Handful of Scientists Obscured the Truth on Issues from Tobacco Smoke to Global Warming.* London: Bloomsbury.

Ou Hongyi: see https://en.wikipedia.org/wiki/Howey_Ou.

Oxford Policy Brief. 2021. "Towards a Declaration for Future Generations." Accessed online https://www.bsg.ox.ac.uk/sites/default/files/2023-01/Policy%20brief%20% E2%80%93%20Toward%20a%20Declaration%20on%20Future%20Generations.pdf (Last accessed September 5, 2023).

Parfit, Derek 1982. "Future Generations: Further Problems." *Philosophy & Public Affairs* 11, no. 2 (Spring): 113–72.

Parfit, Derek 1984. *Reasons and Persons.* Oxford: Clarendon Press.

Parijs, Philippe Van. 1998. "The Disfranchisement of the Elderly, and Other Attempts to Secure Intergenerational Justice." *Philosophy and Public Affairs* 27, no. 4 (Autumn): 292–333.

Party Congress: 中国共产党第十九届五中全会公报. Accessed online at https://www.thepaper.cn/newsDetail_forward_9779332 (Last accessed October 12, 2022).

PBS Newshour: "How the Trump Administration is Dismantling Climate Protections," April 21, 2025 (https://www.pbs.org/video/ trump-agenda-climate-1745271281/).

People's Daily. 2023 (May 4). 总书记心中的新时代好青年. Accessed online at https://paper.people.com.cn/rmrb/html/2023-05/04/nw.D110000renmrb_20230504_2-01.html (Last accessed on September 18, 2023).

Perrez, Frank. Xaver. 1996. "The Relationship Between 'Permanent Sovereignty' and the Obligation Not to Cause Transboundary Environmental Damage." *Environmental Law* (*Northwestern School of Law*) 26, no. 4: 1187–212.

Pollard, Martin Quinn. 2023. "China's Xi Deals Knockout Blow to Once-powerful Youth League Faction." https://www.reuters.com/world/china/chinas-xi-deals-knockout-blow-once-powerful-youth-league-faction-2022-10-26/ (Last accessed September 12, 2023).

Poo Mu-chou. 1998. *In Search of Personal Welfare: A View of Ancient Chinese Religion.* Albany: State University of New York Press.

Purdy, Jebediah. 2015. *After Nature: A Politics for the Anthropocene.* Cambridge: Harvard University Press.

Rawls, John. 1999. *A Theory of Justice.* Cambridge, MA: Harvard University Press.

Revesz, Richard L. 1999. "Environmental Regulation, Cost-Benefit Analysis, and the Discounting of Human Lives." *Columbia Law Review* 4 (May): 941–1017.

Rivoli, Pietra. *The Travels of a T-shirt in the Global Economy: An Economist Examines the Markets, Power, and politics of World Trade.* 2nd edn. Hoboken, NJ: Wiley

Robbins, Paul. 2012. *Political Ecology: A Critical Introduction.* 2nd edn. Oxford: Blackwell.

Robinson, Kim Stanley. 2020. *The Ministry for the Future.* New York: Orbit.

Roethke, Theodore. 1963. *The Far Field: Selected Poems of Theodore Roethke.* New York: Doubleday & Co.

Rosemont, Henry, Jr. 2016. *Against Individualism: A Confucian Rethinking of the Foundations of Morality, Politics, Family, and Religion* (*Philosophy and Cultural Identity*). Lanham, MD: Lexington Books.

Rovelli, Carlo. 2018. *There Are Places in the World where Rules are Less Important than Kindness, and Other Thoughts on Physics, Philosophy, and the World.* New York: Penguin.

Sala, Ilaria Maria. 2024. "Soil is Home to a Vibrant World." *The New York Times*, August 11, A11.

Sanderovitch, Sharon. 2017. *Presence and Praise: Writing the Imperial Body in Han China.* University of California, at Berkeley, Ph.D. dissertation.

Sanft, Charles. 2008/9. "Edict of Monthly Ordinances for the Four Seasons in Fifty Articles from 5 C.E.: Introduction to the Wall Inscription Discovered at Xuanquanzhi, with Annotated Translation." *Early China* 32: 125–208.

Schmitt, Carl. 1927. *The Concept of the Political.* Translated by G. Schwab. Chicago: University of Chicago Press, 1932, expanded 2007, as analyzed in https://plato.stanford.edu/entries/Schmitt (section 3).

Shang Huan 商恒. 2008. *Qin Han jiandu bazhong fazhi wenshu jikao* 秦汉简牍跋中法制文书辑考. Shehui kexue wenxian chubanshe.

Shpancer, Noam. 2010. "You Are a Conformist (That is, You Are Human)." *Psychology Today*, December 5. https://www.psychologytoday.com/us/

blog/insight-therapy/201012/you-are-conformist-is-you-are-human#:~:text=We%20survive%20only%20in%20highly,Conformity%20soothes.

Schnaiberg, A., D. N. Pellow, and A. Weinberg. 2002. "The Treadmill of Production and the Environmental State." In *The Environmental State, Under Pressure* (Research in Social Problems and Public Policy, 10), edited by A. P. Moi and Frederick H. Buttel, 15–32. Oxford, Amsterdam, New York: JAI.

Schumpeter, Joseph. *Capitalism, Socialism, and Democracy*. New York: Harper, 1950.

Sennett, Richard. 2012. *Together: The Rituals, Pleasures, and Politics of Cooperation*. Harmondsworth: Penguin.

Shapiro, Judith. 2001. *Mao's War Against Nature: Politics and the Environment in Revolutionary China*. Cambridge: Cambridge University Press.

Shell. www.shell.com/scenarios (Last accessed September 21, 2022).

Shen Zhongchang 沈仲常. 1979. "'Gao dai tu' huaxiang zhuan zhiyi" 告贷图画像砖质疑, *Kaogu* 考古, 1979, no. 6: 525–7.

Shklar, Judith N. 2019. *On Political Obligations*. New Haven, Yale University Press.

Sivin, Nathan. 1995. "State, Cosmos, and Body in the Last Three Centuries B.C." *Harvard Journal of Asiatic Studies* 55, no. 1 (June): 5–37.

Smil, Vaclav. 1993. *China's Environmental Crisis: An Enquiry into the Limits of National Development*. London: Routledge.

Solnit, Rebecca, and Thelma Young Lutunatabua, eds. 2023. *Not Too Late: Changing the Climate Story from Despair to Possibility*. Chicago: Haymarket Books.

Sommer, Deborah. 2008. "Boundaries of the *Ti* Body." *Asia Major*, 3rd series 21, no. 1: 293–324.

Sun, Jason/ Zhixin, ed. 2017. *Age of Empires: Art of the Qin and Han Dynasties*. New York: Metropolitan Museum of Art.

Spakowski, Nicola. 2021. "'Gender' Trouble: Feminism in China under the Impact of Western Theory and the Spatialization of Identity." In *Feminisms with Chinese Characteristics*, edited by Ping Zhu and Hui Faye Xiao, 37–64. Syracuse: Syracuse University Press.

Stanford Encyclopedia of Philosophy. https://plato.stanford.edu/entries/burke/.

Stanford Encyclopedia of Philosophy. https://plato.stanford.edu/entries/conservatism/.

Stanford Encyclopedia of Philosophy. https://plato.stanford.edu/entries/smith-moral-political/.

Stanford Encyclopedia of Philosophy. https://plato.stanford.edu/entries/locke/.

State Council. 2022 (May 11). State Council Information Office of the People's Republic of China. "Xi tells Chinese Youth to Contribute Energy, Creativity to Rejuvenation." Updated: May 11, 2022 08:59. For the Chinese text, see the *People's Daily* from May 11, 2022. 庆祝中国共产主义青年团成立100周年大会在京隆重举行; accessed online at http://paper.people.com.cn/rmrb/html/2022-05/11/nw.D110000renmrb_20220511_1-01.html (Last accessed September 17, 2023).

Stechemesser, Angela, et al. 2024. "Climate Policies that Achieved Major Emission Reductions: Global Evidence from Two Decades." *Science* 385, no. 6711 (August 22): 884–92.

Stein, Rolf. 1990. *The World in Miniature: Container Gardens and Dwellings in East Asia.* Stanford, CA: Stanford University Press.

Stewart, Douglas J. 1970. "Disfranchise the Old." *New Republic* 29, no. 8: 20–2.

Stone, Christopher D. 1972. "Should Trees Have Standing?—Towards Legal Rights for Natural Objects." *Southern California Law Review* 45: 450–501.

Studley, John. 2018. *Indigenous Sacred Natural Sites and Spiritual Governance.* London: Routledge.

Summit Report. 2022. Publication of the [Helsinki] Committee of the Future 3/2022: The World Summit of the Committees of the Future 2022.

Tan Sor-hoon. 2014. "The Early Confucian Concept of 'Yi' (议)and Deliberative Democracy." *Political Theory* 42, no. 1 (February): 82–105.

Taylor, Charles. 1991. *The Malaise of Modernity.* Toronto: House of Anansi.

TAZ. Nov. 28, 2021. "Es wird Leid geben und Gewalt": see Es wird Leid geben und Gewalt - Literatur, die realistisch bleiben will, muss den

Klimawandel behandeln. Ein Gespräch mit dem Science-Fiction-Autor Kim Stanley Robinson; Accessed online at https://taz.de/Autor-ueber-die-Klimakrise-in-Romanen/!5815427/Source: Es wird Leid geben und Gewalt - Literatur, die realistisch bleiben will, muss den Klimawandel behandeln. Ein Gespräch mit dem Science-Fiction-Autor Kim Stanley Robinson; see https://taz.de/Autor-ueber-die-Klimakrise-in-Romanen/!5815427/ (Last accessed Sept. 16, 2023).

Technical Arts: *Technical Arts in the Han Histories*. 2021. Edited by Mark Csikszentmihalyi and Michael Nylan. Albany: State University of New York Press.

The Economist: "How Games and Game Theory Have Changed the World." June 20, 2024 (anon.).

The New York Times: see NY TIMES.

The World We Want. See United Nations Millennium Development Goals Task Force.

Thomas, Julia Adeney. 2022. *Altered Earth: Getting the Anthropocene Right*. Cambridge: Cambridge University Press.

Threatened Island Nations: Legal Implications of Rising Seas and a Changing Climate. 2013. Edited by Michael B. Gerrard and Gregory E. Wannier. Cambridge: Cambridge University Press.

Toward a Declaration for Future Generations (aka Oxford Policy Brief). 2021. Thomas Hale, et al. Oxford University. Accessed online at https://www.bsg.ox.ac.uk/sites/default/files/2023-01/Policy%20brief%20-%20Toward%20a%20Declaration (pdf).

United Nations. 2015. "Unanimously Adopting Historic Sustainable Development Goals, General Assembly Shapes Global Outlook for Prosperity, Peace." Press release, 7th plenary session, September 25. Accessed online at https://press.un.org/en/2015/ga11688.doc.html, on September 14, 2023.

United Nations Millenium Development Goals Task Force. A Million Voices: The World we Want. 2013–2015. Accessed online at https://www.undp.org/publications/million-voices-world-we-want (Last accessed August 26, 2023).

Urban China 城市中国, Shanghai 2015, issue 70.

Vallor, Shannon. 2016. *Technology and the Virtues: A Philosophical Guide to a Future Worth Having*. Oxford: Oxford University Press.

Wallace-Wells, David. 2019. *The Unhabitable Earth*. New York: Tim Duggan Books (Penguin/Random).

Wang Aiqing 王愛清. 2010. *Qin Han xiangli kongzhi yanjiu* 秦漢鄉里控制研究. Jinan: Shandong daxue chubanshe.

Wang Lihua 王利華. 2014. "Yueling zhongde yu ziran jielü yu shehui jiezou" 月令中的與自然界綠與社會節奏, *Zhongguo shehui kexue* (February): 185–203, 208.

Wang, Michelle H. 2023. *The Art of Terrestrial Diagrams in Early China*. Chicago: University of Chicago Press.

Wang Wentao 王文涛. 2007. *Qin Han shehui baozhang yanjiu: yi zaihuo we zhongde kaocha* 秦汉社会保障研究以灾害为中也的考察. Beijing: Zhonghua shuju.

Wang Zhihe et al. 2014. "The Ecological Civilization Debate." *Monthly Review*, November 1. Accessed online at https://monthlyreview.org/2014/11/01/the-ecological-civilization-debate-in-china/ (last accessed September 18, 2023).

Wannier, Gregory E., and Michael B. Gerrard. 2013. *Climate Change: International Law and Global Governance*, 2 vols. Nomos Verlagsgesellschaft mbH, also available on JSTOR (www.jstor.org/stable/j.ctv941w8s).

Watson, Jesse. 2019. *Paperwork before Paper: Law and Materiality in China's Early Empires (221 BCE-220 CE)*. University of California, at Berkeley, Ph.D. dissertation.

Wei River. 2013. Accessed online at kaogu.cssn.cn/ywb/research_work/excavation_report/201809/W020180907402420204935.pdf; also www.kaogu.cn/en/News/New_discoveries/2013/1026/43140.html.

Well-being Act [of Wales]. 2015. Accessed online at https://www.futuregenerations.wales/about-us/future-generations-act/.

Wells, Matthew. 2016. "Casualties, Regime Type, and the Outcomes of Wars of Occupation." *Conflict Management and Peace Science* 33, no. 5 (November): 469–90.

Weston, Burns H. 2008. "Climate Change and Intergenerational Justice: Foundational Reflections." *Vermont Journal of Environmental Law* 9: 375–430.

Wheatley, Paul. 1971. *The Pivot of the Four Quarters: A Preliminary Enquiry into the Origins and Character of the Ancient Chinese City*. Edinburgh: Edinburgh University Press.

White, Hayden. 1973. *Metahistory: The Historical Imagination in Nineteenth-century Europe*. Baltimore and London: Johns Hopkins University Press.

White, Lynn T., Jr. 1967. "The Historical Roots of Our Ecological Crisis." *Science* 155, no. 3676: 1203–7. Widely available in pdf: https://doi.org/10.1126/science.155.3767.1203.

Whitehead, Alfred North. 1933. *Adventures of Ideas*. New York: Macmillan.

Williams, Bernard. 1993. *Shame and Necessity*. Berkeley, CA: University of California Press.

Williams, James. 1991. *Stand Out of Our Light: Freedom and Resistance in the Attention Economy*. Cambridge: Cambridge University Press.

Williams, Raymond. 1976. *Keywords: A Vocabulary of Culture and Society*. Beckenham, Kent: Croom Helm.

Wilson, Edward O. 1974. *On Human Nature*. Cambridge, M.A.: Harvard University Press.

Wilson, Trenton. 2022. "Response: On Michael Nylan's 'Learning and Emulation in the Early Empires in China.'" October 7.

Xi Jinping. 2017. "Secure a Decisive Victory in Building a Moderately Prosperous Society in All Respects and Strive for the Great Success of Socialism with Chinese Characteristics for a New Era." Delivered at the 19th National Congress of the Communist Party of China, October 18.

Xin Wen. 2022. "The Emperor of Dunhuang: Rethinking Political Regionalism in Tenth Century China." *Journal of Chinese History* 6, no. 1 (January): 43–68.

Xinhua News Agency. 2013 (May 5). "Youth urged to contribute to realization of 'Chinese Dream.'" Accessed online at http://www.china.org.cn/china/2013-05/05/content_28731285.html (Last accessed September 18, 2023).

Xue Mengxiao 薛夢瀟. 2014. "Dong Han xingchun kao" 東漢行春考, *Zhongguo shi yanjiu* 中國史研究 2014, no. 1: 15–33.

Xue Mengxiao 薛夢瀟. 2014b. "Zaoqi Zhongguo de Yuling wenxuan yu Yueling zhidu: yi 'zhengzhi shijian' de zhizuo yu shijian wei zhongxin" 早期中國的月令文獻与月令制度：以政治時間的製作与實踐為中心. Ph.D. dissertation, Wuhan daxue.

Yang Lien-sheng. 1957. "The Concept of Pao as a Basis for Social Relations in China." In *Chinese Thoughts and Institutions*, edited by John King Fairbank, 291–309. Chicago: University of Chicago Press.

"Youth of China in the New Era." 2012. White Paper, Produced by the 18th CPC National Congress, and issued October, 2012.

"Youth Shock Brigade, 1955. "Youth Shock Brigade of the No. 9 Agricultural Producers' Co-operative in Hsinping Township, Chungshan County." *The Socialist Upsurge in China's Countryside*, Chinese edn., Vol. III. Mao Tse Tung Internet Archive. Section 30. Youth. English translation based on Peking Foreign Languages Press 1966.

Zang Zhifei 臧知非. 2022. "'Wang zhang zhao shu' yu Handai yanglao zhidu" 王杖詔書 與漢代養老制度, *Shilin* 史林 2002, no. 2: 35–41.

Zhu Kezhen 竺可楨 [aka Coching Chu]. 1926. "Lun yi sui cha ding *Shangshu* Yao dian si zhongxing zhi niandai" 論以歲差定尚書堯典四仲星之年代. In *Zhu Kezhen quanji* 竺可楨全集, 552–60. Shanghai: Shanghai keji jiaoyu chubanshe, rpt. 2004.

Zuo, Mandy. 2023 (March 16). "China's Xi Jinping Says Ukraine War has Shown the 'Extreme Importance' of Food Security." *South China Morning Post.*

Zuo2. 2023 (March 16). "China Proudly Feeds a Fifth of the Global Population with Only 9 Per Cent of the World's Arable Land." *South China Morning Post.*

Index

"access," defined; see Weiss, Edith Brown
"acquisition and optimization" of resources   xii
"addicted to irreality"   27
"agency" ascribed to persons   xxi–xxii, xxiv, 19, 22
agency; see institutions
AI   128
"air we breathe"   xx, 44
American Relief Administration   3
Analects ascribed to Confucius/Kongzi   21, 44, 81, 155
anarchists   24
Anderson, Greg   54
Anglo-American law   xviii, 1–26; see also Hobbes; Locke; Smith (Adam)
Annals of Mr. Lü (*Lüshi chunqiu*)   52, 57, 62, 80
anti-SLAPP; see SLAPP
Asian Values   xx
"autonomy"   xxi–xxii, 44

Baldwin, James (writer); see "addicted to irreality"
bao 報, defined   52
"Basic Annals" for Wendi   70
Belt and Road   17, 78, 152
bequeathed body" (*yi ti* 遺體)   54
Berry, Wendell (writer)   38, 137
Bickham, Stephen (legal scholar)   114, 123
bilateral agreements   5–6, 15
biodiversity   10, 26, 30, 67, 157, 163
body; see "bequeathed body"; "resonance theories"

body politic   2, 46–60; see also "resonance theories"
Bolsonaro (president)   21
Brazil; see Bolsonaro; Moraes
Brooks, David (political commentator)   xiii, 151
Brundtland Report   23, 83, 86–8, 163
Budyko, M.I. (geophysicist)   134

California   xvi, xxvi, 34, 116, 131
Cambridge History of China   157
Canada   5, 14, 90–1, 95, 164
   Federal Sustainable Development Act   90–1
   "Century Initiative" of Canada   91
capital: "natural" *vs.* "manmade"   18, 20, 79, 125
care of the aged   59, 68, 70, 73–7
care of the disabled   59
care ethics   xv, xix, 37
care of the poor   xx, 40, 59, 71, 77–80
casualty tolerance thresholds   xii, 10, 37
CDR; see Edith Brown Weiss
Cheng Li (China watcher)   112
cheng ren 成人, defined   47–8
Chevron   159
China PRC; see also Mao Zedong; *qi* flows; slogans; Xi Jinping
   "beautiful"   122
   CCP (Chinese Communist Party)   57, 105–6, 152, 153

China experts xvii
Chinese characteristics xx
Chinese exceptionalism xx
Communist Youth League
 106–8, 112–13
 early empires as rich 45
 Five-Year Plans 120, 128
 National People's Congress 105
 since 1949 (PRC) 112–
  13, 125, 149
 Territorial Masterplans
  2021–2035 120
"Chinese-style agriculture"; see Elvin
"choice"; see rational choice,
 game theory
climate change
 consequences of xxii, 25,
  101
 as incontrovertible fact xiii
coal mines, mining xvi, xviii, xxvi,
 16, 18, 115, 129, 149
Cohen, Leonard (singer) 138
Cold War xxvi, 4, 9
collective action 7, 23, 137
colonialism xvii, 5, 41
"Confucian": as anachronistic xiv,
 xix, 44, 54, 69, 155–6
conservation, defined by Weiss 20
cosmos, defined 37, 47, 51, 147
cryonics xvi

d'Ambrosio 155, 157
Danfu (aka Old Duke Danfu, hero)
 46–7
"Daoist" (anachronistic) xix, 14–15,
 44, 54, 147, 155
Darwin, Charles 39, 156; see also
 Social Darwinism
Dawkins, Richard (biologist) 42–3
de-colonizers 4–5
Deng Sui 80
dependence 19, 81
dignity/dignified life 5, 10, 24, 36,
 135, 142, 145

disadvantaged groups (as objects
 of care) xix, 23, 40–1,
 59, 68, 165
distributive acts 71, 78, 89
Documents classic
 "Hong fan"/"Great Plan"
  chap 60–1
 "Pan Geng" chap 41–2,
  46–7, 55–6
Duarte Agostinho and Others
 v. Portugal; see legal
 precedents
Dunhuang 132
Durov, Pavel; see Telegram
Dynamic City Foundation 92

early empires in China; see
 China; pre-unification;
 Qin and Han
Earthjustice; see E-NGO
"ecological civilization" xix, 123,
 127, 154; see also China,
 since 1949
economic rights 26
eco-social intelligence 97
E-NGO 26, 126
Elvin, Mark (social historian)
 65–7
emotional awareness/ maturity 9,
 67, 81, 116, 118, 145; see
 also cheng ren
 as political depression 109
Energy Transfer; see SLAPP
environmental epigenetics xxii
environmental exploitation 11–
 13, 21–2, 66, 80, 118,
 162–3, 165
environmental justice; see justice
environmental law 16, 18–36
Environmental Protection Agency;
 see United States
erga omnes 11
European Court for Human
 Rights 28

European Union   14, 31, 33–5
Extreme Weather Congress   159–60
Exxon Valdez   26

Fedorov, Y.Y. (climatologist)   134, 161
Feinberg, Joel (philosopher)   xxi
FEMA; *see* the United States
Fetal training (*tai jiao* 胎教)   54
Finland   94–6, 129
fireflies   xxvii
First Emperor of Qin   56
Florida   17
Foucault, Michel   19, 27, 100
Four Occupations' Monthly Ordinances   56
Fridays for Future   xiv, 34; *see also* Greta Thunberg, Ou Hongyi
Friedman, Daniel   18
Friedman, Morton   22
Frolov, I.T. (philosopher)   127
future   xiv, xvi, xix, xxi, xxiii, 8–10, 15–26, 29, 31, 37, 42, 48, 52, 63, 83–107, 110–18, 120–3, 127–30, 132–3, 135, 143–4, 146, 149–52, 157, 163, 165

GDP   18
Geaney, Jane (philosopher)   51
German Federal Constitutional Court   31, 89
German Weather Service   159
Gerrard, Michael (legal scholar)   12, 16, 26–7
Global South   23, 100
Golding, Martin (philosopher)   117
Gongyang Tradition   54
Gonsalves, Ralph (prime minister)   84–5
Gorsuch, Neil (Supreme Court Justice)   10

"governance"   4–5, 53–4, 58–9, 73, 78, 97, 100, 105–6, 124, 148, 160
"Great Plan" chap; *see Documents*
"greatly immoral/nefas"   77
Greek playwrights   25
Green Ship   160
Greenpeace   32–4, 165; *see also* NGOs
   SLAPP
greenwashing, defined   xiii, 13, 143
Greta Thunberg   9, 114
Guo Guangwu (historian)   101, 105
Guanzi 管子   42, 56, 80
Guoyu 國語   39, 42, 46, 69, 80

Hahn, short bio   xv
Han emperors
   Hedi   75
   Wendi   70, 73
   Xuandi   55
   Yuandi   78
   Zhangdi   51, 75
Havel, Vaclav (thinker)   138
Hawai'i   8, 17, 31–2, 34
Heilbroner, Robert (eco-economist)   84, 117–18
Held v. Montana   15–16, 28
Hobbes, Thomas (thinker)   1–2, 5, 36, 68
"Hong fan" chap; *see Documents*
Hulsewé, A.F.P.   70
human beings, defined   xxi–xxiv, 2, 21, 27–8, 42, 44, 45, 51, 68, 118, 155; *see also* Nature
Human rights   10; *see also* economic rights; "rights" talk

identity   7, 50, 63
identity politics   xii
imperialist/ colonial racist" agenda   xvii, 4, 15
Inner Canon of the Yellow Emperor   51

Index 197

institutions   x, xiii, xxi, 20, 24, 70, 87, 90, 92, 94, 102–4, 139, 143
"integrity"   xv, xxvii, 2, 5, 10, 36, 110, 119, 143
International Court of Justice   xv, xxiv, xxvii, 8, 14, 24, 161, 166
International Military Tribunals   3, 14, 26, 164
"intertemporal freedom securities"   89
Iroquois Nation of North America   99

Jameson, Fredric (philosopher)   4
"justice"   xii, 2, 8–9, 12, 15, 19, 25, 29–30, 83, 98, 101–3, 105, 111, 131, 144, 161, 166; see also International Court of Justice

Kant, Immanuel (philosopher)   xxv, 5, 144
    Neo-Kantian school   5, 25, 69
Klima Seniorinnen Schweiz   28–9
Kyoto Protocol   164

Langya stele inscription   56
Last Generation   xiv; see also Ou Hongyi
Law
    Domestic, in China   xix, 78, 98, 152
    International   xii, xviii, 3, 5–6, 12, 14, 18, 142, 161, 164 (see also Anglo-American law)
    environmental law
learning; see xue
legal precedents
    in Germany   83–4, 89 (see also German Federal Constitutional Court)

    in South Korea   31
    in Switzerland   28–30
    in the United States   11, 13, 15, 26, 119
"Legalists," as anachronistic   xix, 14, 44
Lepore, Jill (historian)   2
Li Zehou (philosopher)   51
libertarian thought   xvi, xxii, 113, 144
"life-transcending projects"   xx, 145
Locke, John (thinker)   1–5, 8, 12, 36, 144
Lutunatabua, Thelma Young (activist)   137, 143

Maffesoli, Michel (sociologist)   39–40
Malm, Andreas (philosopher)   99
Mandela, Nelson   103
Mao Zedong   xix, 113, 125, 149
    "Away with All Pests"   xix
Marx   12, 124–5
Marxism   123
Merkel, Angela   83
Meta   34–5
Midgley, Mary (philosopher)   11, 43
Mi'kmaq   160
Mingtang   64
Ministry of the Environment (Norway)   83
Ministry of the Future   98–9
Montana; see Held v. Montana
Monthly Ordinances   45, 56–8, 64, 69, 78
Moraes, Alexandre de   36

Narveson, Jan (philosopher)   113, 117
Nature, defined   2, 28, 52, 68, 118, 123, 125, 146–7, 155
neo-liberals   xvi, 10, 15, 21, 24, 117

Neville, Robert   141
NGOs   33, 126; see also E-NGO
Ni Peimin   155, 157
Non-identity Problem   136, 157; see also Parfit
"nourishing the aged"   69, 73, 75; see also care of the aged
Nürnberg trials   3, 37
Nylan, short bio   xv
Nyuen, Ahn Tuan   156, 157

obligations towards future generations   117; see also future
OECD Better Life Index   30, 94
Old Duke Danfu (hero); see Danfu
Oliver, John (comedian)   138
Ou Hongyi (activist)   9
Our Children's Trust   16, 32; see also E-NGO
Oxford University, Policy Brief   97, 100

Pan Yue 潘岳 (bureaucrat)   114
Parfit, Derek (philosopher)   26–7, 114–15, 117, 136, 157
Paris Accords/Climate Conference   23, 90, 129, 165
People's Republic of China; see also China, since 1949
   PRC citizens   xx, 93, 96, 103–4, 148
   Chinese exceptionalism   xx
   Slogans today
      "Asian values"   xx
      "with Chinese characteristics"   xx
      "Two Mountains, Three Phases"   118–19 (see also "ecological civilization")
population registries   58, 71–2
Purdy, Jebediah (legal scholar)   28

qi 氣 flows   43–4, 48, 51, 53, 59; see also "resonance theories"
Qin Shihuang (First Emperor)   56
qun 群 (collective work on behalf of the common good)   49

Radio Canada   159
Radio Free Europe   4
realists   xv, 41, 115
Renki, Margaret (essayist)   xxvii
Repugnant Conclusion; see Parfit
resonance theories   xx, 43, 50, 51, 55, 82
Retreat of the Elephants; see Elvin
RICO laws; see United States
"rites" talk   39, 48, 53, 64, 69, 71, 80, 141
ritual, defined   39
Robbins, Paul (writer)   125
Robert's Rules of Order   38
Robinson, Kim Stanley (novelist); see Ministry of the Future
Rockefeller Foundation   3, 18
Roman empire   xviii, 46, 48, 72
Roman law maxim   xxiv, 72
Rovelli, Carl (physicist)   36–7

Sala, Ilaria Maria   156–7
Schmitt, Carl (philosopher)   81
Schopenhauer (philosopher)   139
seabeds   20
seasonality   55–60
Second Treatise; see Locke
Senior Women; see Klima S.S
Shared socioeconomic pathways SSP   129–32
Shell Oil   12, 127–9
Shun (filial exemplar)   69
SLAPP/anti-SLAPP   33–4
slogans
   Chinese (early empires)
      "Gentleness shown the distant…"   81

"join hearts is to renew
    oneself" 51
"reverently uphold the farmers'
    seasonal round" 73
Smith, Adam (thinker) 2, 9, 22–3
Social Darwinism 24, 37, 41, 81
social media xvii, 35, 45; see
    also zombies
Solnit, Rebecca (activist) 4,
    20, 137, 143
South Korea; see also legal precedents
    Carbon Neutral Act of 2018 31
    National Legislature 31
"sovereignty" 1, 2, 4–5, 15, 21, 162
Soviet Union 3, 127, 134, 135, 161
standard histories 56
"standing" 4, 7–8, 16–17, 28
Standing Rock Sioux 32
stare decisis 15
Stewart, Douglas J. (author) 101
Sultan al Jaber (politician) 138–9
supranational commitments 15
Supreme Court; see United States
Switzerland, government report
    29–30; see also
    Senior Women

Taylor, Charles (philosopher)
    49, 156
TAZ 99
tech giants 34–5, 106; see also
    individual companies
Telegram 34–6
Thunberg, Greta (activist) 9, 114
Tie Feiyan (NPC delegate) 105
TikTok 34–6
"trickle-down" economics xviii
Trump; see USA

United Nations
    UN Millennium Development
        Goals Task Force 84
    UN Sustainable Development
        Goals 84–6, 90,
        125, 163, 165

United States of America;
    see also California;
    Hawai'i; Montana
Agency for Global Media 4
Biden xxvi, 6, 41, 77, 165
Bureau of Land Management
    xxvi
Environmental Protection
    Agency (EPA) 6,
    10, 26, 165
Federal Emergency Assistance
    (FEMA) 17
"patriots" 24, 45
populism (moralizing) 140
Pulp Mills 12
Supreme Court 1, 6–8, 10, 36,
    77, 78, 119, 148
RICO laws 33
National Technical Conference
    on Air Pollution 134,
    161
Trump   xii, xiii, 4, 17, 26,
    34, 139, 165"universal
    [philosophical, moral]
    axioms" xxv, 4, 39–
    40, 111, 156
Universal Declaration of Human
    Rights (1948) 13,
    26, 39, 155
vs. relativism 40, 50
Urban China journal 92–4

value, how to 135
Vienna Convention 5

Wales 85–8, 129
    Assembly of 85–6
    Future Generations
        Commissioner "Well-being
        of Future Generations
        Act" 85–90, 127
Wallace-Wells, David 143, 145–6
Wang Mang (emperor) 70
Weiss, Edith Brown (legal
    scholar) 12, 23, 142–3

well-being   xx, 24, 67, 91–4, 96, 115, 121, 130, 152
"Well-being Act"; *see* Wales
Weston, Burns H. (legal scholar)   18–21, 23
White, Lynn Jr. (historian)   156
White Tiger Discussions (*Bohu tong* 白虎通)   47
Williams, Bernard (philosopher)   xxv, 25
Williams, Raymond   54
Wilson, E.O. (naturalist)   42–3
World Summit of the Committees of the Future   95
World War I   3, 161
World War II   3, 145, 161
Wynn-Williams, Sarah   35

X (formerly Twitter)   34, 36, 102
Xi Jinping   23, 78, 105–8, 112, 118–20, 123, 129, 148
Xiaojing   74
xue 學 (learning and emulation)   52, 68, 81
Xunzi/*Xunzi* (philosopher; text)   42, 48, 49, 53, 56, 63, 68, 71, 74, 80, 81, 146

Yueling; *see* Monthly Ordinances
youth movements; *see* Fridays/Thunberg; Last Generation

Zhuangzi (philosopher)   xvii, 42, 67, 80, 137
zombies   xxiv
Zuckerberg; *see* Meta